M000021395

Take5forHIM:

One-Year Devotionals
for Young Women

Rose Marie Martin

Take5forHIM: One Year Devotionals for Young Women
ISBN: 9781726843737
Copyright ©2018 Rose Marie Martin

Printed by Kindle Direct Publishing, An Amazon.com Company
Available from Amazon.com and other retail outlets.

Permission requests for quotes or information: Take5forHIM@gmail.com

Scripture quotations marked HCSB®, are taken from the Holman Christian Standard Bible®, Copyright © 1999, 2000, 2002, 2003, 2009 by Holman Bible Publishers. Used by permission. HCSB® is a federally registered trademark of Holman Bible Publishers.

Scriptures marked NAS are taken from the NEW AMERICAN STANDARD (NAS): Scripture taken from the NEW AMERICAN STANDARD BIBLE®, copyright© 1960, 1962, 1963, 1968, 1971, 1972, 1973, 1975, 1977, 1995 by The Lockman Foundation. Used by permission. www.Lockman.org.

Scriptures marked NIV are taken from the NEW INTERNATIONAL VERSION (NIV): Scripture taken from THE HOLY BIBLE, NEW INTERNATIONAL VERSION®. Copyright© 1973, 1978, 1984, 2011 by Biblica, Inc.™. Used by permission of Zondervan.

Scriptures marked NKJV are taken from the NEW KING JAMES VERSION (NKJV): Scripture taken from the NEW KING JAMES VERSION®. Copyright© 1982 by Thomas Nelson, Inc. Used by permission. All rights reserved.

Scriptures marked ESV are taken from THE HOLY BIBLE, ENGLISH STANDARD VERSION (ESV): Scriptures taken from THE HOLY BIBLE, ENGLISH STANDARD VERSION® Copyright© 2001 by Crossway, a publishing ministry of Good News Publishers. Used by permission.

Scripture quotations marked CSB®, are taken from the Christian Standard Bible®. Copyright © 2017 by Holman Bible Publishers. Used by permission. Christian Standard Bible®, and CSB® are federally registered trademarks of Holman Bible Publishers.

Cover design by Kat Combs, cover photo by mvp on Unsplash, and author photo by Erin Hansen Images.

Dedicated to the girls who came into my life in the 2014-2015 school year. You know who you are. You bounced into my Covenant Group and sophomore girls' breakout group with bright eyes, long hair, swinging ponytails, big t-shirts, and flip flops. You were eager to make good friend group choices and learn about Jesus. I treasure memories of girls pulling me to the side with, "I need someone to talk to...will you pray for me?" and hugs. And, the girls I've mentored early mornings and mid-afternoons with chicken nuggets and sweet tea at a certain franchise. We've laughed at embarrassments, talked through drama, HOCO dates, seasons of slips, and faith questions. I love you, my adopted daughters.

And, to my forever boyfriend. My heart still races with the "I love you" kisses walking out the door, when my phone lights up a text, and when your car pulls in the driveway. The Valentine's Day devotional "What is Real Love" was inspired by feelings for you. The Friday tradition of homemade chocolate chip cookies were intended for our kids as they grew up. They're in college, but I can't bear the disappointment when there are no cookies. I adore your eyes lighting up like a little kid as you head straight for the cookies.

Intro

Where do I begin writing an introduction to Take5forHIM? God placed me in high school girls' ministry in 2014. It carried into post high school as girls entered college as a way to disciple and keep in touch. You'll read Take5forHIM testimonies during the year, but I absolutely love this age group. <u>This book is specifically written for high school thru college age girls</u>. There's so much shift from freshman year to graduation, and then sort of a repeated pattern between the freshman to college senior. Many changes and transitions during an eight-year span, but oh so similar. Decades may separate us, but I can relate to the same trials because it really hasn't been that long since I was sixteen <smiley face wink>. We learn from others, so absorb the advice and wisdom poured into these pages through personal raw experiences. Life is fast, and as you age, you'll find that some things never change.

We're skipping all over the Bible this year, so get ready to jump from front to back to middle to back. By year-end, the hope is a grass roots understanding of basic Bible stories and God's blueprint for living in the Bible. I've found that many people, including adults, don't know why we practice the things we do in a church service, or have answers to basic faith questions, so you'll also learn what I call the Basics of Christianity. It's a crying shame, but churches and youth groups aren't doing their job to teach your generation.

Also, be emboldened as you read devotionals on strong women in the Bible. I've enjoyed studying the well-known names as well as the women you've got to dig deep to find. Their stories are influential and motivating that anything's possible when God appoints a task.

While 100% against youth groups teaching too much social issues and very little Bible meat, girls need wise advice on pertinent everyday life matters. I'll warn there's a lot about friendship, a lot about partying, and a WHOLE LOT ABOUT DATING, SEX, AND PRAYING FOR YOUR FUTURE HUSBAND. Devotionals on sex are sprinkled throughout the year because it's a hot topic. Sexual immorality is the greatest temptation, so it's addressed regularly to emphasize the importance of a sexually clean life before marriage. Not all girls are blessed with a great mother/daughter relationship, so godly wisdom is communicated in a blunt but loving way. There's truth in the phrase "it takes a village to raise a child."

Looking for a message on a specific topic? Check out the Topic Search on the last page.

Twenty-percent of profits from book sales will be given to two impacting ministries: Amazima Ministries and A Bed 4 Me Foundation. I've been inspired by the female founders of both organizations, but it was a God thing when He placed them in my mind to give monetarily. The story of Amazima's founder Katie Davis captivated me several years ago as I read of her drastic move to Uganda as an 18-year old missionary. Months later, I was flipping through social media and saw a new post by a friend's organization, A Bed 4 Me. The founder is a prodigious woman on a war path to provide beds to kids who are sleeping on the floor or with family members. She's been the hands and feet of Christ as the organization's delivered beds and tailored bedding to kids in her community. I couldn't dream up a better combo to give on my own as we share a love for discipling the future generation. Lastly, up to 10% of profits will be given to missions as boys, girls, men and women around the world are called to spread the gospel. Devotionals on both ministries' founders as well as missions related messages will be read on June 27, 28, 29, and 30th.

Whether beginning on January 1st or during the year, please stick with it for a full year. Don't let dust collect on the cover. Messages are quick and meaningful. Some days will Take5(minutes) and others a one to two-minute thought provoking message to move you in the direction to SEE CHRIST IN EVERYTHING, EVERY DAY!

My prayer for all Take5forHIM young women is that Christ will permeate your soul to mold you into the godly woman He has created you to become! Let's develop into women after God's own heart.

 in Christ,
Miss Rose Marie

JANUARY

A new year; a new you.

"The best is yet to come."

-William Shakespeare

Take5forHIM

JANUARY 1
Prayer for the New Year

Sometimes the best devotionals are what's already been written and sung for a century plus. The below hymn was written in 1925 by Katie B. Wilkinson and based on Philippians 2:5, "Your attitude should be the same as that of Christ Jesus." It's sweet, expressive, and a timeless prayer for a new year.

> May the mind of Christ my Savior live in me from day to day, by his love and power controlling all I do and say.

> May the Word of God dwell richly in my heart from hour to hour, so that all may see I triumph only through His power.

> May the peace of God my Father rule my life in everything, that I may be calm to comfort sick and sorrowing.

> May the love of Jesus fill me as the waters fill the sea; him exalting, self-abasing, this is victory.

> May his beauty rest upon me as I seek the lost to win, and may they forget the channel, seeing only him.[1]

God, let their minds be set on You. I pray YOUR WORD will be embedded on these girls' hearts 24/7. Give them peace as You direct them to serve those who are hurting. Fill them up with Your love and pray many will come to know YOU through these young women. Let their lives exhibit what it means to be a Christian living in this generation. Jesus, may a revival sweep across high school and college campuses, and around the world this year. AMEN.

[1]Wilkinson, Katie B. "May the Mind of Christ, My Savior." *Trinity Hymnal*, Great Commission Publications, Inc., 1990.

Take5forHIM

JANUARY 2
"Go in Peace"

"Then one of the Pharisees invited Him (Jesus) to eat with him. He entered the Pharisee's house and reclined at the table. And a woman in the town who was a sinner found out that Jesus was reclining at the table in the Pharisee's house. She brought an alabaster jar of fragrant oil and stood behind Him at His feet, weeping, and then began to wash His feet with her tears. She wiped His feet with the hair of her head, kissing them and anointing them with the fragrant oil.

When the Pharisee who had invited Him saw this, he said to himself, 'This man, if He were a prophet, would know who and what kind of woman this is who is touching Him—she's a sinner!' Jesus replied to him, 'Simon, I have something to say to you,' 'Teacher,' he said, 'say it.' 'A creditor had two debtors. One owed 500 denari, and the other 50. Since they could not pay it back, he graciously forgave them both. So, which of them will love him more?' Simon answered, 'I supposed the one he forgave more.' 'You have judged correctly,' He told him. Turning to the woman, He said to Simon, 'Do you see this woman? I entered your house; you gave Me no water for My feet, but she, with her tears, has washed My feet and wiped them with her hair. You gave Me no kiss, but she hasn't stopped kissing My feet since I came in. You didn't anoint My head with olive oil, but she has anointed My feet with fragrant oil. Therefore, I tell you, her many sins have been forgiven; that's why she loved much. But the one who is forgiven little, loves little.' Then He said to her, 'Your sins are forgiven.'

Those who were at the table with Him began to say among themselves, 'Who is this man who even forgives sins?' And He said to the woman, 'Your faith has saved you. Go in peace.'" (Luke 7:36-50 HCSB)

What jumps out? There are so many lessons in fifteen verses.

Most likely this woman lived a pretty sleazy lifestyle, but she was OBVIOUSLY ready to make life changes. She was bold to enter the home of a judgy Pharisee because she was not invited. By faith, she believed Jesus was the Son of God. Strong-willed? She was determined to confess, worship, and anoint His feet. Nothing was going to stop her- not even a house full of Pharisees.

Jesus was approachable! He must have had amazing charisma and a laid-back ease that was non-threatening, nor intimidating, but totally welcoming. She took a huge risk walking in the home because she could have been pushed away.

Take5forHIM

Jesus knew what Simon was thinking, 'If He's a prophet, He'd know what kind of woman this is who is touching Him---she's a sinner!" Yep, she was a sinner, but I guess he thought he wasn't?!?!

Then Jesus replied with a parable about two debtors owing money, but the creditor cleared their debts to zero. He compared it to her broken heart versus his lack of action. He looked at her and said, "Your faith has saved you. Go in peace."

Simon and the others watched in dismay and said, "Who is this man who forgives even this slutty woman (paraphrased)?" He's the same one who walked on water, calmed the sea, healed the lame, made the blind man see. Yet, the Pharisees still could not accept Him as their Messiah.

The woman knew the Pharisees were aware of her reputation. She didn't care what they thought because she believed Jesus before she saw Him face-to-face. She had a "Come to Jesus" moment and her life was forever changed.

Sadly, people think they need to get their act together before they can have their own "Come to Jesus" moment. They don't believe they're worthy to step foot in a church building regardless of whether the church advertises "Come as you are." There's a mentality that the church is full of "holier than thou" Pharisees who will look down on them. You are welcome, wherever you show up. You are worthy to meet Jesus just as you are because we are ALL filthy, smelly, stupid sheep---BUT He wants to be Your Shepherd.

Lastly, she confessed with her tears. She didn't say a word, according to the scripture. She wept, washing his dusty feet with her tears, and wiped them clean with her hair. She came READY to confess, worship, and cleanse her soul.

Have you ever heard that people with a rough past are more grateful for the grace of forgiveness than those who have been raised in a Christian home and church? That's the point Jesus made to the Pharisees who lived by strict rituals and book knowledge. THIS WOMAN knew her sins were despicable, but she opened her soul to live for Jesus.

Whatever sins are weighing on your shoulders, let this woman be your inspiration. BELIEVE, GO, CONFESS, SHED TEARS, BOW DOWN TO HIS FEET, WORSHIP, SOAK IN HIS GRACE, AND STAND UP KNOWING YOU HAVE BEEN FORGIVEN. Go in peace BECAUSE HIS SPIRIT HAS BEEN POURED INTO YOUR SOUL, AND YOU'LL NEVER, EVER BE THE SAME.

JANUARY 3

New Year resolutions don't work. Change is hard, but optimistic goals for a new year is a more realistic approach. You can change when you're ready, and it will be a day to day challenge. With Jesus' help and a lot of prayer, you can do anything you set your mind.

Seek God first through scripture, prayer, and reflection. Evaluate yourself and get motivated. He'll give you the strength.

"Let your eyes look forward; fix your gaze straight ahead.
Carefully consider the path for your feet, and all your ways will be established."
(Proverbs 4:25-26 HCSB)

JANUARY 4

Heartstrings can pull into the clouds far from reality. When romance grabs the heart, there's not a clear picture of the guy who has our full attention. That's why it's imperative to listen to the opinions of parents and friends. A neutral observation sees a clear view that intertwined emotions cannot. A heart can be wrapped into a thick utopian perspective of a cloudless blue sky [when there's really not]. Longing for a storybook romance, the negatives are brushed off, and a girl will do everything within her power to make it work. Nobody likes hearing mom say, "He's bad news." A friend says, "He's cheating on you. He's snapchatting with _____ and flirting with _____ in class." Or, maybe worse, "He treats you like dirt! You're a fool to put up with that!" Huhhhh, shaking your head in disbelief. "None of this is true. He loves me and would NEVER."

Girl, hopefully not, but sometimes the only way to wake up to reality is to hear the cold hard truth. Don't ignore the harsh truth hoping he'll change rather than losing him. You deserve the best, so don't waste 18 months, one year, six months, or even a few weeks with a guy who doesn't give you: respect, kindness, compliments, good conversation, special treatment, admiration, laughs, trust, friendship, an easy relationship, love for what's on the inside not outward appearance, same level spiritually, no pressure sexually and a good understanding of that, doesn't bash your friends, gets along well with your family.

Why, oh why, would you settle for anything less? Wisen up and listen to what others say!

"The way of a fool is right in his own eyes,
but a wise man is he who listens to counsel."
(Proverbs 12:15 NAS)

"Let the wise listen and add to their learning,
and the discerning get guidance."
(Proverbs 1:5 NIV)

"Those who trust in themselves are fools,
but those who walk in wisdom are kept safe."
(Proverbs 28:26 NIV)

"Listen to advice and accept discipline, and at the end you will be counted
among the wise. Many are the plans in a person's heart,
but it is the Lord's purpose that prevails."
(Proverbs 19:20-21 NIV)

Take5forHIM

JANUARY 5

Forgive us. You've been wronged, denied, and shafted. Not a particular "us." Not a specific person, group, or church, but you've been injusticed. The modern-day church is not teaching your generation. You've heard GRACE, LOVE, and FORGIVENESS, which are all extremely important, but not about God's character, fearing God, nor His judgment. No wonder there's such a lackadaisical attitude about repeated sin. It's easy to get the general attitude that God is the sweet grandfather upstairs.

No matter how much studying God's Word is encouraged rather than allowing worship songs be fulfillment, scripture is not being poured into your souls. We're guilty of serving a large frothy, iced mocha frapp with whipped cream instead of hot black coffee because it's easier to swallow. You've heard syrupy, watered down self-help messages, and it's pathetic!

Far from a Bible Scholar, but one thing that sticks out is that your age group doesn't know the basics of Christianity and simple Bible stories such as Daniel in the Lion's Den, the talking donkey, the patience of Job, or Queen Esther. Lessons on the Trinity, Jesus' second coming, and Revelation are rarely mentioned. It's a total disgrace!

ADVICE: If you're not in a church that's stirring deeper thinking, strong biblical principles, and convicting sin-- it's time to find another church, get in a Bible Study, or self-teach. Take control and do something about spiritual dehydration.

Living out faith is more than feelings. It's seeing the beauty of salvation woven throughout the Bible. It's embracing the Bible as the Holy Word. It's being thankful for the grace of forgiveness and relishing the sweet friendship with Jesus that's like no other. It's worshipping The Almighty. It's knowing the world will change, but He'll never change over the millenniums of time. It's understanding what was sin 3,000 years ago is a sin in 20__, and there are consequences even if it's not immediate.

It's infuriating because Generation Z isn't hearing this from a pulpit, campus ministry, or youth group. In general, churches are scared to preach the hard stuff because it's unpopular. The result is a dumbed down message that produces shallow minds who become bored easily.

Here's a strong shot of espresso to wake you up!

Peter said, *"Praise the God and Father of our Lord Jesus Christ. According to his great mercy, He has given us a new birth into living hope through the resurrection of Jesus Christ from the dead, and into an inheritance that is imperishable, uncorrupted, and unfading, kept in heaven for you. You are being protected by God's power through faith for a salvation that is ready to be revealed in the last time. You rejoice in this, though now for a short time you have had to struggle in various trials so that the genuineness of your faith- more valuable than gold, which is perishable though refined by fire- may result in praise, glory, and honor at the revelation of Jesus Christ. You love Him, though you have not seen Him. And though not seeing him now, you believe in Him and rejoice with inexpressible and glorious joy, because you are receiving the goal of your faith, the salvation of your souls. Concerning this salvation, the prophets who prophesied about the grace that would come to you searched and carefully investigated. They inquired into what time or what circumstances the Spirit of Christ within them was indicating when He testified in advance to the sufferings and the glories that would follow. It was revealed to them that they were not serving themselves, but you. These things have now been announced to you through those who preached the gospel to you by the Holy spirit sent from heaven. Angels desire to look into these things. Therefore, with your minds ready for action, be serious and set your hope completely on the grace to be brought to you at the revelation of Jesus Christ. As obedient children, do not be conformed to the desires of your former ignorance. But as the One who called you is holy, you also are to be holy in all your conduct; for it is written, 'Be holy, because I am holy.' And if you address as Father the One who judges impartially based on each one's work, you are to conduct yourselves in fear during the time of your temporary residence. For you know that you were redeemed from your empty way of life inherited from the fathers, not with perishable things like silver or gold, but with the precious blood of Christ, like that of a lamb without defect or blemish. He was chosen before the foundation of the world but was revealed at the end of the times for you who through Him are believers in God, who raised Him from the dead and gave Him glory, so that your faith and hope are in God......The grass withers, and the flower falls, but the word of the Lord endures forever." (1 Peter 1:3-25 HCSB)*

JANUARY 6

There's a guy who had the reputation growing up as a sour grape with a bad attitude. As a high school student, he lived a wild lifestyle of alcohol, sex, pot, and was all about himself. He was the class clown and relished being known as Mr. Fun Guy. He participated in a lot of mischief and craved popularity.

After graduation, he got sick of the results of living the secular life, and totally surrendered his life to Jesus. Jesus radiates from his heart, mouth, and on his face. Before and after pictures reveal the makeover. He's amazed how many people said they prayed and cannot believe anyone thought to pray for him.

He's an example why we should NEVER GIVE UP ON ANYBODY. Read Matthew 18:12-14 and Mark 8:34-37.

JANUARY 7

Today's message is for anyone who's lost a parent, a sibling, a grandparent, a special aunt or uncle, a cool cousin, or a bestie. Grief is a chest aching pain all of us will face.

Grief has been described like the ocean. Sometimes it's calm, and other times its waves are so strong it pulls you under until it seems impossible to breathe. The most you can do is swim parallel to the shoreline while riptide currents are strong. It's also been said that time is the great healer although anyone who's experienced the death of a loved one attests that years go by, but the aching and tears never end. A friend in her 40's said upon her son's high school graduation: "My Dad has been gone for 25 years. He never met John, but I so wish he could be here (as her eyes misted and grinned). He'd be so proud of the son I've raised." For every special event, there's an empty seat for the one who's wished could be present.

Everyone has different methods to handle grief. There are times when being alone is soothing, but it's never recommended to over-do isolation. Expressing the heartache with another griever; focusing on the happy memories; and bawling as you laugh and cry together is medicine for the soul.

Hang in there. Sadness represents a whole lotta love that can never be lost or replaced.

> *"My flesh and my heart may fail, but God is the strength of my heart,*
> *my portion forever."*
> *(Psalm 73:26 CSB)*

"Blessed be the God and Father of our Lord Jesus Christ, the Father of mercies and the God of all comfort. He comforts us in all our affliction, so that we may be able to comfort those who are in any kind of affliction, through the comfort we ourselves receive from God. For just as the sufferings of Christ overflows to us, so also through Christ our comfort overflows." (2 Corinthians 1:3-5 CSB)

Take5forHIM

JANUARY 8

We're our worst critics. Sometimes we inflict mental anguish on ourselves. We think we're not good enough. We kick ourselves when we make foolish mistakes. We look in the mirror and criticize the reflection. We compare our failures to others' accomplishments. We dwell on things that don't matter. We second guess decisions. "What if I don't get into _____ College?" "Grrrrr.......I should've studied more." "Why did I waste my time when I should've been _____?" "I thought I was smart, but obviously not- look at my ACT score." "I don't measure up." "I'm not popular." "Why did I just make a fool of myself when I opened my big fat mouth?" "I'm an idiot." "I'm so ugly." "I'm so fat." "I've got grandma's big butt." "I'm so skinny." "I've got a big nose." "My hair is the worst hair of anybody I know." "I need to work out." "I need to lose weight." "I'm not girlfriend material." "I think I'm losing my mind." "I got my parents' worst genes, but my sister got the best of them." "My parents hate me." "God must hate me because nothing ever works out for me." "I HATE MYSELF!" When you cut yourself down, you're "throwin' shade" on God's perfect creation.

Again, YOU are your worst enemy. I guarantee no one or God sees you the way you do when you're at your lowest point. Glorify Him with your life and stop stabbing yourself in the chest. Instead say, "Thank you God for loving me even when I don't like myself!"

If you believe God is sovereign, majestic, holy, righteous, loving, omniscient, omnipresent, omnipotent, that He created the world from nothing- then why would He make a mistake when He created you or anyone else? Ever heard someone referred as a wasted life because they're serving time in prison or they're a crack addict? Not true. He made a perfect creation, but he/she chose the wrong route. Every life has value, but it's a choice how to live.

Psalm 139:1-18 sums up all the reasons why a Christian young woman should be comfortable in her own skin and live with God-given confidence. Read aloud every word.

"You have searched me, Lord, and you know me.
You know when I sit and when I rise; you perceive my thoughts from afar.
You discern my going out and my lying down; you are familiar with all my ways.
Before a word is on my tongue you, Lord, know it completely.
You hem me in behind and before, and you lay your hand upon me.
Such knowledge is too wonderful for me, too lofty for me to attain.
Where can I go from your Spirit?
Where can I flee from your presence?
If I go up to the heavens, you are there; if I make my bed in the depths, you are there.

Take5forHIM

If I rise on the wings of the dawn, if I settle on the far side of the sea, even there your hand will guide me, your right hand will hold me fast.

If I say, 'Surely the darkness will hide me and the light become night around me.' Even the darkness will not be dark to you; the night will shine like the day, for darkness is as light to you.

For you created my inmost being; you knit me together in my mother's womb.

I praise you because I am fearfully and wonderfully made; your works are wonderful, I know that full well.

My frame was not hidden from you when I was made in the secret place, when I was woven together in the depths of the earth.

Your eyes saw my unformed body; all the days ordained for me were written in your book before one of them came to be.

How precious to me are your thoughts, God!

How vast is the sum of them!

Were I to count them, they would outnumber the grains of sand—when I awake, I am still with you." (Psalm 139:1-8 NIV)

None of this is a new revelation, but maybe you desperately needed a kick in the pants! Live for Him and be filled with confidence in your outer beauty, everything you say, do, and believe.

JANUARY 9

"Is not my word like fire?' declares the Lord,
'and like a hammer which shatters a rock?'"
(Jeremiah 23: 29 NAS)

The power of God's Word is mentioned many times, but this is perhaps the most vivid picture. Think about the qualities of fire (warmth, beauty, and destruction, etc.) and the image of a hammer pounding a rock. Read His Word. Soak it in. Grow in your relationship. Without knowing His Word, you will never truly know Him.

*A NOTE ABOUT SHORT DEVOTIONALS. Flipping through Take5forHIM, there's a lot of blank space. Short devotionals are plenteous throughout the year. It wasn't a writer's lazy way to fill in a year-long devotional book but intentional after heavy topics or teaching days to give readers an opportunity to absorb what's been read. The short devos are purposeful days of learning one passage or thoughtful idea to carry throughout the day. Maturing in faith is a process.

Take5forHIM

JANUARY 10

There are times when the only news is bad news, and it comes crashing simultaneously. Times of turbulent weather, massacres, suicides, political chaos, and man-made divisions. Cast out your anxiety and fears with the Light of Christ. With Him, there is hope. While there is still concern and compassion, emotions are not full of oppression because you know Who's in control. Take a deep breath and read these powerful scriptures for assurance that God is sitting on the throne, holds the earth, His people, and you in His loving hands.

"The Lord is near to the brokenhearted; He saves those crushed in spirit."
(Psalms 34:18 HCSB)

"For Christ also suffered for sins, once for all, the righteous for the unrighteous, that He might bring you to God."
(1 Peter 3:18 HCSB)

"Peace I leave with you; My peace I give to you.
I do not give to you as the world gives. Your heart
must not be troubled or fearful."
(John 14:27 HCSB)

"And the peace of God, which surpasses every thought, will guard your hearts and minds in Christ Jesus."
(Philippians 4:7 HCSB)

Memorize Romans 8:31-39. Potent!

Don't let the media's doom and gloom overtake you. Be encouraged by The Almighty God's powerful WORD! Rest in Jesus. Amen & Amen!

Take5forHIM

JANUARY 11

This is the first of countless Old Testament devos throughout the year. The tendency is to shy away from the O.T. due to convoluted stories, gruesome plagues, wars, kings, trials, rituals, and troublesome times. By year end, I hope you'll embrace the richness of the Old Testament as it unfolds God's traits and points to Jesus.

The phrase "being thrown into the lions' den" is used to illustrate a dangerous situation that seems impossible to crawl out alive. Daniel knew up close and personal what it was like to be thrown into a pit of lions.

Daniel's wisdom received the attention of King Darius, the Babylonian king at the time when the Israelites were enslaved- again (hundreds of years after release from Egyptian slavery). There was a group of begrudging men who were jealous of the high-profile job responsibilities the king gave to Daniel, so they schemed a plan when they saw him praying daily in his room to God. They conned the king into enforcing a law that no one could pray except to the king. He marveled the idea by declaring, "IF ANYONE IS CAUGHT PRAYING TO ANOTHER GOD EXCEPT YOUR MAJESTY, THEY'LL BE THROWN INTO A DEN OF LIONS!" All went as planned when the men ratted on David for praying to God. The king was displeased but tried to wiggle out of harming Daniel. The bad guys revisited the king to remind him that once a law is signed, it cannot be revoked. So, the king had Daniel captured.

"'May your God whom you continually serve, rescue you!"' A stone was brought and placed over the mouth of the den. The king sealed it with his own signet ring and with the signet rings of his nobles, so that nothing in regard to Daniel could be changed. Then the king went to his palace and spent the night fasting. No diversions were brought to him, and he could not sleep. At the first light of dawn the king got up and hurried to the lions' den. When he reached the den, he cried out in anguish to Daniel. 'Daniel, servant of the living God,' the king said, 'has your God, whom you continually serve been able to rescue you from the lions?' Then Daniel spoke with the king: 'May the king live forever. My God sent his angel and shut the lions' mouths; and they haven't harmed me, for I was found innocent before him. And also before you, Your Majesty, I have not done harm.' The king was overjoyed and gave orders to take Daniel out of the den, he was found to be unharmed, for he trusted in his God. The king then gave the command, and those men who had maliciously accused Daniel were brought and thrown into the lions' den- they, their children, and their wives. They had not reached the bottom of the den before the lions overpowered them and crush all their bones." (Daniel 6:16-24 CSB)

King Darius was blown away at the sight of the lions who were purring like kittens, so he issued a decree for the people to recognize Daniel's God as the true God. *"For he is the living God, and he endures forever; his kingdom will never be destroyed, and his dominion has no end. He rescues and delivers....." (Daniel 6:26 CSB)*

God rescued Daniel from a ferocious death. The Hebrews were enslaved by the Babylonians because of poor choices, but He had not forgotten them. He saves those who are obedient and call upon His name.

Fourteen generations later, God sent Jesus to rescue those who called upon His name and saved them from eternal damnation. The Old Testament points to Jesus as the people needed a Savior. Savior literally means to be saved or rescued.

Take5forHIM

JANUARY 12

It's in emotionally tense situations when people show their true colors, what they're made of, so to speak. Character shines or caves when the heat rises. A college football championship is a prime example. There are three football players to point out for the good and bad.

First, #52. He and an opposing player mouthed off on the field which resulted in a punch. The referee called a penalty on the team for unsportsmanlike conduct. The head coach expressed disappointment and then the player pouted on the sidelines. Moments later, #52's enragement exploded when an assistant coach apparently commented about the behavior. Teammates pulled him away as he stomped to a bench where another coach met him for a calm down talk. It was unsightly. Millions of viewers saw his true colors. A hot topic, but coaches allowed him back in the game rather than ejecting or benching him. He needed tough love, and the coaches missed a humongous life lesson opportunity which little league coaches and dads could've re-told for years. What did #52 learn?

Mr. Quarterback. Promos featured buff players as if they were on a Hollywood set with fire & smoke flaming behind them. In clips, the QB was in the front center looking like a stallion. When the team was losing 12-0, there was a surprise twist when replaced by a freshman quarterback for the second half of the game. When the camera zoomed over to #1 on the sidelines, he wasn't downcast but smiling on successful plays. The team won, thanks to the freshie. Immediately after the game an anchor rushed to interview #1 for thoughts on the freshman QB's win. "He's destined for stuff like this. He's built for stuff like this. I'm so happy for him, and I'm happy for the team." #1 never wavered support. When the coaches and key players were presented the championship trophy, the new star was on stage. The limelight was ripped from #1 after a successful season, and all eyes were on #15. Did #1 look mad, grim, disgusted, ticked off? No, he celebrated the victory with cheers and pearly whites. He was taken off a pedestal but exhibited noteworthy character.

Lastly, the new star, #15. When interviewed he said, "I want to thank my Lord and Savior Jesus Christ. With Him all things are possible and that's what happened tonight." While it turns many people off when Oscar winners and athletes make proclamation for their fame to honor God; HE GAVE GLORY, HONOR, AND PRAISE TO THE ONE WHO BLESSED HIM WITH THE TALENT. He didn't forget God in the moment. Amen for that!

How do you react under pressure? Do you pitch a fit when called out for a rotten attitude? Would you have composure that is honorable and gracious in a similar situation? Do you recognize God as the One who blessed you with intelligence, talent, riches?

"Finally, brethren, whatever things are true, whatever things are noble,
whatever things are just,
whatever things are pure, whatever things are lovely,
whatever things are of good report,
if there is any virtue and if there is anything praiseworthy —
meditate on these things."
(Philippians 4:8 NKJV)

"The good man out of the good treasure of his heart brings forth what is good;
and the evil man out of the evil treasure brings forth what is evil;
for his mouth speaks from that which fills his heart."
(Luke 6:45 NAS)

"As water reflects the face, so the heart reflects the person."
(Proverbs 27:19 HCSB)

"Everything exposed by the light is made clear,
for what makes everything clear is light.
Therefore, it is said: Get up, sleeper, and rise up from the dead,
and the Messiah will shine on you."
(Ephesians 5: 13-14 HCSB)

Take5forHIM

JANUARY 13

"See then that you walk circumspectly, not as fools but as wise, redeeming the time, because the days are evil. Therefore do not be unwise, but understand what the will of the Lord is. And do not be drunk with wine, in which is dissipation; but be filled with the Holy Spirit, speaking to one another in psalms and hymns and spiritual songs, singing and making melody in your heart to the Lord, giving thanks always for all things to God the Father in the name of our Lord Jesus Christ, submitting to one another in the fear of God." (Ephesians 5:15-21 NKJV)

Partying is so tempting in high school and college. This passage clearly speaks wisdom about the choice to party or not party. Do you want to make wise choices or live foolishly? Don't live for the moment thinking one day you'll straighten up. Fill your friend circle with those who love the Lord and discover the joys of clean living. You'll save yourself a lot of headaches.

JANUARY 14

"Do not fear, for I am with you. Do not anxiously look about you,
for I am your God. I will strengthen you, surely I will help you.
Surely I will uphold you with my righteous right hand."
(Isaiah 41:10 NAS)

Sometimes life throws a curve ball and we feel like giving up- that trapped feeling. Ugh! However, Isaiah 41:10 is such an encouraging verse. If God cares and provides for the birds of the air, of course He's going to take care of His child. Memorize this verse and know He's holding you by HIS RIGHTEOUS RIGHT HAND just as a parent holds the hand of a small child when crossing a busy intersection. He's gripping you by the hand.

JANUARY 15
Giving a 10th

It tends to be low attendance Sunday when a church congregation hears the message is on tithing. Pastors make jokes attempting to loosen the tone, but there's squirming. Why? It's convicting if someone isn't practicing a 10% tithe of their income. People fear they won't have enough money to make ends meet when finances may be stretching paycheck to paycheck anyway.

GOD DOES NOT NEED YOUR MONEY to pay church salaries and the electricity. Tithing is giving back to the Lord who has given everything to you. It's all about trusting that God will be faithful when you give. There are spiritual growth testimonies about how God worked in a family income when the burden was lifted, but tithing should never be with the attitude, "I'm gonna give; therefore, God's gonna bless doubly for my sacrifice."

Money for a teenage and college girl is scant, but I encourage the mentality to give each time cash is earned. Automatically have the mindset- $10 of the $100 goes in the offering plate. You'll never miss the 10%, and you'll rest in the obedience.

"Bring me the full tenth into the storehouse so that there may be food in My house. 'Test Me in this way, says the Lord of Hosts. See if I will not open the floodgates of heaven and pour out a blessing for you without measure. I will rebuke the devourer for you, so that I will not ruin the produce of your land and the vine in your field will not fail to produce fruit,' says the Lord of Hosts." (Malachi 3: 10-11 HCSB)

"Remember this: The person who sows sparingly will also reap sparingly, and the person who sows generously will also reap generously. Each person should do as he has decided in his heart- not reluctantly or out of necessity, for God loves a cheerful giver." (2 Corinthians 9: 6-7 HCSB)

Take5forHIM

JANUARY 16

"There were two farmers who desperately needed rain, and both of them prayed for rain. But only one of them went out and prepared his fields to receive it. Which one do you think trusted God to send the rain? The answer: the one who prepared his fields for it."

This parable is a scene from the Christian movie "Facing the Giants" <u>NOT</u> from the Bible. The story is told by a dedicated prayer warrior who walked the locker lined hallways of a Christian school praying daily for the students. The downtrodden football coach needed encouragement during a losing season. Mr. Bridges, the prayer warrior, walked into the coach's office and blessed him with a parable based on Philemon 1:22 which was written by Paul while he was in prison in Rome not knowing if he would ever be released. Paul trusted God to provide a way to be released.

"But, meanwhile, also prepare a guest room for me,
for I trust that through your prayer I shall be granted to you."
(Philemon 1:22 NKJV)

"I know your works. See. I have set before you an open door,
and no one can shut it, for you have little strength, have kept My word,
and have not denied My name."
(Revelation 3:8 NKJV)

Mr. Bridges: "Which one are you? God will send the rain when He is ready. You need to prepare your field to receive it."[2]

Prepare for a flood. Pray big, bold prayers for a revival of hearts. Nothing is too big for God. He may not answer exactly as prayed, but His ways are higher and His ways are better.

Are you ready to receive God's blessings? PREPARE FOR A FLOOD!

[2]*Facing the Giants*. Dir. Alex Kendrick. Perf. Alex Kendrick, Shannen Fields, Tracy Goode, James Blackwell, Bailey Cave, Jim McBride, Jason McLeod. Samuel Goldwyn Films, Destination Films, 2006. DVD.

Take5forHIM

JANUARY 17

TRUE or FALSE? Friend problems go away when you get older.

I recently lost a 25-year friendship. We didn't have a heated argument or split hairs over politics. We've been through many trials, joys, her divorce, raising kids, college football games, and visits. We don't talk often, but we always pick up where we left off because we know each other so well.

So, what happened? She didn't die although it feels like it. She re-married after fourteen years as a single, hard-working, career mom. It was a quick romance which I fully supported because she's a level headed, godly woman. She prayed for years regarding the possibility of a second marriage. Specifically, she prayed for a perfect situation and obviously God-ordained or she wanted no part of it. Their love at first sight story sounded like an answered prayer. However, I received the following email after she received a Take5forHIM weekly devo.

"I need to be removed from your list. _____ and I have decided to say goodbye to friends from our life before we knew each other and only have mutual friends in our new life together. You have to give up a lot of things in order to have what you want most. I am sure you understand."

Tears streamed down my face. Astonished, I read the devastating email repeatedly. Goodbye to friends? She's saying goodbye to me? Do the bride and groom think old friends will intrude on their happiness? I live seven hours away. NO, I don't understand! I was shocked and in disbelief. Why is this happening? I felt like I received a dreaded death phone call.

I replied in less than 10 sentences and I left voice mail messages. *(No reply)*

In a brief paragraph, she slammed the door shut. It felt cold, final, and it hurts like HELL!

Many relate because friends come and go like seasons. People change, and you cannot control others. You're responsible for yourself, so how you handle conflict is up to you. You're called to love a friend at all times- even if her behavior is irrational. Represent Christ well in all that you say. And, no matter what, don't stop praying for a sister in Christ.

"Therefore, God's chosen ones, holy and loved, put on heartfelt compassion, kindness, humility, gentleness, and patience, accepting one another and forgiving one another if anyone has a complaint against another. Just as the Lord has forgiven you, so you must also forgive."
(Colossians 3:12-14 HCSB)

Take5forHIM

JANUARY 18

What does it mean to refer to Jesus as the cornerstone?

"For through Him we both have access by one Spirit to the Father. So then you are no longer foreigners and strangers, but fellow citizens with the saints, and members of God's household, built on the foundation of the apostles and prophets, with Christ Jesus Himself as the cornerstone. The whole building, being put together by Him, grows into a holy sanctuary in the Lord. You are also being built together for God's dwelling in the Spirit." (Ephesians 2:18-22 HCSB)

In ancient building (and even today), the cornerstone was the first stone set in the construction of the foundation. Jesus is the foundation of the church. Without Him, the Christian church would not exist. He is THE CORNERSTONE.

You can't "just believe in God," you must put hope, trust, belief in Jesus as the cornerstone of your life FIRST- before all else. Many believe in God, but they may not be committed to Jesus. A Christian cannot believe one without the other.

Verses such as Ephesians 2:20-22 depict our union with Jesus.

"Jesus told them, 'I am the way, the truth, and the life.
No one comes to the Father except through Me.'"
(John 14:6 HCSB)

JANUARY 19

Little lambs and images of grown sheep are cute, sweet, innocent, and sometimes humorous with all of their heavy wool and stick-like legs.

Now, the truth. Sheep aren't known to be smart animals, and there are Bible passages comparing people to sheep [and Jesus as a shepherd]. There's always one in the bunch who veers off in the wrong direction, but the shepherd guides him back to the flock. Regardless, the shepherd faithfully loves and cares for a sheep's every need anyway, and in many ways.

"We all went astray like sheep; we all have turned to our own way; and the Lord has punished Him for the iniquity (wickedness, sin, immoral, bad behavior) of us all." (Isaiah 53:6 HCSB)

Remember the parable of the lost sheep? *"Then Jesus told them this parable: 'Suppose one of you has a hundred sheep and loses one of them. Doesn't he leave the ninety-nine in the open country and go after the lost sheep until he finds it? And when he finds it, he joyfully puts it on his shoulders and goes home. Then he calls his friends and neighbors together and says, 'Rejoice with me; I have found my lost sheep.' I tell you that in the same way there will be more rejoicing in heaven over one sinner who repents than over ninety-nine righteous persons who do not need to repent."* (Luke 15:3-7 NIV)

A shepherd protects his flock with an ointment repellant to deter bugs from nesting in the nose membranes. Without it, the gnatty-like pests nest and hatch a wormy larvae in noses. The sheep find a tree and literally beat their heads against it until they beat themselves to death.

During mating season, male sheep will have their heart set on a particular girl, but another guy has his eyes on the same beautiful ewe. Determined to fight for the one they each love, they battle by ramming their horns at full force. The violent match is often fatal. The shepherd sees this coming during mating season, so he lathers male horns with an oily substance to prevent horns from locking up, making them slippery. The bucks give up easily out of frustration. They're too dumb to realize the horns could be a weapon on any part of the competitor's body. And, the ewe chooses the buck with the best personality <smile>.

Sheep are dirty, filthy, smelly animals with hot wool coats. They enjoy cooling off in a stream, but they can drown easily because their wool gets weighty. Their good shepherd uses the crook of his staff to pull him safely to land just as he does when he wanders from the flock.

Take5forHIM

I'm a dirty, rotten, stupid, smelly sheep, and so are you. We want to be beautiful, dress well, and have gorgeous, shiny, long, tangle-free blonde hair. Even if we appear polished on the outside, we're flawed on the inside. Nobody's perfect. We sin because humans sin. We all have hurts. Everybody's a little weird and persnickety. We all have bugs flying around in our heads that need beating out. Jealousy rears its ugly head when another girl is talking to our guy. We're living in the flesh, and it's easy to stray from our Father. We need God to guide our decisions and protect us from harm. Have you ever wondered what it would be like if you never knew there was a God or Jesus? Spend time thinking about what life would be like without The Good Shepherd. We'd be a mess, and life is hard as it is!

The Lord is my shepherd;
I shall not want.
He makes me to lie down in green pastures;
He leads me beside the still waters.
He restores my soul;
He guides me in the paths of righteousness
For His name's sake.
Even though I walk through the valley
of the shadow of death, I fear no evil;
For Thou art with me;
Thy rod and Thy staff, they comfort me.
Thou dost prepare a table before me in the presence of my enemies;
Thou hast anointed my head with oil;
My cup overflows.
Surely goodness and lovingkindness will follow me
all the days of my life;
And I will dwell in the house of the Lord Forever."
(Psalm 23 NAS)

JANUARY 20
Deborah

It was a male dominated world in biblical times. Men held leadership roles, and women shut their mouths and took care of the home. They were to be seen and unheard, so it was very unusual when a woman named Deborah became a judge.

Background: When the Israelites reached the Promised Land, God raised up judges to keep the people in check with the laws He had laid out for them in Exodus.

In Joshua 3, God told Joshua to drive out the Canaanites, Hittites, Hivites, Perizzites, Girgashites, Amorites & Jebusites because their bad influences would be devastating to His people- and they were easily strayed anyway. God gave specific instructions, but they started worshiping Canaanite gods and marrying into their tribes even though God warned against it. Some worshiped God and other gods at the same time. Every time God raised up a new judge, they would straighten up and then fall back into sin and rebellion. Then the cycle would repeat.

Twelve Judges governed Israel in this period: Othniel, Ehud, Shamgar, Deborah, Gideon, Tola, Jair, Jepthah, Ibzan, Elon, Abdon, and Samson.

There's not a lot of info on Deborah except that she was a prophetess and the wife of Lappidoth, but she was also called a mother in Israel (Judges 5:7). She was respected by the people and Barak, the commander of the Israelite army. She pushed Barak to deploy 10,000 men to fight in the battle against Jabin, king of Canaan- specifically Jabin's commander Sisera. Barak was scared of the Canaanites' 900 iron chariot army, but Deborah was a faithful woman of God and said she'd go with him. Read below as a strong female leader encouraged a male commander that the Lord would win the battle and turn Sisera into the hands of a WOMAN!

"Barak said to her, 'If you will go with me, I will go. But if you will not go with me, I will not go.' 'I will go with you,' she said, 'but you will receive no honor on the road you are about to take, because the Lord will sell Sisera into a woman's hand.' So Deborah got up and went with Barak to Kedesh. Barak summoned Zebulun and Naphtali to Kedesh: 10,000 men followed him, and Deborah also went with him......It was reported to Sisera that Barak son of Abinoam had gone up Mount Tabor. Sisera summoned all his 900 iron chariots and all the people who were with him from Harosheth of the Nations to the Wadi Kishon. Then Deborah said to Barak, 'Move on, for this is the day the Lord has handed Sisera over to you. Hasn't the Lord gone before you?' So Barak came down from Mount Tabor with 10,000 men following him. The Lord threw Sisera, all his charioteers, and all his army into confusion with the sword before Barak. Sisera left

Take5forHIM

his chariot and fled on foot. Barak pursued the chariots and the army as far as Harosheth of the Nations, and the whole army of Sisera fell by the sword; not a single man was left." (Judges 4:9-16 HCSB)

Then, Sisera fled on foot to hide. He went to a woman named Jael's home. She let him inside her home, gave him a glass of milk, and then killed him while sleeping by hammering a peg into his temple! OUCH!!! Barak went to Jael's home searching for Sisera, and she showed him the dead body with a tent peg nailed through his forehead.

Under Deborah's leadership, she nudged Barak that the Lord would drive out the forces of Jabin's army if he did exactly as the Lord directed. *"The power of the Israelites continued to increase against Jabin king of Canaan until they destroyed him." (vs. 24 HCSB)* Americans are accustomed to military men and women on the battlefield, but it was uncommon for a woman in those times to be involved. Yay for Deborah! Another reason men should listen to a woman <smile>.

JANUARY 21

*"But He said to them, 'Where is your faith?' And they were afraid,
and marveled, saying to one another, 'Who can this be? For He commands
even the winds and water, and they obey Him!'"*
(Luke 8:25 NKJV)

The disciples were in the boat with Emmanuel (God is with us), yet they were afraid when the storm came. The waves were rocking the boat and the rain was pouring. Jesus was peacefully sleeping when the disciples awakened him.

The disciples had witnessed amazing miracles but feared for their lives. Did they think Jesus would let them drown? Where was their faith? Did they believe in His power only when it involved others and not their own well-being?

In life's storms are you going to trust Him to calm the turbulence by stretching out His arms or are you going to flip out?

JANUARY 22

Character. Class. Christ-centered.

If unacquainted with First Lady #41, let me introduce an extraordinary woman. Although she's in the great grandmother league and lived to be 92 years old, Barbara Bush's character is ageless. Although Take5forHIM devos are normally written on women in the Bible, this spectacular lady's life mirrored a great biblical figure. Being the wife of a U.S. President is honorable, but the three C's are the best adjectives.

Mrs. Bush's popularity outweighed her husband's Presidential ratings. She didn't like the attention because she preferred her "superman" to be favored. Known as "the enforcer" by family members, her warm personality, graciousness, humbleness, and God & family first priorities are traits of a phenomenal role model. White hair, faux pearls, beautifully weathered wrinkles, and laugh lines made her a work of art. Her down to earth nature welcomed everyone she met, and every photo reflects a woman who radiated from the inside out.

Her memoir is highly recommended for all young women. The book is a treasure even if you're not a Republican. The autobiography captures early life thru post White House years, and the book's Preface is *so Barbara*. She penned her book as the story of a privileged life, but there's no mention of silver and gold because she valued a wonderful life overflowing with family, friends, and events which included both. The Preface is full of witty comments about her weight and the beauty of shedding "a good tear or two" because "love brings a tear," and "in a life of privilege there are lots of tears."[3] The dialogue emulated a modest woman who never patted herself on the back but praised others for their part in pulling together her life story.

In a society full of ME-ism, we can learn a lot from a high-profile woman who would've never posted her literacy campaign success or a fake portrait to raise herself on a high pedestal. Many in our generation wear a mask of numero uno's perfect life and seek fame through thousands of social media followers.

LESSONS:
-Be humble and let others give the kudos.
-Let popularity be the last thing sought.
-Priorities of God & family first will bring joy of the privileged life not found in wealth or "likes."

"Therefore we do not lose heart. Though outwardly we are wasting away, yet inwardly we are being renewed day by day. For our light and momentary troubles are achieving for us an eternal glory that far outweighs them all. So we fix our eyes not on what is

Take5forHIM

seen, but on what is unseen, since what is seen is temporary, but what is unseen is eternal.

For we know that if the earthly tent we live in is destroyed, we have a building from God, an eternal house in heaven, not built by human hands. Meanwhile we groan, longing to be clothed instead with our heavenly dwelling, because when we are clothed, we will not be found naked. For while we are in this tent, we groan and are burdened, because we do not wish to be unclothed but to be clothed instead with our heavenly dwelling, so that what is mortal may be swallowed up by life. Now the one who has fashioned us for this very purpose is God, who has given us the Spirit as a deposit, guaranteeing what is to come.

Therefore, we are always confident and know that as long as we are at home in the body we are away from the Lord. For we live by faith, not by sight. We are confident, I say, and would prefer to be away from the body and at home with the Lord. So, we make it our goal to please him, whether we are at home in the body or away from it." (2 Corinthians 4:16 - 5:9 NIV) (A passage read at Barbara Bush's funeral, April 2018.)

[3]Bush, Barbara. *Barbara Bush a Memoir*. New York, London, Toronto, Sydney, Tokyo, Singapore, Lisa Drew Books, Charles Scribner's Sons, ©1994.

Take5forHIM

JANUARY 23

It feels like yesterday, but I was the victim of a mean girl attack in the summer following 7th grade. To say kids are resilient is hogwash because the memory dredges pain.

Under the circumstances, names have been changed to protect the identity of the mean girls. It was a slower life back then without social media and cells in a small South Georgia town without a lot to do during summer months. So, I was excited in July when Sandy invited about ten friends to a spend-the-night birthday party at her new house. Like all middle school girls, I was self-conscious what to wear to the party, so I bought a new pair of shoes that day. I remember the weird hunch that something didn't feel right when Mama dropped me off, although the first half of the night was fun. After pizza and cake, the girls headed upstairs. Sandy had the new vinyl soundtrack for the release of "Grease". Girls yacked about favorite movie scenes and sang every word of the songs. There were lots of giggles until bedtime. We stayed upstairs in the playroom and guestroom. The parents' master bedroom was secluded from the second floor. Troubled started when Sandy decided who was staying in which room. I cannot remember who was in the room with me, but there was a definite division between the two groups. My roommates and I were suspicious that something was up after sudden exclusion. We were asleep when the others burst into the dark room and targeted me with an awful smelling concoction. I don't know if it was poured, spooned, or brushed into my hair but it was an awful odor. They ran out laughing. The roomies turned on the lights. My hair, clothes, and sleeping bag were a mess with a salmon colored stinky goo which we later found out the main ingredients were toothpaste and ketchup. I really needed a shower, but I just changed clothes and tried to rub out the thick paste with a wet washcloth. Inferiority flooded as I sat on-guard in the dark barely street-lit room. I felt isolated as we whispered about the incident. They were certain the meanies were scheming more mischief. It was a restless night and, yes, the little witches preyed on me again later with similar goo. It was awful, and I questioned "why me" because Sandy and I had been besties until she moved out of my neighborhood. It was a long night of uneasiness, and the mean girls had a blast threatening raids by murmuring outside the doorway and opening/shutting doors for hours.

Sandy's mom was a super sweet, happy, perky, pretty, friendly lady. Breakfast was awkward. Miss Trina chit-chatted and tried to make us laugh while she served breakfast, but everyone was hush mouth. I always loved Miss Trina, but she couldn't make me smile that morning. She was clueless about the night. Sandy adamantly said, "Everybody's got to leave by 10 a.m." I couldn't wait to get outta there, but I left barefooted because, no surprise, my new sandals were missing. Grrrrrr...

Take5forHIM

I shyly told the gist of the story to Mama on the car ride home. I needed a little justice, but she didn't go to bat when I needed her the most. She never said anything to Miss Trina, and I dreaded when school started back. It haunted 8th grade and I was super glad when the school zones separated me, Sandy, and the other mean girls in 10th grade (high school).

Have you been victimized? Ugh, it's the worst feeling ever. I stored it deep because I didn't get sympathy from my own mother who swept it under the rug and brushed off the reason we were no longer friends as "they moved out to Sunny Hill Subdivision." It was never addressed, so I harbored skepticism in future friendships after my best friend since pre-school had made me a laughing stock.

The point to be made is that kids, teenagers, and adults can be vicious. Friendships are never repaired after bullying. Esteems are damaged and hurt feelings are rooted. If you're a victim of any wrong-doing, stick up for yourself. Don't stand for it. If it happens on campus, report it to a school administrator. If you're harassed at work, file a complaint with a manager or higher. If you're a minor, tell a parent to take action to end the annoyance. And, please, don't ever, EVER mistreat another human being with such evil spiritedness. Nobody deserves to be bullied. No one!

" *A bruised reed he will not break, and a smoldering wick he will not snuff out.*
In faithfulness he will bring forth justice."
(Isaiah 42:3 NIV)

"The one who walks with the wise will become wise,
but a companion of fools will suffer harm."
(Proverbs 13:20 HCSB)

"You have heard that it was said, 'You shall love your neighbor and hate your enemy.'
But I say to you, love your enemies, bless those who curse you, do good to those who
hate you, and pray for those who spitefully use you and persecute you, that you may
be sons of your Father in heaven; for He makes His sun rise on the evil and on the good,
and sends rain on the just and on the unjust." (Matthew 5:43-45 NKJV)

In addition, read 1 Peter 2:1-5.

Take5forHIM

JANUARY 24

"As Jesus was walking beside the Sea of Galilee, he saw two brothers, Simon called Peter and his brother Andrew. They were casting a net into the lake, for they were fishermen. 'Come, follow me,' said Jesus, 'and I will send you out to fish for people.' At once they left their nets and followed him.

Going on from there, he saw two other brothers, James son of Zebedee and his brother John. They were in a boat with their father Zebedee, preparing their nets. Jesus called them, and immediately they left the boat and their father and followed him." (Matthew 4:18-22 NIV)

"As Jesus went on from there, he saw a man named Matthew sitting at the tax collector's booth, 'Follow me,' he told him, and Matthew got up and followed him.

While Jesus was having dinner at Matthew's house, many tax collectors and sinners came and ate with him and his disciples. When the Pharisees saw this, they asked his disciples, 'Why does your teacher eat with tax collectors and sinners?'

On hearing this, Jesus said, 'It is not the healthy who need a doctor, but the sick. But go and learn what this means: 'I desire mercy, not sacrifice.' For I have not come to call the righteous, but sinners.'" (Matthew 9:9-13 NIV)

"Jesus went up on a mountainside and called to him those he wanted, and they came to him. He appointed twelve that they might be with him and that he might send them out to preach and to have authority to drive out demons. These are the twelve he appointed: Simon (to whom he gave the name Peter), James son of Zebedee and his brother John (to them he gave the name Boanerges, which means "sons of thunder"), Andrew, Philip, Bartholomew, Matthew, Thomas, James son of Alphaeus, Thaddeus, Simon the Zealot and Judas Iscariot, who betrayed him." (Mark 3:13-19 NIV)

Also read John 1:35-51 on the calling of other disciples.

Can you imagine dropping everything to follow a complete stranger who said, "Come, follow me. I'll make you fishers of men." Fishers of men meant they were going into the people business with Jesus to save souls. Also note that Jesus didn't choose rigid religious leaders as disciples. The twelve were not perfect by any means. As a matter of fact, after listening to Jesus teach daily, sharing meals, praying, living life, and predictions of death, they didn't truly make sense of who He was (or understand the parables or teachings) until the resurrected Jesus walked in the room on the third day- showing scarred hands and feet. It's perplexing that it took the resurrection for the

Take5forHIM

men to grasp Jesus, but aren't we the same way? We question, question, question. We want more proof than the living word of the Bible.

Thousands of years later, Jesus is still calling disciples. There's no need to stand in the Campus Quad shouting, "Thou shalts and thou heathens you're going to hell if's...." Be a disciple where God has planted: homes, apartments, dorms, friend circles, sororities, campus organizations, jobs, and study groups. Don't shove it down throats. Jesus didn't. He discipled to the sinners rather than the holy-roller self-righteous guys. The sick know they need a doctor (Matthew 9:12-13).

JANUARY 25

Nothing's worse than having hopes, dreams, and expectations that never come to fruition. It's a heartbreak and disappointment when you pray for something that looks promising that God will answer favorably, yet it doesn't work out. Tears are shed and sleep is lost- all because a plan didn't turn out as hoped and prayed. It's hard to accept that God slammed the door. It's tough to swallow when you were asking for something that made good sense and seemed so right.

There's not a scientific formula for recovery. We've all been there, but trust in God's promises for a better plan. Time and trust.

Read Proverbs 3:5 and Isaiah 40:31.

"And again,
I will put my trust in Him."
(Hebrews 2:13 NIV)

JANUARY 26

Jesus traveled throughout Galilee teaching crowds and healing the sick. News disseminated fast as people were talking about His teaching and the miracles. Many followed to hear more. It was rare to have walking teachers trekking from place to place spreading the good news of God, and the things He said was unlike anything they had heard from strict Jewish leaders. He came to a place where there was a crowd, so he walked up a mountainside in order for them to hear and see Him better. The teachings of Chapters 5, 6 and 7 are known as the Sermon on the Mount which essentially laid out how converted Christians are to live. The first twelve verses of Chapter 5 are known as the Beatitudes which means supreme blessedness [that comes with the Christian lifestyle].

"Now when Jesus saw the crowds, he went up on a mountainside and sat down. His disciples came to him, and he began to teach them.

The Beatitudes
He said:
"Blessed are the poor in spirit,
 for theirs is the kingdom of heaven.
Blessed are those who mourn,
 for they will be comforted.
Blessed are the meek,
 for they will inherit the earth.
Blessed are those who hunger and thirst for righteousness,
 for they will be filled.
Blessed are the merciful,
 for they will be shown mercy.
Blessed are the pure in heart,
 for they will see God.
Blessed are the peacemakers,
 for they will be called children of God.
Blessed are those who are persecuted because of righteousness,
 for theirs is the kingdom of heaven.

Blessed are you when people insult you, persecute you and falsely say all kinds of evil against you because of me. Rejoice and be glad, because great is your reward in heaven, for in the same way they persecuted the prophets who were before you." (Matthew 5:1-12 NIV)

Jesus didn't pound laws but pointed them to complete dependence on God- hopeful encouragement for God's people.

Take5forHIM

JANUARY 27

The next section of the Sermon on the Mount:

"You are the salt of the earth. But if the salt loses its saltiness, how can it be made salty again? It is no longer good for anything, except to be thrown out and trampled underfoot. You are the light of the world. A town built on a hill cannot be hidden. Neither do people light a lamp and put it under a bowl. Instead they put it on its stand, and it gives light to everyone in the house. In the same way, let your light shine before others, that they may see your good deeds and glorify your Father in heaven." *(Matthew 5:13-16 NIV)*

This has nothing to do with the slang term "salty" used today. The Urban Dictionary defines salty as angry, agitated, upset, as well as someone who is mean, annoying, and repulsive.[4] Here, Jesus is calling us to be the seasoning of the earth by not hiding your Christianity. We're pegged to share the gospel and exhibit love through acts of kindness; therefore, being the salt and light in a dark world.

[4]"Salty." *Urban Dictionary*, 2011, /www.urbandictionary.com/define.php?term=Salty.

Take5forHIM

JANUARY 28

Some believers argue they don't need to go to church. They're settled to worship, pray, and read scripture in the comfort of their homes- in front of the TV if they choose. It's true that faith is built on a one-on-one relationship with God, accessible anywhere, but anti-church-goers miss out on shared unity with other believers and the public worship experience. They also lack spiritual bonding time in the joys and struggles of life. The regular routine can be easily procrastinated over time due to Sunday Morning Sickness.

Unfortunately, the church can sometimes be viewed negatively by the world as a business. Churches with the right motives are: building God's kingdom, spreading his message, ministering to the lost, feeding His sheep, being the Body of Christ.

"Let the message about the Messiah dwell richly among you,
teaching and admonishing one another in all wisdom,
and singing psalms, hymns, and spiritual songs,
with gratitude in your hearts to God."
(Colossians 3:16 HCSB)

"For where two or three are gathered together in my name,
I am there among them."
(Matthew 18:20 CSB)

Take5forHIM

JANUARY 29

God is so good- GREAT- AMAZING. It's cool to see Him shining on faces, building bonds between Christians. Lives so intertwined in relationships and how various situations play out. Someone asked, "How can you see Him in so much? I cannot." I'm far from righteous or a perfect Christian, but believe that by reading the Bible, dependence, and spending time in prayer, one naturally sees Him in much of the day.

Delight in Him and look for sightings.

"And one called out to another, 'Holy, Holy, Holy is the Lord of Hosts.
His glory fills the whole earth.'"
(Isaiah 6:3 HCSB)

Jesus said, "Go home to your people and report to them what great things
the Lord has done for you, and how He had mercy on you."
(Mark 5:19 NAS)

"But ask the animals, and they will teach you, or the birds in the sky,
and they will tell you, or speak to the earth, and it will teach you,
or let the fish in the sea inform you. Which of all these does not know that the
hand of the Lord has done this? In his hand is the life of every creature
and the breath of all mankind."
(Job 12:7-10 NIV)

JANUARY 30

"Brothers and sisters, we do not want you to be uninformed about those who sleep in death, so that you do not grieve like the rest of mankind, who have no hope. For we believe that Jesus died and rose again, and so we believe that God will bring with Jesus those who have fallen asleep in him. According to the Lord's word, we tell you that we who are still alive, who are left until the coming of the Lord, will certainly not precede those who have fallen asleep. For the Lord himself will come down from heaven, with a loud command, with the voice of the archangel and with the trumpet call of God, and the dead in Christ will rise first. After that, we who are still alive and are left will be caught up together with them in the clouds to meet the Lord in the air. And so we will be with the Lord forever. Therefore encourage one another with these words."
(1 Thessalonians 4:13-18 NIV)

Death, funeral home visitation, and funerals are unpleasant. There's sadness and a sickening as you stand over the casket paying final respects to a loved one, maybe an elderly grandparent, while Aunt Polly remarks, "Doesn't she look beautiful." Your thought: "No, she looks white as a sheet and my Granny never wore thick cake-like makeup." Ugh! Then, sad songs are sung at the funeral while everyone stares at the closed casket and Granny's glamour shot photo on an easel. The pastor, Brother Billy, depends on a written script as if he's reading verbatim what Aunt Polly and Uncle Tom typed. Grrrr! The scene at the graveside is also solemn, tearful, and quiet. It's a somber event.

Granny loved the Lord, attended church her entire life, and frequently spoke of Jesus. Based on the above passage from 1 Thessalonians and other uplifting passages about crossing over from this life to heaven, why should a funeral for a Christian be tearful? It should certainly be a celebration of their life and the life they are living throughout eternity! Praise God that Granny put her trust in the Lord Jesus Christ as her Savior. Praise God for the legacy, memories, and eight-layer chocolate cakes! Praise God the body in the casket is just the shell of a 95-year old decaying body, but her spirit is alive and youthful in the presence of the Lord Jesus Christ today. The tears are absolutely natural because family and friends will sincerely miss her but rejoice. Granny's home.

The true tears and mourning are when attending a non-believer's funeral.

JANUARY 31

"Your eyes saw my unformed body;
all the days ordained for me were written in your book
* before one of them came to be.*
How precious to me are your thoughts, God!
* How vast is the sum of them!*
Were I to count them,
* they would outnumber the grains of sand-*
* when I awake, I am still with you.*

If only you, God would slay the wicked!
* Away from me, you who are bloodthirsty!*
They speak of you with evil intent;
* your adversaries misuse your name.*
Do I not hate those who hate you, Lord.
* and abhor those who are in rebellion against you?*
I have nothing but hatred for them;
* I count them my enemies.*
Search me, God, and know my heart;
* test me and know my anxious thoughts.*
See if there is any offensive way in me,
* and lead me in the way everlasting.*
(Psalm 139:16-24 NIV)

Psalm 139 was written by David. The previous fifteen verses describe God's ever presence with David (and all people). Verses 16 and following illustrates how you were knitted by God's hands, and He knows every aspect of your being. In the last lines (search and know my heart), David asked God to reveal any ounce of sin so that he could live gloriously for the Lord.

Nothing can be concealed. He knows all, but an occasional appraisal is recommended because it's easy to be unaware of our own motives. God, uncover deep dark sins which are sometimes glossed as innocent because it's never said aloud. Thoughts are secret sins of the heart. Change us, O Lord.

Take5forHIM

FEBRUARY

*"Don't look back;
you're not going
that way."*

-Mary Englebreit,
Graphic Artist

Take5forHIM

FEBRUARY 1

What does the Bible say about God's Word?

"Is not My WORD like fire, declares the Lord?
And like a hammer which shatters a rock?"
(Jeremiah 23:29 NAS)

"In the beginning was THE WORD, AND the Word was with God,
and THE WORD WAS GOD."
(John 1:1 NAS)

"The Word became flesh and took up residence among us.
We observed His glory, the glory as the One and Only Son
from the Father, full of grace & truth."
(John 1:14 HCSB)

"For the word of the Lord is right, and all His work is trustworthy."
(Psalm 33:4 HCSB)

"For whatever was written in earlier times was written for our instruction,
that through perseverance and the encouragement
of the Scriptures we might have hope."
(Romans 15:4 NAS)

"Whoever believes in me, as scripture has said,
rivers of living water will flow from within them."
(John 7:38 NIV)

"Your Word is a lamp for my feet, and a light on my path."
(Psalm 119:105 HCSB)

"He wore a robe stained in blood, and His name is the word of God."
(Revelation 19:13 HCSB)

"All Scripture is God-breathed and useful for teaching, rebuking,
correcting and training in righteousness, so that the servant of God
may be thoroughly equipped for every good work."
(2 Timothy 3:16-17 NIV)

Take5forHIM

*"For THE WORD of God is living and effective and sharper
than any double-edged sword...."
(Hebrews 4:12 HCSB)*

*"The grass withers, the flower fades,
but the word of OUR GOD stands forever."
(Isaiah 40:8 NIV)*

God's word is rich.
It's comforting.
It's refreshing to the soul.
'Nuff said.

Take5forHIM

FEBRUARY 2
College Anxiety- "Be Still"

On the edge of anxiety for the big reveal.
Who will get accepted to _____University?

"Be still and know I am GOD."

This is the time of year many eager high school seniors have circled on their hearts' calendars. There will be tears of disappointment, tears of excitement, and lots of....."What's Plan B?.......I don't have a Plan B!"

"Be still and know I am GOD."

This is a big moment in the life of a high school senior.

College readers recall the pressure of the college search. They have memories of the victorious moment when they were accepted to their prized school of choice or the agonizing process of elimination. Most agree that despite where they landed for four years, they love it and it's where they were meant to be.

On the flip side, underclassmen haven't arrived to this climatic time in life, so they "just don't get it." They're trying to figure out what to wear to the Sadie's Dance because standardized test scores and college searches seem "a long way away." Seniors have already lived the underclassmen moments of being still and knowing God is in control when facing decisions such as whether to take accelerated courses, college classes, or home school. This is a huge time of trusting God for guidance, too.

"Be still and know I am GOD."

You're a wreck! You have butterflies, sleepless nights, nail biting, and sassy episodes with your parents as you inch towards receiving an acceptance notification. You've put all your hopes, dreams, and focus in one place. It's hard to practice patience.

"Be still and know I am GOD."

Seniors, how are you going to react if you don't get into _____ University? Will life be over? Is Plan B to stomp your feet in anger, kicking and screaming?

"Be still and know I am GOD."

Take5forHIM

Your plan may be _____ University, but God's plan may set you on a different course. If you don't get accepted into your top choice, are you going to swallow your pride believing God's Plan B is better? If it's God's will, it will be. If it's not [HIS WILL], then you will have no choice but to move forward. It's the process in your Walk with Christ. This may be your season to learn how to

"Be still and know I am GOD."

He gave you the brains, the talent, and the words for essays. You put your best in an application and now it's out of your control. His best is where He's already placed you—now and in the future.

The full verse is: *"Be still, and know that I am God; I will be exalted among the nations, I will be exalted in the earth."*
(Psalm 46:10 NIV)

The context of the 46th Chapter of Psalms is regarding God being our refuge in a time of trouble such as in wars and national conflict. Regardless of family conflicts, anxiousness, depression, stress, national threats, chemo treatments, flunking a class, regretting a huge mistake, or trying to figure out Plan B--the phrase applies to every situation in life as we wait on God in the stresses of life. He is sovereign! Praise Him if you get into your #1 college choice. Praise Him if you don't!

Wait silently, be patient, and let His plan unfold as He directs your path.

"Look at the birds of the air: they do not sow or reap or store away in barns, and yet your heavenly Father feeds them. Are you not much more valuable than they?"
(Matthew 6:26 NIV)

"Trust in the Lord with all your heart and lean not on your own understanding; in all ways submit to Him, and He will make your paths straight."
(Proverbs 3:5-6 NIV)

Take5forHIM

FEBRUARY 3

WARNING: SENSITIVE TOPIC!

There are misconceptions about what's physically A-O-K in intimacy. What's the limit? What is God's limit? What does the Bible say is the limit?

It's true that the Bible does not give specifics on certain sexual acts and whether it's approved. First, use common sense. What makes it unobjectionable to be touched or touch a sexual body part? The purpose is for intimacy, exploration, and pleasure-correct? Your levelheadedness agrees so there's the answer. It's not admissible.

Any sexual activity outside the bonds of marriage is considered sexual immorality and impurity. There are plenty of verses that specify sexual immorality.

Read Colossians 3:1-11; 1 Corinthians 7:8-9; 1 Corinthians 6:15-20; 1 Corinthians 10:6-13; 1 Thessalonians 4:3-8.

These are only a few, but there are more. The Bible is very clear-cut. Are you going to believe God's Word stands throughout time as His best for you OR are you going to believe what the world (or a guy) tells you?

Take5forHIM

FEBRUARY 4

Girls, a social life is applauded, but nobody is going to love and care as much as a parent's unconditional love. Family dynamics vary, but it's predictable your parents hanker for good talks and a fruitful bond with their daughter. A relationship cannot be one-sided. It takes two whether it's a friendship, romantic, marriage, or family. There are areas of your life that aren't shared with even the best of friends due to trust issues or to keep it light. At your age, it's normal to reserve feelings as far from the spectrum as possible from Mom and Dad. However, parental wisdom and life experiences are natural resources as you seek guidance for pending decisions to accomplish tasks. Don't be prideful, stubborn, tight lipped, and too independent to ask for navigation or a listening ear.

Sling an ax to shatter the concrete wall causing division. Shock Mom or Dad by plopping down on the sofa, turning off the computer, and converse about what's filling your head. They crave valuable time. Impossible? You: "But, you don't know my blankety blank Mom (or Dad)!" If the bond was demolished years ago, grab glue to plaster the fragments. Reconstruction is past due. Don't isolate. Swallow your pride. GO TO MOM, DAD, or both. Open-up.

"Do two walk together, unless they have agreed to meet?"
(Amos 3:3 ESV)

"Remember your leaders, those who spoke to you the word of God.
Consider the outcome of their way of life, and imitate their faith."
(Hebrews 13:7 ESV)

Take5forHIM

FEBRUARY 5

"Who can separate us from the love of Christ? Can affliction or anguish or persecution or famine or nakedness or danger or sword? As it is written: "Because of You we are being put to death all day long; we are counted as sheep to be slaughtered. No, in all these things we are more than victorious through Him who loved us. For I am persuaded that not even death or life, angels or rulers, things present or things to come, hostile powers, height or depth, or any other created thing will have the power to separate us from the love of God that is in Christ Jesus our Lord." (Romans 8:35-39 HCSB)

You cannot lose your salvation. Once you've committed to Jesus, He will not let you go. You may stray away for a while, but He'll draw you back. His love is irresistible and there's nothing to compare.

FEBRUARY 6
"No God ~ No Peace;
Know God ~ Know Peace"

In his 20's, this bumper sticker slogan was on the back of my husband's white convertible. On the first day of a new job, his boss saw his car in the parking lot. The next day he beamed and rejoiced. He said, "I knew you were a Christian without asking, and the bumper sticker confirmed it."

God's word says, *"They will know we are Christians by our walk."* Does your demeanor reflect Christianity without verbally proclaiming it? Read 2 Thessalonians 1:6-10, *"They will know we are Christians by our love."*

FEBRUARY 7

Last week, we read Psalm 139 for a powerful depiction of God's character. *The HCSB (Holman Christian Standard Bible) translation of verse 5 is: "You have encircled me. You have placed your hand on me."* He goes everywhere you go and never leaves your side. He encircles YOU. He has placed HIS hand on YOU!

God, we pray for physical and emotional protection. Keep this girl in the safety of Your hand. Guide and protect her as she swims unknown waters. Chart her path. Amen.

FEBRUARY 8

"Here I am."

Genesis 22:1: God said Abraham's name and he replied, "Here I am." In other words, "God, I'll do what you ask. I trust you." Again, in verse 11 when the angel of the Lord called his name at the moment he was about to slay his son Isaac, Abraham said, "Here I am." That shows obedience. Abraham didn't understand what was going on, but he submitted to God's calling to do whatever asked even if he didn't understand the "why."

In a dream, God called Jacob's name. He answered, *"Here I am." (Genesis 31:11 NAS)*

At the burning bush, God called Moses' name and he responded, "Here I am."

God called boy-aged Samuel's name three times. He didn't recognize it as God's voice but thought it was Eli. Eli suggested it may be the Lord. So, when the Lord called his name a fourth time, Samuel's response was, *"Speak, for your servant is listening." (1 Samuel 3:9 HCSB)* Here I am!

Prophet Isaiah heard the voice of the Lord saying, *"'Who shall I send? Who will go for us?'" (Isaiah 6:8 HCSB)* Isaiah's response? You got it, *"Here am I. Send me!" (HCSB)* From there, Isaiah was sent to share God's word with the northern tribes of Israel.

The Lord got the attention of a follower named Ananias in a vision to go speak to Saul [future name is Paul] to lay hands on him to regain his sight as confirmation of Jesus' calling upon him. Ananias' first response was, *"Here I am, Lord." (Acts 9:10 HCSB)* When the Lord explained what he was to do, he first resisted because of Saul's rebellion against the Jesus movement. Ananias obeyed. Saul's eyesight was restored and Saul (Paul) was committed to Jesus. Ananias was blessed as an intercessor for God's heart change in Saul.

How about you? Has God called your name to take action? What was the reply? Are you ready, available and willing to say, "Here I am, Lord?"

FEBRUARY 9

"Jesus answered [the woman], 'Everyone who drinks this water will be thirty again, but whoever drinks the water I give them will never thirst. Indeed, the water I give them will become in them a spring of water welling up to eternal life.' The woman said to him, 'Sir, give me this water so that I won't get thirsty and have to keep coming here to draw water.' He told her, 'Go, call your husband and come back.' 'I have no husband,' she replied. Jesus said to her, 'You are right when you say you have no husband. The fact is, you have had five husbands, and the man you now have is not your husband. What you have just said is quite true.' 'Sir,' the woman said, 'I can see that you are a prophet. Our ancestors worshiped on this mountain, but you Jews claim that the place where we must worship is in Jerusalem.' 'Woman,' Jesus replied, 'believe me, a time is coming when you will worship the Father neither on this mountain nor in Jerusalem. You Samaritans worship what you do not know; we worship what we do know, for salvation is from the Jews. Yet a time is coming and has now come when the true worshipers will worship the Father in the Spirit and in truth, for they are the kind of worshipers the Father seeks. God is spirit, and his worshipers must worship in the Spirit and in truth.' The woman said, 'I know that Messiah is coming. When he comes, he will explain everything to us.' Then Jesus declared, 'I, the one speaking to you- I am He." (John 4:13-26 NIV)

Our physical bodies will always hunger and thirst daily. There's no changing the fact that we need food and drink to sustain us. In this passage, Jesus told the woman that He's our spiritual nourishment. Set aside at least 30 minutes daily to read The Word and pray. Busy schedule? Give God a slice of the day, and He'll provide plenty of time in exchange to get chores and homework completed. Give it a try!

Take5forHIM

FEBRUARY 10

A dot on a time line represents our short time on earth. The line represents eternity. Live for the line not the dot. *"But seek first His Kingdom and His righteousness; and all these things shall be added to you." (Matthew 6:33 NAS)*

Principles for Living- Day One:
Prayer- Pray without ceasing. (*Ephesians 6:18*)

Forgive- so you can be forgiven. (*Luke 6:37*)

Reputation- Always do the right thing. *"A good name is more desired than great riches." (Proverbs 22:1 NAS)*

Live the golden rule- Love the Lord your God and love your neighbor more than yourself. (*Mark 12:30-31*)

Choose friends carefully. They shape who you are. Ask, is this person encouraging me to live for the line or the dot? (*1 Corinthians 15:33*)

Vision- Begin with the end in mind- set short term goals to reach the vision. The ultimate vision is to hear Christ say, *"Well done good and faithful slave." (Matthew 25:21 NAS)*

Marriage- Marry your best friend- the rest will sort itself out. (*1 Corinthians 13:4-8*)

Work- Do not focus on making money. Instead focus on your area of giftedness (organization, sales, creativity, hospitality, nursing, etc.) and pursue your passion. Money may follow giftedness mixed with passion, but satisfaction never follows the pursuit of money. (*Proverbs 23:4-5*)

FEBRUARY 11

Principles for Living- Day Two:

Attitude- You can't control your circumstances, but you can control your attitude about the circumstance. Bloom where you're planted. *(Philippians 4:11-13)*

Money- Give the first 10%, save the next 10%, and consider wisely what to do with the rest. *(Matthew 6:19-21)*

God's Word- At the end of the day, everything worth knowing is in the Bible. Use it as an instruction manual for living well. *(Proverbs 3:13-15; 2 Timothy 3:16)*

Humility- Clothe yourself in humility so that God may be glorified through life. God gives grace to the humble, but disgrace to the proud. *(James 4:6)*

Decisions- When in doubt- "Do I go to the party?" "Do I go on the trip?" Make your default answer yes- go- do- act (as long as it's morally right). Most of the time you will be glad you did. *(Matthew 4:18-22)*

Margin- In the busyness of living well, leave plenty of margin. It's often in the margin that God does His best work. *(Hebrews 4:9-11)*

Endurance- Leave it all on the field. No matter the results, you always win when you give life your best. *(2 Timothy 4:7)*

Honesty- Always be honest, it's the best policy. *(Leviticus 19:36; Proverbs 12:17)*

Laughter- Enjoy the journey whether hard or easy. Laughter is good medicine. *(Proverbs 17:22)*

(I thank my dear friends who craft bookmarks for high school graduates with Principles of Living they penned. It sums up great advice for all.)

Take5forHIM

FEBRUARY 12

Do you ever pray for your future husband or dream of who he will be, what he'll look like, wedding day dreams? Pray NOW for your husband. Pray that he'll be a God-loving, God fearing, decision making man. Pray for a strong spiritual leader for your family. Pray that he's being raised in a Christian family rooted in biblical principles. Pray he will be a significant financial provider, but not obsess over a career. Pray for his faithfulness to a lifetime marriage together.

"Husbands, love your wives, just as Christ also loved the church and gave Himself up for her; that He might sanctify her, having cleansed her by the washing of water with the word, that He might present to Himself the church in all her glory, having no spot or wrinkle or any such thing, but that she should be holy and blameless. So husbands ought also to love their own wives as their own bodies. He who loves his own wife loves himself; for no one ever hated his own flesh, but nourishes and cherishes it, just as Christ also does the church." (Ephesians 5:25-29 NAS)

FEBRUARY 13
What is faith?

*"Now faith is confidence in what we hope for and
assurance about what we do not see."*
(Hebrews 11:1 NIV)

Non-believers will ask, "How can you believe in something you cannot see?" This tough question can be answered by simply giving your testimony. Profess what you believe, why, and how you came to faith.

Jot it down in the space below.

FEBRUARY 14
What is real love?

When your heart races when his name pops up on your phone ~ NOT BOASTING ~ Wanting to call him when you have good news ~ A shoulder to cry on ~ Love is making compromises and being okay with it ~ Someone to laugh with over the dumbest things ~ Sharing life ~ Someone you cannot imagine EVER separating from ~ UNSELFISH ~ Loving his family like your own ~ Lighting up when you see him across the room ~ Comfortable in silence ~ Talks non-stop ~ Accepting he's not perfect but he's perfectly imperfect to you ~ Having healthy arguments ~ Someone to share your innermost thoughts ~ Dream together ~ Saying you're sorry ~ Forgiving and Forgetting ~ Not Jealous ~ Kindred Spirits ~ Completing his sentence before he finishes ~ PATIENCE ~ Loving what's on the inside ~ KIND ~ Loves in the darkest of times ~ Supportive ~ DOES NOT BRAG ~ Shares the same faith ~ DOES NOT PROVOKE ANGER ~ Cannot spend enough quality time together ~ There's never enough time together ~ Laughing ~ Making chocolate chip cookies every Friday because it makes him smile----the quickest way to a man's heart is food ~ Envisions the future together ~ Loves despite sickness even if it's terminal ~ Loves more ~ PRAYING TOGETHER ~ Constantly falling deeper in love ~ Becomes your best friend over years of time as life experiences bond ~ IS NOT ARROGANT ~ Endures heartache ~ NOT JEALOUS of the time he spends with his dog (a guy's best friend) ~ Loves in the valleys and the mountains of life ~ DOES NOT HOLD GRUDGES ~ When there are no words to describe your feelings ~ Encourages ~ Does not criticize ~ Sets goals ~ FAITHFUL ~ Would never cheat because once is too much ~ Just being there ~ Lifts your spirits ~ Thinking the same thought at the same time ~ Not afraid to confide ~Happy for one another's successes ~ Loves despite the failures ~ POSITIVE ~ Eyes only for him---total tunnel vision ~ Speaks highly to friends about one another ~ COMFORTABLE ~ Having fun doing nothing together ~ Loves even if the bank account is depleted ~ Works as a team ~ When you can't be mad for very long ~ Hurts when he hurts/joyful when he's happy ~ Makes decisions together ~ Does not overpower the other ~ Agree to Disagree ~ Appreciates each other's differences ~ DOES NOT USE A HARSH TONE OF VOICE ~ DOES NOT ABUSE- PHYSICALLY OR EMOTIONALLY ~ When you crane your neck looking for his car to pull in the driveway ~ Loving even if you are miles apart ~ Trusting him when you are apart ~ Listening to boring, mundane details of his day and loving every boring, mundane detail ~ Loving his "scent" when he walks out of the room ~ Cleaning up after him without complaining ~ Wanting to go the extra mile to see him for a few minutes because it's worth it ~ A spontaneous purchase – his favorite candy at the checkout aisle- and giddy when you give it to him ~ Crying together ~ Praying for him ~ Reaching for a hug or a touch to encourage ~ The unspoken words to give him space after a rough day ~ Knowing what to say without saying a word ~ Not trying to out-do one another ~ Knowing how to argue ~ Appreciating the grey hairs and wrinkles ~ Not letting the sun go down without saying, " I was wrong" ~ Not being EMBARRASSED ~ Seeing the sunny side of life together ~ Being personality opposites and appreciating the differences ~ Confidence that you can conquer anything together ~ Thinking he's the best looking guy in the world even if he's really not "so cute" to anybody else ~ Being married and never using the word divorce ~ COMMITMENT ~ Dependent in a healthy way ~ Missing him when you attend a party without him ~ CONTENT ~ Just as happy to eat a bowl of cereal or a steak dinner as long as you're sharing a meal together ~ Raising a family ~ Seasons of life ~ Sticking it out for LIFE.

It's the love month so now is a good reminder that anybody can fall in love, but not everybody is committed for life. Don't get your heart entangled with a guy who doesn't match up to your high expectations for a lifetime love.

Real love is: Grandma and Grandpa who grew old together.

Read 1 Corinthians 13 :4-7, coined as "The Love Chapter."

FEBRUARY 15

Recently, a dark cloud was hanging over my head. The day started with social media sending me over the edge. With shaky fingers and an attitude, "That's it! I'm deleting my apps and re-gaining lost time in my days by not getting caught up in others' lives." It was a band-aid for the moment. But, it wasn't enough....

I was jarred. I hid stress during the work day by staying focused, talking very little to co-workers, and watching the clock for the magic moment I could dash out. I left on a stormy afternoon crying out to God as the windshield wipers wiped away the pouring rain. The weather was fitting. Thankfully no one was home that afternoon, so I walked straight to the bed, crawled under layers of blankets, and cried my eyes out for at least an hour. I cried and evaluated what upset me. To the outside world, it may be silly, but it got under my skin. The tears lead to other matters to pray until the pillow was drenched, and my eyes were swollen like golf balls. I was a mess when my family came home, and they probably wondered what the heck was wrong with Mom. I perked up as the evening progressed, and the next day, *"Because of the Lord's great love we are not consumed, for His compassions never fail. They are new every morning; great is Your faithfulness." (Lamentations 3:22-23 NIV).* It was a new day and perspective.

Crying is good, y'all! Guys think we're full of drama and girly hormones, but they'd be better off if they closed their bedroom doors and had a good cry, too. Guys are infamous for not admitting frustrations until they blow their top instead of shedding tears. It's not a sign of weakness but humbleness that you've reached a limit you cannot bear alone. It's unhealthy to pin up emotions and push them aside. When you put a post-it note on it, feelings get buried under a stack that never gets handled.

The solution is always to give it to God! Go in your inner room and let it all out! Let crocodile tears flow as you ask God to work in the cloud that's hanging over your head (Matthew 6:6). Cry under the blankets or face down on the floor but give it to the One who sent His only Son to earth to walk with the distressed to save souls from hopelessness! Jesus came to serve the hurting in a broken world.

You are not a cry baby! You are a beautiful young woman who has human feelings that need to be released.

"Sing to Yahweh, you His faithful ones, and praise His holy name. For His anger lasts only a moment, but His favor, a lifetime. Weeping may spend the night, but there is joy in the morning."
(Psalm 30:5 HCSB)

Also: Psalm 107:6.

Take5forHIM

FEBRUARY 16

"Charm is deceitful, and beauty is vain.
But a woman who fears the Lord, she shall be praised."
(Proverbs 31: 30 NAS)

There's too much emphasis on physical appearance when the One who created us could care less about the outer self. Beauty comes from within, and we'll radiate an indescribable beauty as we grow closer to Christ.

Take5forHIM

FEBRUARY 17
Your Worth

"Are not two sparrows sold for a copper coin? And not one of them falls to the ground apart from your Father's will. But the very hairs of your head are all numbered. Do not fear therefore; you are of more value than many sparrows."
(Matthew 10: 29-31 NKJV)

If God cares so much for the well-being of a little bird and He knows how many strands of hair cover your head, why worry about the future or your value? Deliberate on that one.

FEBRUARY 18

Read Proverbs 31:10-31.

Why wait until you're an official adult (18 years old or a working woman) to aspire by the standards of a Proverbs 31 woman? Whether God's plan is to be a wife and mother or live singlehood, your goal should be to exemplify Proverbs 31.

Some of the text is difficult to identify in today's world, but the meat and potatoes is:
-Strive to be an excellent wife. She's more valuable than jewels.
-Trustworthy and loyal to a husband.
-She enjoys cooking, taking care of the home, and family- even if it means less sleep to get it all done.
-She reaches out to the needy and is a good example to her kids to do the same.
-She is positive and has a great outlook on the future.
-Above all, she loves the Lord!

FEBRUARY 19

"Therefore, everyone who hears these words of mine and puts them into practice is like a wise man who built his house on the rock. The rain came down, the streams rose, and the winds blew and beat against that house; yet it did not fall, because it had its foundation on the rock. But everyone who hears these words of mine and does not put them into practice is like a foolish man who built his house on sand. The rain came down, the streams rose, and the winds blew and beat against the house, and it fell with a great crash. When Jesus had finished saying these things, the crowds were amazed at his teaching, because he taught as one who had authority, and not as their teachers of the law." (Matthew 7:24-28 NIV)

Jesus' parables were unlike any teaching the people had ever heard. They were accustomed to the pounding of the law instead of life application. His parables are visual and relatable. This passage is a practical reminder that Christ is the solid rock and that all other ground is sinking sand. The ways of the world pull us in so many directions, but He provides a steady foundation.

Beach houses are a dream come true for many. The scenic view and serenity cannot be beaten- until a hurricane threatens. Definitely not calling out beach homeowners as fools, but when the storm surge floods into a shoreline it doesn't matter how high the pilings are beneath the house. If there's enough water and wind, the soft sand erodes, and the house succumbs. Insurance companies charge higher premiums for annual property insurance on beach property versus inland homes for a good reason. It's a fact that there's a high cost for dreamy living which cautions to be temporal and unstable. A repeated re-build for a steadier foundation may/may not be successful when the next storm hits land.

While waterfront beach homes weren't built in Jesus' day, His teaching is rational. He must've had a stage presence when He spoke. Envision a kind, gentle spirit, strong voice, an instant friend to all, an easy listening delivery, and an evident leader. He communicated to the people in a way that got them thinking. Over two thousand years later, His messages are timeless.

Take5forHIM

FEBRUARY 20
Hannah

The story of Hannah (the first two chapters of 1st Samuel) describes a young woman with exceptional character, faith, and dedication.

Background: There's tremendous discord in Old Testament stories when a man has more than one wife (Abraham, Hagar & Sarah; Jacob, Rachel & Leah, etc.). Hannah was married to Elkanah who was also married to Peninnah. Elkanah and Peninnah had children, but Hannah did not. It's horrible, but Peninnah is referred as Hannah's rival and that she bitterly pointed out her infertility. It was not a good situation. Plainly, God's best has always been for a man to have one wife.

Each year, the Israelites went to a nearby place called Shiloh to make their annual sacrifice to the Lord. This was most likely one of the annual festivals such as Passover. Elkanah gave portions of the sacrifice to Peninnah, and all of their sons and daughters. To Hannah, he would give a double portion "for he loved Hannah, but the Lord had closed her womb." Since she didn't have children, a double portion signified his special love for her.

While at Shiloh, she was distraught because she longed for a child. Elkanah tried consoling by asking why she was crying. He questioned whether she thought having ten sons was better than him which was totally insensitive for a husband to say to his barren wife. Why do you need kids when you have the love of your life?!?! She went to the Lord's house to pray. She was at the end of her rope and cried out to God. *"Deeply hurt, Hannah prayed to the Lord and wept with many tears. Making a vow, she pleaded, 'Lord, if you will take notice of your servant's affliction, remember and not forget me, and give your servant a son, I will give him to the Lord all the days of his life.'" (1 Samuel 1:10 HCSB)* Of all things, the priest Eli saw Hannah praying only with her lips moving and accused her of being drunk. She respectfully told him she was pouring out her soul to the Lord, asking for a son.

After leaving the temple, it's written that her face was no longer sad. The weight of the childless burden had been placed in the Lord's hands. It was a turning point.

The Lord answered her prayer by giving her a son, Samuel. After weaning him from nursing around 3 years old, she took him to the temple at Shiloh. She reminded Eli that she was the woman who prayed for a son, promising to give him back to the Lord to live and serve Him as long as he lived. She left her son with Eli, and Samuel grew into the godly man he was destined to become. What a strong woman to drop off her only child to be raised under the care of a priest!

Take5forHIM

Chapter two is Hannah's beautiful prayer worshipping the Lord. She belted out strong words praising Him as holy, the one and only judge, the giver, the provider, the rock, the creator of the world, the protector of His children, and verse 10, *"And He will give strength to His king. And will exalt the horn of His anointed."* (1 Samuel 2:10 HCSB) Many scholars believe she is prophetically speaking of God's everlasting kingdom under the future Messiah.

She's never mentioned after Chapter 2, but she was blessed with three sons and two daughters in addition to Samuel who grew up in the temple (verse 21).

Hannah showed a composed persona. She wasn't sassy with Peninnah for taunting remarks regarding infertility. And, she didn't answer Eli with a sharp tongue after insinuating she was drunk. Instead, she talked her walk without lashing back during distress. Many times, our mouths are brutal when we're stressed out. In lieu of harsh words, her mouth poured out to God to give her the desire of her heart.

"My heart exults in the Lord; My horn is exalted in the Lord,
My mouth speaks boldly against my enemies,
Because I rejoice in Thy salvation.
There is no one holy like the Lord,
Indeed, there is no one besides Thee,
Nor is there any rock like our God."
(1 Samuel 2:1-2 NAS)

"In the day of prosperity be happy. But in the day of adversity, consider—
God has made the one as well as the other so that man may
not discover anything that will be after Him."
(Ecclesiastes 7:14 NAS)

Take5forHIM

FEBRUARY 21

Take a few minutes to read Daniel 3- the story of Shadrach, Meshach and Abednego. Then, back up to Daniel 2:46-49 for the backdrop on the coolest guys in the Bible. This is a simple Bible story, but the lessons run deep.

King Nebuchadnezzar crafted a 90'x9' gold statue and commanded the people to bow down to worship the statue at the sound of horns, lyre, and other instruments. Anyone who did not worship the manmade gold statue would be thrown into a fiery furnace. Some Chaldeans took the opportunity to point out Shadrach, Meshach, and Abednego who were not obeying the king's command. Nebuchadnezzar questioned the three men and gave the ultimatum of blazing hot fire if they didn't worship the statue he created. The men were bold and spoke their feelings before hearing the trumpets.

"'Nebuchadnezzar, we don't need to give you an answer to this question. If the God we serve exists, then he can rescue us from the furnace of blazing fire, and he can rescue us from the power of you, the king. But even if he does not rescue us, we want you as king to know that we will not serve your gods, or worship the gold statue you set up.'" (Daniel 3:16-18 CSB)

The king didn't let them get the best of him, so the three men were bound and thrown immediately into the blaze. The king exclaimed, *"'Look! I see four men, not tied, walking around in the fire unharmed; and the fourth looks like a son of the gods.'"* *(Daniel 3:25 CSB)* The king approached the furnace door and called their names, and they walked over to him. Their hair was not singed; robes were not burned; and there was no smoky smell of fire. The king was absolutely astounded they were not affected, so he praised the God of the threesome! He decreed if anyone denounced God, they would be mistreated.

Our human nature wants God to save us before we're thrown in a fiery pit. We don't want to endure pain, so we pray ahead of time. "God, please don't let _____ happen. Protect me!" Many times, God allows bad times to come, but He's in the fire (or lion's den) with us. When the trial is over, we're stronger and more dependent. There are blessings when standing in a "bonfire."

*Scholars believe the fourth man in the fire was an angel or the pre-incarnate Son of God (pre-incarnate means before life or birth). How can that be? The Trinity of God the Father, God the Son, and the Holy Spirit have always existed. God SENT HIS ONLY SON to live on earth and He dwelled among us.

Take5forHIM

FEBRUARY 22
No Regrets

There's a sweet love story tucked in the depths of the fire breathing dragon and killing scenes in "The Hobbit" series: Tauriel and Kili.

In a defining moment in "Desolation of the Smaug", Kili courageously told Tauriel that he's not ashamed to express his feelings. Legolas made eye contact with her and poignantly said she's needed elsewhere, so she shied away just as in previous encounters. Torn with what to do, she turned back to look at Kili who wasn't giving up on their future. He placed a shiny stone in her palm and said, "Keep it as a promise."[5]

In the Battle of Five Armies, Kili died a gruesome death by the beast Bolg. Tauriel was distraught as she knelt beside Kili. She looked up at Thranduil and said, "If this is love I do not want it. Take it from me, please…. Why… does it hurt so much?" He replied, "Because it was real." Then she kissed her dead love goodbye.[6]

Such a tear jerker! They cared for one another, but never acted on it partly because she was an elf and he was a dwarf. Then it was too late.

We assume "one day" will come, but there's never a guarantee because others step in, circumstances change, and time is lost. Sometimes we must be the one to force a phone call, text, visit, or make a plan. Why assume the guy you're crushing will take action?

But not just in romantic love, also times such as: 1) resolving a friendship, 2) encouraging a depressed friend, 3) doing the right thing at the right moment, 3) visiting an elderly grandparent, or 4) befriending someone labeled as a misfit.

Don't fear rejection. Don't procrastinate. Don't live life with regrets, wishes, and "what if's," so take the first step!

"And just as you want people to treat you,
treat them in the same way."
(Luke 6:31 NAS)

"Love must be without hypocrisy. Detest evil; cling to what is good.
Show family affection to one another with brotherly love.
Outdo one another in showing honor."
(Romans 12:9-10 HCSB)

Take5forHIM

"Many a man proclaims his own loyalty, but who can find a truthworthy man? A righteous man who walks in his integrity— How blessed are his sons after him."
(Proverbs 20:6-7 NAS)

"A new commandment I give to you, that you love one another, even as I have loved you, that you also love one another. By this all men will know that you are my disciples, if you have love for one another."
(John 13:34-35 NAS)

"Beloved, let us love one another, for love is of God; and everyone who loves is born of God and knows God. He who does not love does not know God, for God is love."
(1 John 4:7 NKJV)

[5]*The Hobbit, The Desolation of Smaug.* Dir. Peter Jackson. Perf. Ian McKellen, Martin Freeman, Richard Armitage, Benedict Cumberbatch, Evangeline Lilly, Lee pace, Luke Evans, Stephen Fry, Ken Stott, James Nesbitt, Orlando Bloom. Warner Brothers Pictures, 2 December 2013.
[6]*The Hobbit: The Battle of the Five Armies.* Dir. Peter Jackson. Perf. Martin Freeman, Ian McKellen, Richard Armitage, Evangeline Lilly, Lee Pace, Luke Evans, Benedict Cumberbatch, Ken Stott, James Nesbitt, Cate Blanchett, Ian Holm, Christopher Lee, Hugo Weaving, Orlando Bloom. Warner Brothers Pictures, December 2014.

Take5forHIM

FEBRUARY 23

"Get up! Go to the great city of Ninevah and preach against it
because their evil has come up before me."
(Jonah 1:2 CSB)

Stop and read Jonah 1:1-3:10.

The prophet Jonah was given an exclamation point command from God to go- and go right this minute. Instead, Jonah tried to escape God by boarding a ship in the opposite direction. He panicked because he presumed a mission to the Ninevites was forlorn. So, God brewed a storm causing the boat's captain to question Jonah's part in bringing on turbulent weather. The men threw Jonah overboard to save their lives from perishing [and to calm the water]. Jonah was spared from drowning and gulped by a large fish (a whale?). He lived inside the whale for three days while he prayed and submitted to God's will before the whale delivered him to dry land.

The Lord again said, "Get up and go!" This time, Jonah went straight to the king and told him that the Lord said they must change their wicked ways, or the city would be demolished in forty days. The king took the message seriously by decreeing a mandatory food fast to call upon the name of the Lord, hoping the Lord may change his mind about destroying the city. The people obeyed the king's order, and God pardoned them from destruction. Mercy and grace.

Jonah was obedient, the king took it to heart, and so did the people. The end? Nope. In Chapter 4, Jonah was angry because he expected to watch the city burn down as he sat on the sidelines. The mission trip was successful, yet he pouted when God forgave the heathens so easily. Jonah stewed bitterly because the Assyrian city was an enemy to Israel. He knew of God's great mercy and compassion but couldn't understand why the Lord would have mercy on any territory other than Israel. He felt excessive guilt over his feelings and wanted to die for it. Jonah escaped to a shady place to settle.

"Then the Lord God appointed a plant, and it grew over Jonah to provide shade for his head to rescue him from his trouble. Jonah was greatly pleased with the plant. When dawn came the next day, God appointed a worm that attacked the plant, and it withered. As the sun was rising, God appointed a scorching east wind. The sun beat down on Jonah's head so much that he almost fainted, and he wanted to die. He said, 'It's better for me to die than to live.' Then God asked Jonah, 'It is right for you to be angry about the plant?' 'Yes, it's right!' he replied. 'I'm angry enough to die!' So the Lord said, 'You cared about the plant, which you did not labor over and did not grow. It appeared in a night and perished in a night. But may I not care about the great city

Take5forHIM

of Ninevah, which has more than a hundred and twenty thousand people who cannot distinguish between their right and their left, as well as many animals?' (Jonah 4 CSB)

The Gentiles in Ninevah were unaware of God before Jonah's arrival. God grew the plant to provide shade from the scorching heat, and then killed it as a means of teaching Jonah the lesson of His mercy towards the spiritually lost Ninevites. Bible commentaries explain that God showed Jonah his desire for all nations to receive salvation- not only the Hebrews (later known as Israelites; now as the Jews). Hundreds of years later, God sent Jesus to teach grace, mercy, and forgiveness to all.

FEBRUARY 24

An observation is that high school and college girls are uptight about academics around the clock. Don't stress over school and don't overload yourself or your stress can only be blamed on yourself. Time is too precious. *"Be anxious for nothing, but in everything by prayer and supplication with thanksgiving let your requests be made known to God."* (Philippians 4:6 NAS)

Take a breather. Add something to your day that differs your normal routine. Go to a new coffee shop or plan an activity you've never experienced. Rock climbing, rafting, hiking? Stress relievers.

FEBRUARY 25

Ever thought about how truly disgusting it is for a girl to hook up with one guy after another? It's not only promiscuous, it's gross. This is going to be graphic, but the thought of bodily fluids of the mouth and genitals and hands all over bodies, and then that girl doing the same sexual activities with another guy the next weekend. There's a good chance the guys have also had multiple sex partners, too. Ewwww! What's the difference in the promiscuity of a college girl versus that of a hooker [besides money]? Harsh, but thought stirring.

"Or do you not know that your body is a temple of the Holy Spirit who is in,
whom you have from God, and that you are not your own?
For you have been bought with a price;
therefore, glorify God in your body."
(1 Corinthians 6:19-20 NAS)

"Run from sexual immorality! Every sin a person can commit is outside the body.
On the contrary, the person who is sexually immoral sins again his own body."
(1 Corinthians 6:18 HCSB)

Paul said, "Now to the unmarried and the widows I say: It is good for them
to remain unmarried, as I do. But if they cannot control themselves,
they should marry, for it is better to marry than to burn with passion."
(1 Corinthians 7:8-9 NIV)

Take5forHIM

FEBRUARY 26

God promises to:
Love you- *John 3:16*
Give you eternal life- *1 John 5:11-13; John 10:10*
Hear your prayers- *2 Chronicles 7:14*
Give your life purpose- *Romans 12:1-2*
Guide- *Psalm 32:8*
Give wisdom- *James 1:5-6*
Makes you courageous- *Isaiah 41:10*
Give peace- *Philippians 4:6-7*
Comfort- *2 Corinthians 1:3-4*
Meet needs- *Hebrews 4:16*

FEBRUARY 27

Younger minds memorize and retain better than older brains. The more it's read, the more it's recalled. The importance of knowing scripture cannot be emphasized enough. Today, write a verse on an index card. Pull it out wherever you go during the day/week. Say it over and over until it sinks. Begin with the familiar John 3:16 or a more challenging verse. As faith grows, you'll depend on scriptures more to get through a hard day or witnessing to a friend. Thankfully, the Word is easily accessible on smart phones if the printed Bible is not nearby. We're spoiled by convenience, but it can never be robbed from your mind.

Next week, add another verse while not forgetting the first week's, and so on as weeks stack up. It's a great exercise as a small group, too.

FEBRUARY 28

Need a guide to charge up your prayer life? Pray by the ACTS model.

A is for Adoration. God is a magnificent and holy God. Show adoration for God, your Heavenly Father.
C- Confession. Ask for forgiveness for the known, secret, and unaware sins.
T- Thanksgiving. Thank God for all He has done and will do.
S- Supplication. Ask God to heal, work, wisdom, and anything on your heart.

FEBRUARY 29

More prayer advice. As scripture is memorized, add verses to prayers.

Dear Heavenly Father,
"Holy, Holy, Holy. The whole earth is full of your glory." (Isaiah 6:3 NAS) We are in awe of the beauty that You've made. Every blade of grass, the sun and stars, and Heaven that awaits us. You alone are worthy to be praised.

Forgive us for ___<insert sins>___. We have not loved our neighbors as ourselves nor been kind, tender-hearted, and forgiving, as You have forgiven us. May we increase and abound in love for one another and for all (1 Thessalonians 3:12). Strengthen our hearts so that we will be blameless and holy when we stand before You. Reveal our wrong-doings so that we will walk in Your path.

Create clean hearts and renew a right spirit within us (Psalm 51:10). Stir an affection to love You with all of our hearts, souls, strength, and might (Luke 10:27). May we rise up to be strong women who set an example in the privacy of homes and the public. Convict us before slander comes off the tongue to see the best in others and use our mouths to encourage one another and build each other up. *"Let no corrupt word proceed out of your (our) mouth, but what is good for necessary edification, that it may impart grace to the hearers." (Ephesians 4:29 NKJV)* God, use us in a genuine way that doesn't turn peers off from Christianity. Draw others to You through the modeling of our faith that they will see joyful living.

God, we pray to seek You first and not make boyfriends, finances, friends, jobs, college, money, stuff, or anything else come before you as an idol. Show us how to live by revealing Your magnificence and authority. Reign over our lives as Lord.

Fill us up, Holy Spirit. Amen.

MARCH

"See Christ in
everything, every day!"

-Take5forHIM

MARCH 1
Ashes, Lent, & Giving up Chocolate

Ash Wednesday is the first day of Lent as Easter approaches. Here are VERY basic answers about the season leading up to why we're called Christians.

Why does Easter fluctuate between March and April? Easter is determined by the first full moon after March 21. The date was established in 325 A.D. by the Council of Nicaea.

What is Ash Wednesday? Ash Wednesday is the first day of Lent. Easter Sunday's date is first established and then back up the calendar 46 days which is always a Wednesday. (Some explain it by calculating back 40 days excluding Sundays – 40 is the symbolic time of testing seen throughout the Bible. For example, rain for 40 days and nights during The Flood; the Israelites spent 40 years in the wilderness; Jesus fasted for 40 days in the desert and then was tempted by Satan.)

Lent is a time to repent sins and focus on Jesus' death and resurrection.

Why are ashes marked on the forehead during on Ash Wednesday service? Many Christians attend a church service in which ashes are rubbed on the forehead in the sign of a cross. Traditionally, the pastor will say something like, "We are born from dust and will return to dust." This is based on Genesis 3:19.

"By the sweat of your brow you will eat your food until you return to the ground,
since from it you were taken; for dust you are and to dust you will return."
(Genesis 3:19 NIV)

"Then the Lord God formed a man from the dust of the ground and breathed into his
nostrils the breath of life, and the man became a living being."
(Genesis 2:7 NIV)

Do you have to give up chocolate, sweets, soft drinks during Lent? No! Jesus made the ultimate sacrifice, so you do not have to "give up" a favorite food or social media. However, some denominations are very strict about abstaining. The purpose of a fasting is a reminder that Jesus sacrificed for you. I gave up chocolate one Lent. I cheated and couldn't do it- no will-power. That was the last time, and I'm OK with it although I have a lot of respect for those who do "give up" something. It's a personal decision.

How do Mardis Gras and Fat Tuesday relate to Ash Wednesday? Mardis Gras is the

Take5forHIM

French term for "Fat Tuesday." It's always the day before Ash Wednesday. Fat Tuesday can be traced to medieval Europe. The tradition followed France and later to New Orleans. Fat Tuesday is a day of feasting before 46 days of fasting. In other words-- eat, drink & be merry before 46 days without.

Is Easter more important than Christmas? Christmas is a favorite time of year, but we should celebrate Easter year-round as it was the single day in history that saved us from our sins. When Jesus died on the cross, He bled as the ultimate perfect lamb for the sins of the world. On the third day when He rose from the grave and walked out of the tomb, He crushed the sting of death. Think of Him rising against Satan and the people who crucified Him. He could have fought the death penalty. He could have come down from the cross- not even been nailed. Instead, He suffered, bled, and died on the cross to show His majesty and power on the third day. There is no other religion who serves a living, risen Savior.

Jesus' birth is a beautiful story of God coming to earth in a quiet, humble way as a baby to grow and live among us (Emmanuel- God is with us). And, His death & resurrection is also a touching story of God's Son humbly dying on the cross to save the world of their sins. And even more beautiful than that, the story of Jesus did not end because He's alive. Death could not hold Him in the grave, and He will reign forever!

What does it mean when people say the Spirit is living in us? Before Jesus' death and resurrection, people went to temples to pray. At Pentecost (see Acts 2), the formality ended, and a relationship began which is ah-mazing! Technically, people could have prayed to God anytime, anywhere because He was always there. But, the veil was torn at the moment of his death. The veil in the temple separated the people from the altar of God, so the torn veil symbolized the end of the separation between us and God. When you become a Christian, His spirit dwells in you.

"But God, who is rich in mercy, because of His great love with which He loved us, even when we were dead in trespasses, made us alive together with Christ (by grace you have been saved), and raised us up together, and made us sit together in the heavenly places in Christ Jesus, that in the ages to come He might show the exceeding riches of His grace in His kindness toward us in Christ Jesus." (Ephesians 2:4-7 NKJV)

"It was now about noon, and darkness came over the whole land until three, because the sun's light failed. The curtain of the sanctuary was split down the middle. And Jesus called out with a loud voice, 'Father, into Your hands I entrust my spirit.' Saying this, He breathed His last." (Luke 23:44-46 HCSB)

Hopefully this simplicated your questions!

Take5forHIM

MARCH 2

"Let us hold unswervingly to the hope we profess,
for He who promised is faithful.
And let us consider how we may spur one another
on toward love and good deeds,
not giving up meeting together, as some are in the habit
of doing but encouraging one another."
(Hebrews 10:23-25 NIV)

Don't let go of the truth of Jesus, God's only Son. Don't turn your back on Him, but cling tightly to the Bible and what you believe to be truth. Hold on unswervingly (not wavering).

MARCH 3
Leah: The Unbeloved

Isaac and Rebekah had two sons, Jacob and Esau. Their story is a biggie in itself. Esau was furious over their dad's inheritance, so Jacob fled from home to go live with their Uncle Laban. Jacob fell in love with his cousin Rachel. Laban said, "You can marry her if you work seven years for free." Jacob was so infatuated that he agreed. When the seven years was up, Uncle Laban said they could marry. At the wedding, the bride wore a veil which was customary. The next morning, he woke up in bed with the wrong bride. HE HAD BEEN TRICKED INTO MARRYING HER OLDER SISTER LEAH! Jacob was livid, but Laban justified that Leah was the oldest and he shouldn't have given the younger daughter in marriage before her. He said he could marry the girl of his choice if he worked another seven years, so love bitten Jacob agreed to another seven years.

The sisters bickered and didn't get along sharing the same husband, and Jacob favored his first love. Leah was not known to be the pretty sister, and she felt quite unloved knowing she had been pawned off to a man who didn't love her in return. Leah was blessed with children while Rachel was barren which caused even more friction. Sadly, after Leah and Jacob's first son Reuben was born she said, *"The Lord has seen my misery; surely my husband will love me."* When the second son was born she said, *"Because the Lord heard that I am unloved, He has therefore given me this son also."* After the third son was born, she hoped Jacob would be more attached to her because she had birthed three sons. When the fourth son, Judah, was born her attitude changed saying, *"This time I will praise the Lord."* (Genesis 29:31-35 HCSB)

Interestingly, God honored the first marriage as the inheritance line to Jesus NOT through the girl of his dreams nor Jacob's favored son Joseph (the first son of his beloved). Leah, the wife who struggled with inferiority and feeling unloved, was the multi-great grandmother of the Messiah. Judah, the one she praised God for giving, was Jesus' ancestor. This poor woman got the bad end of the stick from the beginning when her Dad slipped her in as Jacob's wife. Whatever sisterhood bond she had in the past ended at that moment. She obviously developed feelings for Jacob over time and with each child, she hoped to find favor in his sight. Through her hardship in a dysfunctional home, she turned to God and praised Him for the fourth son. Leah's heart changed and that must have pleased God so much that the honor of the future King Jesus came from Judah whose name means "praise."

Who thinks the Bible is boring?
Look up the following passages: Genesis 35:23-26; Genesis 49:10; Numbers 24:1; Psalm 60:7 and 108:8, God calls Judah His "scepter."

Take5forHIM

MARCH 4

Drugs are raging. You know that more any adult. Drugs and death caused by o.d.'ing are too common. What the heck is going on? What happened to those sweet faces from elementary school who are now walking the halls of high school glazed over and stoned at 8 a.m.? It's an epidemic! It's heartbreaking! Many wonder why HASN'T ANYBODY REACHED OUT TO WAKE THEM UP?

It begins with a couple of friends who are adventurous and bored. Someone can be book smart, but still be willing to "try it." "What's one time?" "It's just for fun?" "It's just weed." Weed is just the beginner, and it is an addictive drug. Then it may be coke, heroine, and meth. Drugs are a big vacuum trap that becomes a daily habit quickly.

Nobody intends to become dependent. There's not a hashtag called #addictiongoal. It's no different than being pulled into a rip current. They test the water even though there are double red flags. They're aware they shouldn't step foot, but it's a gorgeous day and the water looks calm from the shore. They go out and all the sudden cannot get back to the white sandy beach. They furiously try swimming back, but the current pulls them farther out. They've heard that swimming parallel to land is the best way to safety, but they just want to stay above water. They panic. Their lungs can't take it any longer, so they succumb to death by drowning. Drugs are no different. Why test the water when there are double red flags?

Another harsh reality: Drug users have no idea if the drugs are mixed in the correct ratios. Sounds weird to say but true; therefore, the improper mixes cause overdosing and other extremities. The dealers DO NOT CARE! They could care less about safety, they just want to sell it. If they get caught, it won't be because they mixed drugs incorrectly. They're not licensed pharmacists! Their business is to make a buck to support their lifestyle habits and keep themselves fed. Satan is loving dragging each one down the miry pit of hell on earth. He wants to kill, steal and destroy.

Don't get sucked into a dangerous riptide you cannot swim out! It's a rough life, and you cannot be certain you'll swim to safety. Fill your mind with good stuff and far away from: trying to be cool; trying to fit in with a certain group; trying to fill a void; trying to numb pain. Nothing, absolutely nothing, will satisfy your soul except Jesus! Be addicted to Jesus!

"The thief comes only to steal and kill and destroy;
I have come that they may have life,
and might have it abundantly."
(John 10:10 NAS)

Take5forHIM

MARCH 5
Not a Prophet

"In the past God spoke to our ancestors through the prophets at many times and in various ways, but in these last days he has spoken to us by his Son, whom he appointed heir of all things, and through whom also he made the universe. The Son is the radiance of God's glory and the exact representation of his being, sustaining all things by his powerful word. After he had provided purification for sins, he sat down at the right hand of the Majesty in heaven. So he became as much superior to the angels as the name he has inherited is superior to theirs." (Hebrews 1:1-4 NIV)

Although Abraham, Isaac, Jacob, and Moses all seem to be way up there in the religious realm, Jesus is above all. He was not a prophet or called to do a certain task. He is King of Kings and Lord of Lords, God's one and only Son. He is superior to these men, prophets, and angels; God in the flesh.

MARCH 6

Paul said in his letter to the Philippians, "I have learned to be content in whatever circumstances I am. I know both how to have a little, and I know how to have a lot. In any and all circumstances I have learned the secret of being content- whether well fed or hungry, whether in abundance or in need. I am able to do all things through Him who strengthens me." (Philippians 4:11-13 HCSB)

Can you say the same?

MARCH 7

"For to which of the angels did He ever say,
'You are my Son; today I have become your Father.'"
(Hebrews 1:5 HCSB)

In the Bible, angels are appointed as messengers or to travel ahead. Most Jews believed angels were divine, but the author of Hebrews is teaching that Jesus was God's Son, fully man/100% God. Divine.

MARCH 8
Being Humble with Giving

Jesus said, "Be careful not to practice your righteousness in front of others to be seen by them. If you do, you will have no reward from your Father in heaven.

So when you give to the needy, do not announce it with trumpets, as the hypocrites do in the synagogues and on the streets, to be honored by others. Truly I tell you, they have received their reward in full. But when you give to the needy, do not let your left hand know what your right hand is doing, so that your giving may be in secret. Then your Father, who sees what is done in secret, will reward you." (Matthew 6:1-4 NIV)

Give quietly without seeking recognition. An anonymous gift comes from the heart.

MARCH 9

"And when you pray, do not be like the hypocrites, for they love to pray standing in the synagogues and on the street corners to be seen by others. Truly I tell you, they have received their reward in full. But when you pray, go into your room, close the door and pray to your Father, who is unseen. Then your Father, who sees what is done in secret, will reward you. And when you pray, do not keep on babbling like pagans, for they think they will be heard because of their many words. Do not be like them, for your Father knows what you need before you ask Him." (Matthew 6:5-8 NIV)

Huh??? Did that sound familiar? Did you look back at yesterday's message thinking today's was a repeat? Almost, but Jesus transitioned from talking about giving humbly- not like a showman; to praying humbly- not like a phony.

Have you ever been in a room when someone starts praying and it rolls like a memorized speech? Don't misunderstand, one can have the gift of speaking articulate, heartfelt prayers. Then there are fervent prayers which lack sincerity. It's in the tone of voice.

When praying aloud in a group, it's OK if you get tongue tied, disconnect with random sentences, and reach in the air for a lost train of thought. God knows pure genuineness from the fake. It's not for an audience approval, but for His ears.

Take5forHIM

MARCH 10

Jesus said this is how to pray:

The Lord's Prayer
"Our Father who art in heaven,
Hallowed be Thy name.
Thy kingdom come.
Thy will be done,
On earth as it is in heaven.
Give us this day our daily bread.
And forgive us our debts, as we also have forgiven our debtors.
And do not lead us into temptation, but deliver us from evil. For thine is the kingdom,
and the power and the glory forever. Amen." (Matthew 6:9-13 NAS)

Take5forHIM

MARCH 11

Have you ever gazed at a beautiful sunset? Been in awe of the beauty of mountains? Let the calming sound of the waves put you in a trance? Stood still at the sight of a rainbow? There are so many picturesque scenes every day of God's creations. Scenes that cause one to say, "How can anyone not believe in the God and Creator of the Universe when they see that?!?!?!"

"For since the creation of the world His invisible attributes,
His eternal power and divine nature,
have been clearly seen, being understood through
what has been made, so that they are without excuse."
(Romans 1:20 NAS)

MARCH 12
Touching the Hem

Jesus was on his way to heal a man named Jairus' dying daughter when...

"While He was going, the crowds were nearly crushing Him. A woman suffering from bleeding for 12 years, who had spent all she had on doctors yet could not be healed by any, approached him from behind and touched the hem of His robe. Instantly her bleeding stopped.

'Who touched Me?' Jesus asked.

When they all denied it, Peter said, 'Master, the crowds are hemming You in and pressing against You.'

'Someone did touch Me,' said Jesus. 'I know that power has gone out from Me.' When the woman saw that she was discovered, she came trembling and fell down before Him. In the presence of all the people, she declared the reason she had touched Him and how she was instantly cured. 'Daughter,' He said to her, 'your faith has made you well. Go in peace.'" (Luke 8:43-48 HCSB)

Can you imagine having your period for 12 years? Bible scholars believe this is the type of bleeding implied. A bleeding woman was shunned as unclean and regarded spiritually unworthy in the religious community. So "unclean" that anything she touched was also considered dirty. We dread five to seven days, every 28 days. Can you imagine no tampons or disposable maxi pads, but cloth that has been hand washed and hung to dry many times? No laundry detergent, just boiled water? Life was hard! Most likely the woman was also very moody, grumpy, whiny, tired, and hard to live with! She had been to a multitude of doctors, yet she believed if she could just weave through the crowd, Jesus could heal her. She was desperate.

She was weak and discouraged after 12 years of doctors who could not help. In their ancient day of medical care, we cannot fathom what she physically endured as doctors examined and prescribed remedies. What was impossible for man to heal, was possible for Jesus even if she only touched His garment.

What if......Envision being so sick that you rushed to the medicine cabinet for ibuprofen? The med becomes your hope because your head feels like it's going to crack wide open. The med doesn't relieve the pain, so you pop another one and drink caffeine. Then your Mom goes to the pharmacist asking for a better medication. It doesn't work. The next day you go to the doctor, but he's unsure what more can be done. Then you wait four days for a second opinion with a highly recommended

Take5forHIM

physician. Every day is more miserable than the one before. On appointment day, you wait an hour and then another 30 in the examination room. The doctor comes in, asks 20 questions, examines, and suggests something new. Days later, the pain has not subsided. Imagine how low her spirits must have been after 12 years of let-downs that nothing cured her from bleeding. When she heard of Jesus' miracles, she may have left home with all the strength and determination left in her body to get to Him. She had run out of options, and she took a huge risk funneling in the crowd with those who may have recognized her as "the bleeding woman."

Not only did she know she was immediately healed, He knew power had gone out from His body. A bit fearful to be singled out, she admitted being the one. Our gentle Savior called her "daughter" and proclaimed that her faith healed her. Any protests from the mob were silenced when He called her daughter- not woman. Worthy to be called daughter by the Son of God was music to her ears. This sent a message that men and women are created equal in the eyes of God. Generally speaking, women were considered lower class to men in those times. Something we take for granted, but a woman in B.C. days did not.

Applying her story---
We want life to be good, but our definition of good is not guaranteed. Whether it's physical affliction or what seems an impossible life crisis, S—T—R—E—T—C---H your arms to meet Jesus where you are. His perfect plan may not be physical healing, but to heal spiritual wounds. He gives our lives purpose and hope for a glorious life in Heaven----free of all diseases ---by putting our faith in Him.

"What is impossible with men is possible with God."
(Luke 18:27 HCSB)

Take5forHIM

MARCH 13

If anyone slaps the religious label on your forehead, rectify your preference is be known as a Christ follower. You don't want to be known as religious, rigid, and ritualistic. You want to be grounded; live a moral life that honors the Lord; one who stands up for God's ways; exhibit an attitude which glorifies God; integrity that reflects Christian ideals; speech and conduct that's admirable- all which echo Jesus.

"For by grace you have been saved through faith; and that not of yourselves, it is the gift of God; not as a result of works, that no one should boast. For we are His workmanship, created in Christ Jesus for good works, which God prepared beforehand, that we should walk in them."
(Ephesians 2: 8-10 NAS)

MARCH 14
Cussin'

My Daddy once said, "There ain't nothing worse than a pretty girl cussin'!" It's like two things that don't mix: cereal and water; water and grease; orange juice and toothpaste; a girl and potty mouth.

Cursing mirrors the heart. When someone is mad, bitter, angry, hateful- that black heart comes pouring out of the mouth. Therefore, a beautiful girl is suddenly very unattractive in eyes of the beholder and her Creator.

What's worse than any four-letter word? Saying "J-C," "G-D," or any other form of slander against our God. He is the one and only true God, the creator of every living thing seen & unseen, your Creator. He is Majestic, Holy, Righteous, Omniscient, the Alpha & Omega, Almighty God, King of Kings, the Author of Salvation. He is worthy of respect.

Whether you're frustrated, angry, or in temptation- take a deep breath and hold your tongue. It's just wrong, and pastors should be preaching full sermons on the Third Commandment; however, I cannot ever recall hearing one. God shows unlimited grace and mercy, but the name above all names deserves reverence.

Some bicker that words like "gosh," "darnit," "gee whiz," "dad-gummit," "frickin" are just as bad as saying the real word. Once, I got an earful from a preachy guy who scolded me for saying "Oh my gosh" and "golly." I snapped back an apology but let him know he was on the verge of legalism. For me, it's southern slang, and not intended to be irreverent. The best counsel is to examine your mouth as to whether it needs detoxing. You'll know better than anyone.

"You shall not take the name of the Lord your God in vain,
for the Lord will not leave him unpunished who takes His name in vain."
(Exodus 20:7 NAS) The Third Commandment

"A good man brings good things out of the good stored up in his heart,
and an evil man brings evil things out of the evil stored up in his heart.
For the mouth speaks what the heart is full of."
(Luke 6:45 NIV)

"May these words of my mouth and this meditation of my heart
be pleasing in your sight, Lord, my rock and my redeemer."
(Psalm 19:14 NIV)

Take5forHIM

MARCH 15

Take5forHIM is not proposed to be the only source of spiritual enrichment [because the thirst for more can never be quenched]. There are topics on these pages that nobody else wants to touch, and hopefully the "tell it like it is" approach is fresh and vital. There are, however, stupendous books available as additional aids for solid theology. Avert from authors who merely shout optimism instead of a higher level of teaching. Pursue deeper knowledge- even if it's over your head.

The below prayer was extracted from a book of combined prayers written by Puritans during the 1800's, "The Valley of Vision." There's not one prayer that's better than the next. They're fabulous and gripping. The Puritans exhibited humility and confidence in their faith. Their prayers resonate solid theology, staunch, devout, and a continuous desire for deeper knowledge. It's satisfying to reckon the different levels of spirituality. Generations have been zealous for Jesus. Their intense contemplations have been written on paper and preached in pulpits. Reading a prayer like this one whips up excitement for our infinite God who listens to His sheep's prayers.

Thou Great I AM,

Fill my mind with elevation and grandeur at the thought of a Being
  with whom one day is a thousand years,
  and a thousand years as one day,
A mighty God, who amidst the lapse of worlds,
  and the revolutions of empires,
  feels no variableness,
  but is glorious in immorality.
May I rejoice that, while men die, the Lord lives;
  that, while all creatures are broken reeds,
  empty cisterns,
  fading flowers,
  withering grass,
  he is the Rock of Ages, the Fountain
  of living waters.
Turn my heart from vanity,
  from dissatisfactions,
  from uncertainties of the present state,
  to an eternal interest in Christ.
Let me remember that life is short and
  unforeseen,
  and is only an opportunity for usefulness;
Give me a holy avarice to redeem the time,

Take5forHIM

so that I may feed the hungry,
clothe the naked,
instruct the ignorant,
reclaim the vicious,
forgive the offender,
diffuse the gospel,
show neighbourly love to all.
Let me live a life of self-distrust,
dependence on thyself,
mortification,
crucifixion,
prayer.[7]

[7]Bennett, Arthur (Editor). *The Valley of Vision: A Collection of Puritan Prayers and Devotions*. The Banner of Truth Trust, 1975, 2002, 2003. Print.

MARCH 16
Throwing Stones

"At dawn, he went to the temple complex again, and all the people were coming to Him. He sat down and began to teach them.

Then the scribes and the Pharisees brought a woman caught in adultery, making her stand in the center. 'Teacher,' they said to him, 'this woman was caught in the act of committing adultery. In the law Moses commanded us to stone such women. So what do You say?' They asked this to trap Him in order that they might have evidence to accuse Him.

Jesus stooped down and started writing on the ground with His finger. When they persisted in questioning Him, He stood up and said to them, 'The one without sin among you should be the first to throw a stone at her,'

Then He stooped down again and continued writing on the ground. When they heard this, they left one by one, starting with the older men. Only He was left, with the woman in the center. When Jesus stood up, He said to her, 'Woman, where are they? Has no one condemned you?'

'No one, Lord,' she answered.

'Neither do I condemn you,' said Jesus. 'Go, and from now on do not sin anymore.'

Then Jesus spoke to them again (the people who He was originally teaching), saying, 'I am the light of the world. He who follows Me shall not walk in darkness but have the light of life.'" (John 8:1-12 HCSB)

Who are we to judge when we are all sinners?

Unlike the bleeding woman who sought Jesus to be healed (Luke 8:43-48) and the woman who washed His feet with her tears (Luke 7:36-50), the adulterous woman was brought to Him. She didn't come on her own free will, so her situation was totally different. She was shameful as she was drug by a group of men to be judged after being caught "in the act." She may have worn little clothing or a skimpy blanket that barely covered her. Embarrassing and humiliating!

Women were condemned for being caught in bed with another man's wife or just hooking up for the night. In their culture, women were to be seen and not heard- inferior to men. Even though it takes two to tango, the man got off the hook because he was not the sinner- in man's eyes.

Take5forHIM

The Pharisees were thrilled to bring the woman to Jesus because they couldn't wait to hear what the man many claimed to be the Son of God would say. They were looking for any way they could slap Him with a blasphemy charge. The Pharisees were quick to brutally hurt and maybe kill her with pebbles right off the ground but were oblivious to their own hearts of stone. Instead, Jesus started writing in the dusty sand with his finger although it's unknown what He wrote. With calmness and a lack of condemnation towards the woman, He convicted them of the sin in their hearts that whoever is without sin should cast the first stone. This was not what they expected. As they walked away, maybe they thought, "This is useless. We cannot get Him to cave in, not even raise His voice."

She and Jesus were left standing there. He asked where they went and if anyone stoned her. She said, *"No one."* He replied, *"Neither do I [condemn you]." (HCSB)*

The big take away that's rarely pulled out is the phrase, *"Go, and from now on do not sin anymore."* Jesus-told-her-to-go-and-sin-no-more. He forgave and expected her to turn away from adultery. Christ redeems us when we ask forgiveness, but He expects us to walk from the sin- TO CHANGE. Be so repulsed by sin, so thankful that He deluged grace over you, that you have no desire to go back to old ways. Be nauseated by former sin.

After Jesus told her to sin no more, He went back to teaching the people before being interrupted. The next words out of His mouth were, *"I am the light of the world. He who follows Me shall not walk in darkness but have the light of life." (John 8:12 HCSB)*

Take5forHIM

MARCH 17

All you need is Jesus. It's true, but kinda not. Jesus should be our number ONE, but we need PEOPLE, too. The brick and mortar of a church building isn't pertinent, but a community of believers and to hear God's Word on a regular basis are essentials. Ultimately, we need people whether it's in a church or social setting. We need like-minded friends _and_ those God's placed in our lives who are much different so that we can provide an across the board view of what being a Christian is all about.

A college girl once said, "I have so many friends of different backgrounds because I'm involved in so many organizations on campus. I think God just wants me to show them love. We're all sinners and we all have different kinds of sin, so I just listen and love [rather than preach]." She's learned much about life, compassion, and redemption by having a wide variety of friendships.

We're not meant to be alone. PEOPLE NEED PEOPLE. People need you! Don't preach-just LOVE, LISTEN, and answer questions biblically.

"For where two or three gathered in my name, I am there among them."
(Matthew 18:20 HCSB)

"When Job's three friends heard of all this evil that had come upon him,
they came each from his own place, Eliphaz the Temanite, Bildad the Shuhite
and Zophar the Naamathite. They made an appointment together to come
to show him sympathy and comfort him."
(Job 2:11 ESV)

"A man of many companions may come to ruin,
but there is a friend who sticks closer than a brother."
(Proverbs 18:24 ESV)

"Two are better than one, because they have a good reward for their toil.
For if they fall, one will lift up his fellow. But woe to him who is alone when
he falls and has not another to lift him up!"
(Ecclesiastes 4:9-10 ESV)

Take5forHIM

MARCH 18

"...whatever is true, whatever is honorable, whatever is just, whatever is pure, whatever is lovely, whatever is commendable..."
(Philippians 4: 8 HCSB)

Recently someone posted this verse on social media. It's invigorating after scrolling through pictures, political rants, bragging rights. Use your phone to encourage others.

*Follow Take5forHIM on social media for spiritual encouragement and ministry updates.

Take5forHIM

MARCH 19

Broken relationships cause sleepless nights, tossing and turning, headaches, and other emotional effects. Do you have an unsettled relationship? Confrontation is agonizing. Adults struggle with apologies, too. It's even more laborious to reach out to mend hard feelings with someone who has wronged you.

End the stress. Be the peacemaker. What does the Bible say? Read Matthew 5:9, Matthew 7: 12, 1 Thessalonians 5: 13, Mark 11:25.

*A NOTE ABOUT PROVIDING SCRIPTURE TEXT. I spoil girls with many typed verses for reading convenience, but it's therapeutic to mix it up by searching verses on your own. The objective is to get in THE WORD.

MARCH 20

Abram (later known as Abraham) was promised to father a great nation and that his old-aged barren wife Sarai (later known as Sarah) would have a son. Sarai became impatient when she didn't become pregnant, so she took matters in her own hands by telling Abraham to have sex with her maidservant Hagar (Genesis 16:1-4). He agreed, and Hagar became pregnant. An angel of the Lord appeared to Hagar and said,

"You have conceived and will have a son. You will name him Ishmael, for the Lord has heard your cry of affliction. This man will be like a wild donkey. His hand will be against everyone, and everyone's hand will be against him; he will settle near all his relatives." (Genesis 16:11-12 CSB)

There was horrendous rivalry between Sarah and Hagar, especially after the birth of Isaac. She told Abraham that her son Isaac would not be a co-heir with Ishmael and to send Hagar and "her" son out of "their" land. Abraham was stressed out, so he talked to God about Sarah's insistence.

"But God said to Abraham, 'Do not be distressed about the boy and about your slave. Whatever Sarah says to you, listen to her, because your offspring will be traced though Isaac, and I will also make a nation of the slave's son because he is your offspring." (Genesis 21:11-13 CSB)

The next morning, Abraham sent Hagar and their fourteen-year old son away. Hagar wept loudly when she and Ishmael were out in the wilderness alone.

"God heard the boy crying, and the angel of God called to Hagar from heaven and said to her, 'What's wrong, Hagar? Don't be afraid, for God has heard the boy crying from the place where he is. Get up, help the boy up, and grasp his hand, for I will make him a great nation.' Then God opened her eyes, and she saw a well. So she went and filled the waterskin and gave the boy a drink. God was with the boy, and he grew; he settled in the wilderness and became an archer. He settled in the Wilderness of Paran, and his mother got a wife for him from the land of Egypt." (Genesis 21:17-21 CSB)

The land that was given to Ishmael is what's known as the Arab nation, and he's said to be the father of the Muslim faith. Ishmael's land was divided into Twelve Tribes (see Genesis 17:20) just as there were Twelve Tribes of Israel from Abraham's grandson thru Isaac, Jacob. The boundaries of their lands are specified in Numbers 34:1-12. Both sons fathered large territorial nations.

Take5forHIM

There's always been conflict between Israel and the Arab nation throughout the Bible and it roars still today. They've bickered and fought over land and have held a grudge over Abraham's sons by different mothers (see Genesis 16:11-12 above). Hagar was sort of the innocent bystander in the family collision but told that her son would father a great nation, and God kept the promise. Arabs are blessed with sitting on a wealth of oil, which is one of the world's greatest fuel suppliers. Hagar's son was blessed with a nation, but not a father.

Think deeper on today's lesson. What effects did Sarah's mating tactic have on the region's history? Do you think it was right/wrong of Sarah to make the suggestion? Should Abraham have consulted God before having sex with another woman? Referring to Genesis 21:11-13, why did God tell Abraham to do whatever Sarah said? Do you think Ishmael stored up anger against his father which fueled fire between the two nations over thousands of years? How do you think he became the father of Muslims?

MARCH 21

May the road rise to meet you,
May the wind be always at your back.
May the sun shine warm on your face,
The rains fall soft upon your fields.
And until we meet again, May God hold you in the palm of His hand.
May God be with you and bless you,
May you see your children's children.
May you be poor misfortune,
Rich in blessings,
May you know nothing but happiness from this day forward.
May the road rise to meet you
May the wind always be at your back,
May the warm rays of sun fall upon your home,
And may the hand of a friend always be near.

May green be the grass you walk on,
May blue be the sky above you,
May pure be the joys that surround you,
May true be the hears that love you.
-Author Unknown

MARCH 22

"You shall love the Lord your God with all your heart and
with all your soul and with all your mind."
(Matthew 22: 37 ESV)

We were created to worship. Are you going to worship the King of Kings or are you going to worship yourself, your car, your friends, your stuff? It's hard to digest but take a personal assessment. Verse 38 following says, "This is the greatest and most important commandment." All of this was said right out of Jesus' mouth. Let's worship Jesus!

MARCH 23

Isaiah 53, referred as the Suffering Servant Passage, is one of the most well predicted and detailed passages describing Jesus' life, death, and resurrection. Take a few minutes to read the entire chapter.

> *"But he was pierced through for our transgressions,*
> *He was crushed for our iniquities;*
> *the chastening for our well-being fell upon Him,*
> *and by His scourging we are healed..."*
> *(Isaiah 53:5 NAS)*

Words like transgressions and iniquities are foreign words in our everyday language. Transgression is an act that goes against a law, rule, crime, or code of conduct. Iniquity is immoral and extremely unfair behavior.

MARCH 24
Praise God Almighty,
They Were Free at Last!

We sing praise songs about chains falling off, being set free, deliverance from the bondage of sin, and walking through the split sea. Such lines are referencing the release of the Hebrews (a.k.a. the Israelites and later known as the Jews) from 430 years of Egyptian slavery, led by Moses and brother Aaron. The Hebrews were God's chosen people. God told Abraham he would be the father of a great nation and his descendants would greatly multiply. Years later, they became slaves in Egypt and mistreated with long days of hard physical labor. The Hebrews thought they had been forgotten by God.

Moses came into the picture as a baby who's saved by the grace of God when all Hebrew baby boys were ordered to be killed because the Pharaoh said the Hebrew population was increasing too rapidly. By faith, Moses' mother put him in a basket in the Nile River not knowing Pharaoh's daughter would rescue the child and raise him in the palace. As an adult, Moses was proud of his heritage and preferred not to be considered royalty. Via a burning bush, God told Moses to plea with the current Pharaoh to free the Hebrews. Moses stuttered and questioned his leadership ability, but God didn't let him wiggle out. It's a long story, but the Egyptians suffered through a horrible series of Ten Plagues because every time Moses & Aaron went to Pharaoh requesting the people to be freed, he flat out said "NO!" So, the country endured water turned to blood, frogs, swarming gnats, dead cattle, awful open sores, locusts, hail, complete darkness, and lastly the death of the first-born males in every single home.

In Exodus 12, God descriptively told Moses & Aaron about a new tradition for their people. He gave specific instructions: kill a lamb, how to cook, eat, and dispose of the bones. God told them to brush the blood of the slain lambs above and around the doors of their homes so that when He comes over Egypt to sweep death of the first males (the last plague), He would not bring death to the Hebrews. He furthermore said this would be called the Passover feast and it shall be celebrated every year throughout the generations and told how God spared lives with the blood-stained doorframes. This was the first step of the Exodus (great departure) release from slavery. The Hebrews did exactly as God said. There was a great wailing of grief throughout Egypt as first-born males died that evening, including the Pharaoh's son. Pharaoh sent word for the Hebrews to "GET OUT," SO THE WORD SPREAD QUICKLY TO THE 600,000 HEBREW MEN PLUS WOMEN AND CHILDREN (totalling about 2 million). They fled on foot with their belongings and livestock.

Take5forHIM

There was trouble when Pharaoh regretted the decision, so he sent his army to go after them. When they almost reached the Red Sea, Moses and the Hebrews saw the Egyptians approaching. They feared, but Moses held out his staff which God had given him to perform miracles and the sea parted. Amazingly, there was dry sand as the 2 million crossed the Red Sea literally running for their lives. Once the last person reached the other side, the Egyptian army was already on the open path. When the Hebrews were safely on land, the sea merged and drowned the army.

The Hebrews WERE FREE!! THEY CRIED, CHEERED, HUGGED, PRAISED THE LORD, AND BOWED DOWN TO WORSHIP THEIR GREAT GOD. "THEIR CHAINS FELL OFF," THEY WERE SET FREE. HALLELUJAH!!!

Freedom by the blood, grace, & redemption of the Lord Jesus Christ is a visual parallel of Passover and the Hebrews' freedom.

Although it may seem fictitious, never doubt the miraculous story of the Red Sea. Today's Jews affirm the story and take the Passover observance very seriously. Our belief that Jesus is the Messiah separates us from equivalent religious beliefs, but Jews and Christians embrace this narrative—which we believe foreshadows Jesus' coming.

The Israelites killed the Passover lambs next to the front door where they were about to sprinkle the blood. When they painted the blood with the brush, they first touched the top horizontal part of the doorframe, then each side post (the vertical sides). In doing this, they went through the motions of making the sign of a bloody cross, the prophecy of another Passover sacrifice to come centuries later. Thus, the door was "sealed" on all four sides with the blood of the lamb.[8]

When the blood dripped from the top of the door to the ground, it was a symbol of Jesus whose blood would drip from his body nailed on the cross to below his feet. Isn't that the coolest thing ever?

"And you shall take a bunch of hyssop, dip it in the blood that is in the basin, and strike the lintel and the two doorposts with the blood that is in the basin. And none of you shall go out of the door of his house until morning."
(Exodus 12:22 NKJV)

Jesus said, "'I am the door. If anyone enters by me, he will be saved and will go in and out and find pasture.'"
(John 10:9 ESV)

[8]Rosen, Ceil and Moishe. *Christ in the Passover: Why is this night different?*. Moody Press. 1978, 31-32.

The Jewish traditions of the Passover feast are intriguing. For years, I've enjoyed the book "Christ in the Passover" as an enlightening source to learn more about the traditions, foods, and rituals. Jews are unaware that almost everything about the feast points to Jesus. Messianic Jews (Jews who have become Christians) embrace the Jewish and Christian holidays as a full circle enhancement celebrating Israelite heritage and God's son being born to die as a final sacrifice for their sins.

A prominent food term is unleavened bread (matzo is most well-known food item).

> The leaven in yeast is what causes dough to puff up and rise. In the Bible, leaven was a symbol of sin. The unleavened bread represented the sweetness and wholesomeness of life without sin. It foreshadowed the sinless, perfect life of the Messiah, who would come to lay down His life as God's ultimate Passover Lamb. They ate it at the first Passover to represent starting fresh from Egypt to walk as a new nation before the Lord.[9]

"Seven days you shall eat unleavened bread, and on the seventh day there shall be a feast to the Lord. Unleavened bread shall be eaten for seven days; no leavened bread shall be seen with you, and no leaven shall be seen with you in all your territory. You shall tell your son on that day, 'It is because of what the Lord did for me when I came out of Egypt.'" (Exodus 13:6-8 ESV)

> The matzo bread is a flat, unleavened like wafer. The baker pricks the dough with a fork and rolls lines down the dough with something similar to a pizza cutter to prevent even the slightest bit of rising. Since educated on the meanings and symbolism, we correlate the matzo to verses such as: "But He was pierced because of our transgressions, crushed because of our iniquities; punishment for our peace was on Him, and we are healed by His wounds"(some translations say stripes) (Isaiah 53:5) and Zechariah 12:10.[10]

Isn't it bodacious how God instituted these rituals thousands of years ago and it's still practiced by Jewish people today?

[9]Rosen, Ceil and Moishe. *Christ in the Passover: Why is this night different?*. Moody Press. 1978, 28-30.
[10]Rosen, Ceil and Moishe. *Christ in the Passover: Why is this night different?*. Moody Press. 1978, 70.

Take5forHIM

MARCH 27

Why are Jews called God's chosen people? Did He care about the other people in Bible times? Are Jews still his favorites?

God told Abraham he would be the father of many nations. His grandson Jacob's name was changed to Israel (Genesis 32:28). The Hebrews were then called Israelites, and the Twelve Tribes of Israel were formed from Jacob's sons. The land was divided and named for each tribe. The word Jew derived from Judah, one of the tribes centered in Jerusalem. Hebrew, Israelite, and Jew are used synonymously to describe the descendants of Jacob.

> God created every living soul and He cares about every living soul. He chose Israel to teach all nations about Himself- to be an example and witness to the existence of the one true and living God: "Ye, are my witnesses, saith the Lord, and my servant whom I have chosen...I, even I, am the Lord...ye are my witnesses, saith the Lord, that I am God." Isaiah 43:10-12[11]

The Israelites drifted many times which disappointed God. The Old and New Testament stories of bouncing back and forth to God are no different than people today. They were the people God made a covenant with to be an example of true followers, but their sinful natures were no different than anyone who has ever lived.

So, who are God's favorites? God loves everyone because He uniquely created all people. His desire is for all to acknowledge Him as their God. He hears the prayers of His people, those who have accepted Him as their Lord and Savior. Jews, Gentiles, and all nationalities who have chosen to follow Him for thousands of years. Heaven is adorned by those who called upon Him as the Lord their God.

"The Lord is near all who call on Him, to all who call on him in truth. He fulfills the desire of those who fear Him; He also hears their cry and saves them. The Lord preserves all who love him, but all the wicked He will destroy. My mouth will speak the praise of the Lord, and let all flesh bless his holy name forever and ever." (Psalm 145:18-21 ESV)

[11]Rosen, Ceil and Moishe. *Christ in the Passover: Why is this night different?.* Moody Press. 1978, 7.

Take5forHIM

MARCH 28

What does it mean to have the fear of the Lord? It's not a negative or nervous phrase such as "I'm shaking in my boots!"- fearing God is gonna strike. Rather, fear is: reverence, respecting His Holy Name, awe, adoring, honoring, having full confidence, thankfulness, and trust in the Lord. "Fear of the Lord" is mentioned hundreds of times in the Bible. It is utter acknowledgement and surrender to God as Lord over your all.

Discover a better understanding of fear by reading the following verses: Proverbs 1:7; Proverbs 8:13; Ecclesiastes 12:13; Job 28:28; Psalm 33:8; Proverbs 14:27; Proverbs 14:26; Psalm 25:14; Deuteronomy 10:12; Psalm 111:10; Psalm 86:11; Luke 1:50; Proverbs 19:23; Acts 10:35; Proverbs 2:1-6; Psalm 145:19; Exodus 20:20; Deuteronomy 31:12; Acts 9:31.

"The fear of the Lord is the beginning of wisdom;
All those who practice it have a good understanding.
His praise endures forever!"
(Psalm 111:10 ESV)

MARCH 29

"Life is like a camera. Focus on what's important; capture the good times; develop from the negatives. If things don't work out, take another shot."

"Is the glass half full or half empty?"

"Two men looked out a prison window. One saw bars, the other stars.

Jesus said there will be hardships, right? How you handle losing the car keys; nixed from a scholarship; a girl getting the attention of the boy you like; poor tips one night of bussing tables; forgetting a homework assignment; getting fired because you didn't show up for work (wrote the wrong work schedule down for the week)- is all matter of perspective. Whether it's a genetic disposition, there's no reason to get so bent out of shape that cuss words come off your lips. Make up your mind that mishaps will not rob your joy.

Job (pronounced Jobe) in the Bible is a great one to study when it comes to extreme adversity. Job was a godly man who experienced one trial after another. He lost everything- money, family, health yet gained patience. He asked "why" often, but his character emerged. In Job Chapter 2, his body was covered with boils (terrible sores). His wife asked, *"'Do you still hold fast your integrity? Curse God and die!' But he said to her, 'You speak as one of the foolish women would speak. Shall we receive good from God, and shall we not receive evil?' In all this, Job did not sin with his lips."* (Job 2:9-10 ESV)

It's effortful to stay on the positive side when the feedback from others is negative, but Job persevered because he maintained the correct perspective that God was in the middle of it with a purpose. *"In all this, Job did not sin with his lips."*

Verses to point to when an attitude arises:
> *"Now who is there to harm you if you are zealous for what is good?"*
> *(1 Peter 3:13 ESV)*

"Either make the tree good and its fruit good, or make the tree bad and its fruit bad, for the tree is known by its fruit. You brood of vipers! How can you speak good, when you are evil? For out of the abundance of the heart the mouth speaks. The good person out of his good treasure brings forth good, and the evil person out of his evil treasure brings forth evil. I tell you, on the day of judgment people will give account for every careless word they speak, for by your words you will be justified, and by your words you will be condemned." (Matthew 12:33-37 ESV)

Take5forHIM

MARCH 30

The Lord's Supper, commonly known as Communion, is a ritual all Christian churches participate on a regular basis as a remembrance of Jesus' death on the cross. It's also referred to as the Last Supper as it was Jesus' last meal with the disciples, which happened to be their Passover meal (Matthew 26:17).

Denominations have different guidelines about who can participate in Communion. Some pastors announce that only those who are in Christ can partake of the elements; some say all are welcome to the table. The bread and the wine (usually grape juice) are symbolic and very meaningful for the believer. It's a time in which believers are quiet, reflective, and prayerful about the sacrifice Jesus made for us.

"As they were eating, Jesus took bread, blessed and broke it, gave it to the disciples, and said, 'Take and eat it, this is My body. Then He took a cup, and after giving thanks, He gave it to them and said, 'Drink from it, all of you. For this is the blood that establishes the covenant; it is shed for many for the forgiveness of sins. But I tell you, from this moment I will not drink of this fruit of the vine until that day when I drink it in a new way in My Father's kingdom with you.' After singings psalms, they went out to the Mount of Olives." (Matthew 26:26-30 HCSB)

*The metaphor of the body and blood are figuratively speaking- not literal.

Like oftentimes when Jesus spoke allegorical terminology, the disciples didn't understand the meaning or the unfolding of events within the next 24 hours and three days later.

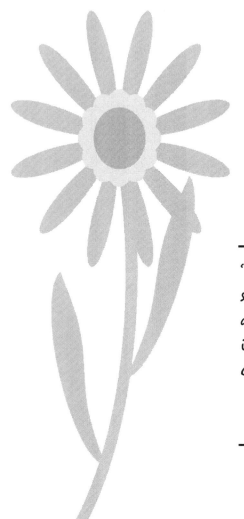

APRIL

"The cross shows us the seriousness of sin— but it also shows us the immeasurable love of God."

-Billy Graham

Take5forHIM

APRIL 1

Do you fully understand why Jesus had to die on the cross?

I've been a Christian most of my life, but I didn't understand until recent years when it was simply explained. I stop and think really, really hard about it every now and then so that I can wrap my head around it because the concept is hard to understand in our culture. So here goes....

In Bible times, they sacrificed perfect sheep as an offering to God during the Passover which commemorates the liberation of the Israelites from Egyptian slavery (Read Exodus 14- crossing the Red Sea). The sheep was the pre-cursor of the perfect sacrifice- Jesus. God was very clear to Moses and Aaron the rules for the Passover meal which included not breaking any bones of the lamb which was sacrificed (Exodus 12:46). It was their belief system, and their way of worshipping God to give Him thanks for freeing them from slavery.

Jesus' death was prophesied that the perfect lamb would be slain, and His bones would not be broken (John 19: 36 & 37). That's why you hear the phrase referring to Jesus as "the Lamb of God- the one who takes away the sin of the world" (John 1:29), first called so by John the Baptist. Jesus was the final sacrifice. Because God is so perfect in all His ways, Jesus was crucified on the Passover. He paid the ultimate price on the cross for our sins- liberating us from the bondage of sins.

At the moment of His death, the veil of the temple which separated us from God was torn (see Matthew 27:51). In those days, people went to the synagogue to pray and even then, there was a curtain separating one from the altar. He died so that we can live in unity with the triune of the Holy Father, Son & the Holy Spirit.

"He protects all of his bones; not one of them is broken."
(Psalm 34:20 HCSB)

"Jesus let out a loud cry and breathed His last. Then the curtain of the sanctuary was split in two from top to bottom. When the centurion, who was standing opposite Him, saw that He breathed His last, he said, 'surely this man was God's Son.'"
(Mark 15:37-39 HCSB)

"But he was wounded for our transgressions;
he was crushed for our iniquities;
upon him was the chastisement that brought us peace,
and with his stripes we are healed."
(Isaiah 53:5 ESV)

Take5forHIM

APRIL 2

"It was now about noon, and darkness came over the whole land until three in the afternoon, for the sun stopped shining. And the curtain of the temple was torn in two. Jesus called out with a loud voice, 'Father, into your hands I commit my spirit.' When he had said this, he breathed his last. The centurion, seeing what had happened, praised God and said, 'Surely this was a righteous man.' When all the people who had gathered to witness this sight saw what took place, they beat their breasts and went away. But all those who knew him, including the women who had followed him from Galilee, stood at a distance, watching these things." (Luke 23:44-49 NIV)

The significance of the curtain splitting in the temple at the moment of Jesus' death is enormous. Here's the historical background.

At the time, the holy temple in Jerusalem was the center of Jewish life. It was the place where animal sacrifices and worship according to the Law of Moses was followed faithfully. It's uncertain the curtain's exact measurements, but Jewish writings indicate it was around 60 feet high and a heavy four inches thick. The book of Exodus says it was elaborately made of blue, purple and scarlet fine twisted linen (Exodus 26). The curtain separated the Holy of Holies- the earthly dwelling place of God's presence- from the rest of the temple where men were allowed to worship. Only the high priest was allowed to go behind the curtain (or veil) once each year for the Jewish Day of Atonement Festival (Exodus 30:10; Hebrews 9:7) to enter into God's presence for all of Israel and make atonement for their sins (Leviticus 16).

The Book of Mark says that the earth shook, the rocks split, and the curtain was torn at Jesus' death <Goose Bumps>. The torn veil symbolized the changed religious system of the Law. Jesus' sacrifice, the shedding of His own blood as the perfect Passover Lamb on the cross, and His foretold resurrection opened the door to God without any curtains dividing us from the Holy One (Matthew 17:22-23, Matthew 20:18-19, Matthew 26:31-32). No temple made with hands could separate us from God from that day forward. The built temple was actually destroyed by the Romans in 70 A.D.

> *"The God who made the world and everything in it,*
> *being Lord of heaven and earth,*
> *does not live in temples made by man."*
> *(Acts 17:24 ESV)*

Hallelujah! We don't walk miles to a temple to pray. We enter the Holy of Holies, so to speak, any time of day by praying to our Lord Jesus. He's walking in and beside us always.

Take5forHIM

APRIL 3

"Later, Joseph of Arimathea asked Pilate for the body of Jesus. Now Joseph was a disciple of Jesus, but secretly because he feared the Jewish leaders. With Pilate's permission, he came and took the body away. He was accompanied by Nicodemus, the man who earlier had visited Jesus at night. Nicodemus brought a mixture of myrrh and aloes, about seventy-five pounds. Taking Jesus' body, the two of them wrapped it, with the spices, in strips of linen. This was in accordance with Jewish burial customs. At the place where Jesus was crucified, there was a garden, and in the garden a new tomb, in which no one had ever been laid. Because it was the Jewish day of Preparation and since the tomb was nearby, they laid Jesus there." (John 19:38-42 NIV)

Who was this man, Joseph of Arimathea who asked to bury Jesus?

"Now when evening had come, there came a rich man from Arimathea, named Joseph, who himself had also become a disciple of Jesus."
(Matthew 27:57 NKJV)

"Joseph of Arimathea, a prominent council member, who was himself waiting for the kingdom of God...."
(Mark 15:43 NKJV)

"Now there was a man named Joseph, from the Jewish town of Arimathea. He was a member of the council, a good and righteous man who had consented to their decision and action; and he was looking for the kingdom of God."
(Luke 23:50-51 ESV)

Other than these verses, scholars believe he was a high counselor, a voting member of the Sanhedrin which officially wanted Jesus condemned to death. They considered Jesus as blasphemous in his claims to be the Son of God. There's speculation that Joseph did not agree to push Pontius Pilate to have Jesus crucified, but believed Jesus was the Messiah.

Joseph's burial fulfilled the prophecy in Isaiah 53, "And they made his grave with the wicked and with a rich man in his death, although he had done no violence, and there was no deceit in his mouth."
(Isaiah 53:9 ESV)

So, who is Nicodemus in the John 19 passage? He was also a member of the Jewish ruling council. His one-on-one encounter with Jesus can be read In John 3. Look forward to a devo on his story on May 16.

Take5forHIM

APRIL 4

Fun fact: The books of Matthew, Mark, Luke, and John are called the Books of the Gospels. Each book tells of Jesus' birth, life, death, and resurrection. Many of the same stories are in all four books, but with slightly different accounts. During Easter season, thumb through all four books to read through Holy Week from Palm Sunday to Easter.

APRIL 5

Regarding yesterday's message that all four gospels are similar with slightly different accounts, so is true on Resurrection Day. Who found the empty tomb? Mary Magdalene- definitely. Who was with her? A couple of the books say Mary, the mother of James, or "the women" which is assuming it's both Marys. There are also variations of Mary seeing a gardener who was Jesus, angels, and a young man (an angel) sitting inside on the right side of the tomb. Don't get hung up on what was the true account. The nuts and bolts: THE TOMB WAS EMPTY!

"When the Sabbath was over, Mary Magdalene, Mary the mother of James, and Salome bought spices so that they might go to anoint Jesus' body. Very early on the first day of the week, just after sunrise, they were on their way to the tomb and they asked each other, 'Who will roll the stone away from the entrance of the tomb?' But when they looked up, they saw that the stone, which was very large, had been rolled away. As they entered the tomb, they saw a young man dressed in a white robe sitting on the right side, and they were alarmed. 'Don't be alarmed,' he said. 'You are looking for Jesus the Nazarene, who was crucified. He has risen! He is not here. See the place where they laid him. But go, tell his disciples and Peter, He is going ahead of you into Galilee. There you will see him, just as he told you.' Trembling and bewildered, the women went out and fled from the tomb. They said nothing to anyone, because they were afraid." (Mark 16:1-8 NIV)

The Jewish people observe the Sabbath from sundown on Friday until sundown on Saturday evening. This passage indicates that they waited until dawn the next morning to go to the tomb to anoint the dead body with oils and spices [to cover the decaying stench]. This was a common practice among Jews.

Matthew's account was that the chief priests and the Pharisees asked Pilate for a guard to watch the tomb for three days because Jesus said he would rise again in three days. They feared his body would be stolen by the disciples who would claim he had risen. Pilate sent a guard to keep watch. The guard was most likely a very strong, well-armed soldier type who took the job seriously. The rock is described as heavy and cumbersome. There's no way the women could unroll the stone, nor could anyone have gotten past the guard.

Hallelujah, the tomb was empty! He is risen; He is risen, indeed!

Take5forHIM

APRIL 6

Why do Christians observe the Sabbath on Sunday instead of Saturday as in the Bible? Since the creation, God established the seventh day as the day of rest. All throughout the Bible, Saturday (or the seventh day) is observed as the holy day of the week set aside for rest. You guessed it, because Jesus rose from the dead on a Sunday, the first day of the week, it became the new day of celebration. Jesus' resurrection changed everything.

"Therefore, just as sin entered the world through one man, and death through sin, and in this way, death came to all people, because all sinned—

To be sure, sin was in the world before the law was given, but sin is not charged against anyone's account where there is no law. Nevertheless, death reigned from the time of Adam to the time of Moses, even over those who did not sin by breaking a command, as did Adam, who is a pattern of the one to come.

But the gift is not like the trespass. For if the many died by the trespass of the one man, how much more did God's grace and the gift that came by the grace of the one man, Jesus Christ, overflow to the many! Nor can the gift of God be compared with the result of one man's sin: The judgment followed one sin and brought condemnation, but the gift followed many trespasses and brought justification. For if, by the trespass of the one man, death reigned through that one man, how much more will those who receive God's abundant provision of grace and of the gift of righteousness reign in life through the one man, Jesus Christ!

Consequently, just as one trespass resulted in condemnation for all people, so also one righteous act resulted in justification and life for all people. For just as through the disobedience of the one man the many were made sinners, so also through the obedience of the one man the many will be made righteous." (Romans 5:12-19 NIV)

Take5forHIM

APRIL 7

The Beginning of the Church: Day One

"When the day of Pentecost came (the formal beginning of the Christian church), they were all together in one place. Suddenly a sound like the blowing of a violent wind came from heaven and filled the whole house where they were sitting. They saw what seemed to be tongues of fire that separated and came to rest on each of them. All of them were filled with the Holy Spirit and began to speak in other tongues as the Spirit enabled them.

Now there were staying in Jerusalem God-fearing Jews from every nation under heaven. When they heard this sound, a crowd came together in bewilderment, because each one heard their own language being spoken. Utterly amazed, they said: 'Aren't all these who are speaking Galileans? Then how is it that each of us hears them in our native language? Parthians, Medes and Elamites; residents of Mesopotamia, Judea and Cappadocia, Pontus and Asia. Phrygia and Pamphylia, Egypt and the parts of Libya near Cyrene; visitors from Rom (both Jews and converts to Judaism); Cretans and Arabs- we hear them declaring the wonders of God in our own tongues!' Amazed and perplexed, they asked one another, 'What does this mean?' Some however, made fun of them and said, 'They have had too much wine.'" (Acts 2:1-13 NIV)

Pentecost or the Feast of Weeks was a Jewish holiday recognized fifty days after Passover as the harvest celebration commemorating God's provision and sustenance of His people. The Hebrew term for Pentecost (Feast of Weeks) is Shavuot. Exodus 23:16, Deuteronomy 16:10, Leviticus 23:15-21 describe how the holiday should be observed.

After reading several commendable articles, there's more significance than realized. There were numerous pilgrims in Jerusalem (see verses above) observing the Feast of Weeks. Jewish holidays were taken very seriously, so many traveled to their Holy City as it was a faithful custom to do so. Interpret this passage as a day of world evangelization not as the day of speaking in unknown tongues. It's said that 3,000 people were harvested into the kingdom of God on that day.

Take5forHIM

APRIL 8

The Beginning of the Church: Day Two

"Then Peter stood up with the Eleven, raised his voice and addressed the crowd: 'Fellow Jews and all of you who live in Jerusalem, let me explain this to you; listen carefully to what I say. These people are not drunk, as you suppose. It's only nine in the morning! No, this is what was spoken by the prophet Joel:

'In the last days, God says, I will pour out my Spirit on all people. Your sons and daughters will prophesy, your young men will see visions, your old men will dream dreams. Even on my servants, both men and women, I will pour out my Spirit in those days, and they will prophesy. I will show wonders in the heavens above and signs on the earth below, blood and fire and billows of smoke. The sun will be turned to darkness and the moon to blood before the coming of the great and glorious day of the Lord. And everyone who calls on the name of the Lord will be saved.'

'Fellow Israelites, listen to this: Jesus of Nazareth was a man accredited by God to you by miracles, wonders and signs, which God did among you through him, as you yourselves know. This man was handed over to you by God's deliberate plan and foreknowledge; and you, with the help of wicked men, put him to death by nailing him to the cross. But God raised him from the dead, freeing him from the agony of death, because it was impossible for death to keep its hold on him. David said about him:

'I saw the Lord always before me. Because he is at my right hand, I will not be shaken. Therefore my heart is glad and my tongue rejoices; my body also will rest in hope, because you will not abandon me to the realm of the dead, you will not let your holy one see decay. You have made known to me the paths of life; you will fill me with joy in your presence.'

'Fellow Israelites, I can tell you confidently that the patriarch David died and was buried, and his tomb is here to this day. But he was a prophet and knew that God had promised him on oath that he would place one of his descendants on his throne. Seeing what was to come, he spoke of the resurrection of the Messiah, that he was not abandoned to the realm of the dead, nor did his body see decay. God has raised this Jesus to life, and we are all witnesses of it. Exalted to the right hand of God, he has received from the Father the promised Holy Spirit and has poured out what you now see and hear. For David did not ascend to heaven, and yet he said, 'The Lord said to my Lord: Sit at my right hand until I make your enemies a footstool for your feet.'

'Therefore, let all Israel be assured of this: God has made this Jesus, whom you crucified, both Lord and Messiah.'

Take5forHIM

When the people heard this, they were cut to the heart and said to Peter and the other apostles, 'Brothers, what shall we do?' Peter replied, 'Repent and be baptized, every one of you, in the name of Jesus Christ for the forgiveness of your sins. And you will receive the gift of the Holy Spirit. The promise is for you and your children and for all who are far off—for all whom the Lord our God will call.' With many other words he warned them; and he pleaded with them, 'Save yourselves from this corrupt generation.' Those who accepted his message were baptized, and about three thousand were added to their number that day." (Acts 2:14-41 NIV)

Peter was sorta the first preacher who preached his first sermon. Can you imagine 3,000 converts in one day? And, when the people left Jerusalem after the Feast of Weeks (Pentecost), they went back to their homelands as new believers in the Lord Jesus Christ. Thus, world evangelization began as more and more Jews and Gentiles (anyone who is not Jewish) heard about the risen Messiah.

APRIL 9

The Beginning of the Church: Day Three

"They devoted themselves to the apostles' teaching and to fellowship, to the breaking of the bread and to prayer. Everyone was filled with awe at the many wonders and signs performed by the apostles. All the believers were together and had everything in common. They sold property and possessions to give to anyone who had need. Every day they continued to meet together with glad and sincere hearts, praising God and enjoying the favor of all the people. And the Lord added to their number daily those who were being saved." (Acts 2:42-47 NIV)

This was a new chapter for Jews as they were accustomed to teachings of laws which were handed to Moses. Jews didn't abandon their heritage, this was an enhancement and fulfillment because Jesus was the Messiah they waited for hundreds of years. While there was persecution from non-believing Jews who didn't understand because their ears were not open to this new faith, Peter and the apostles' ministry began to spread rapidly. Their new identity label was not Jew but Christian.

APRIL 10

The outcome after hearing extreme, diverse opinions while flipping news channels on the boob tube? ONE BIG HEADACHE. Even Christians squabble knit picky theological differences such as: Was creation literally a six day 24-hour time increment or were the six days on another time scale? Did Jesus share the same blood as Mary or did God place Jesus in her womb; therefore, was Mary strictly the human vessel to carry the Messiah? Debates on whether God pre-destined (or elected) who would become Christians or is salvation open to all? If so, is it due to God's omniscience because He already knows who will choose Him? Did the Great Flood really cover the entire world, and did Noah's family re-populate earth? Brilliant scholars contest their reasonings at conferences worldwide. Does any of it matter in the big picture? Is it going to make a difference in your salvation and eternal destination? (Answer: No)

Our God is mysterious, infinite, and HOLY. Man's eagerness for answers is natural, but regardless of how logical some of the scholars' conclusions, we'll never know the answers to many intellectual controversies. What we know of God is in His Word; the rest will be discovered in eternity.

"Even as he chose us in him before the foundation of the world, that we should be holy and blameless before him. In love he predestined us for adoption as sons through Jesus Christ, according to the purpose of his will." (Ephesians 1:4-5 ESV)

"So then, as through one trespass there is condemnation for everyone, so also through one righteous act there is life-giving justification for everyone." (Romans 5:18 HCSB)

"This is how the birth of Jesus the Messiah came about; His mother Mary was pledged to be married to Joseph, but before they came together, she was found to be pregnant through the Holy Spirit." (Matthew 1:18 NIV)

"But you, be fruitful and multiply; spread out over the earth and multiply on it.' Then God said to Noah and his sons with him, 'Understand that I am establishing my covenant with you and your descendants after you, and with every living creature that is with you- birds, livestock, and all wildlife of the earth that are with you- all the animals of the earth that came out of the ark. I establish my covenant with you that never again will every creature be wiped out by floodwaters; there will never again be a floor dot destroy the earth.'" (Genesis 9:7-11 CSB)

"God called the light Day, and the darkness he called Night. And there was evening and there was morning, the first day." (Genesis 1:5 ESV)

Take5forHIM

APRIL 11

"I in them, and You in me; that they may be made perfect in one,
and that the world may know that You have sent Me,
and have loved them as You have loved me."
(John 17:23 NKJV)

We are the body of Christ. We are family. This doesn't imply that all Christians are going to be instant friends, but we're unified.

The best friends you'll ever have are ones with similar interests. It's so true with Christian friends. Sharing highs and lows with a kindred spirit in Christ is the best BFF.

APRIL 12

It's enraging how adults are appalled by high school drinkers, but when their own kids enter college, it's suddenly accepted "because that's what college kids do!" I've been around parents who giggle about their kids turnin' 'em up. Well, here's a heavy dose of what's not swell!

Buzzing is one thing, but puking brains out is NOT. The fun is over when you're cleaning up sloppy projectile vomit off the walls and floor after you've run to the johnny to puke for the fourth time. There's nothing glamorous about wiping up the night's dinner of green beans, bacon, cornbread, chocolate ice cream, and your sober friend (OR MOM) does not find it cute at 2:20 a.m. The sight and smell are repugnant.

Now, for a 30-second advertisement. DO NOT GET BEHIND THE WHEEL OF A CAR OR LET ANYONE WHO IS UNDER THE INFLUENCE OF ALCOHOL DRIVE YOU HOME. Not only is there a prime chance of a DUI (a $10,000 mistake plus community service plus counseling plus an insurance premium increase plus attending a class where mothers of drunk drivers give DUI violators an earful about how their child was killed by a drunk driver), did you know you can register as legally drunk up to 5 hours after the last drink? Yep, the liver metabolizes approximately 1 ounce of alcohol per hour. The average person's blood alcohol level from one ounce of alcohol will rise to .015. A blood alcohol level of .08 is the legal limit for driving. FACTS!

If you haven't experienced a drunken state of losing self-control, remember, it's ugly and there's a price to pay at the end of the night when the bed is spinning or hanging on the toilet. The raunchy day following is wasted, too.

Party Girls: If you own this book and read the devotionals, then you are SET APART. You're either seeking to know Jesus or you know Him but choosing a double-life. Let's face it, nothing in the Bible means anything to the unbeliever. You, my dear, have at least an ounce of His Spirit living in you.

"See that you don't look down on one of these little ones, because I tell you that in heaven their angels continually view the face of My Father in heaven. For the Son of Man has come to save the lost. What do you think? If a man has 100 sheep, and one of them goes astray, won't he leave the 99 on the hillside and go and search for the stray? And if he finds it, I assure you: He rejoices over that sheep more than over the 99 that did not go astray. In the same way, it is not the will of your Father in heaven that one of these little ones perish." (Matthew 18:10-14 HCSB)

Take5forHIM

APRIL 13

<u>The Apostles Creed</u>
I believe in God, the Father almighty,
creator of heaven and earth.
I believe in Jesus Christ, his only Son, our Lord,
who was conceived by the Holy Spirit
and born of the virgin Mary.
He suffered under Pontius Pilate, was crucified, died,
and was buried; he descended to hell.
The third day he rose again from the dead. He ascended to heaven
and is seated at the right hand of God the Father almighty.
From there he will come to judge the living and the dead.
I believe in the Holy Spirit, the holy catholic church,
the communion of saints, the forgiveness of sins,
the resurrection of the body, and the life everlasting. Amen.[12]

If you've attended a traditional church service, most likely you've recited affirmations of faith such as The Apostles Creed. The Creed was written by a Council in Milan to Pope Siricius around 390 A.D., and it sums up the Christian faith.

It doesn't take many weeks of reciting a creed with a congregation for it to get implanted deep in the brain- as if a button is pushed and the robot speaks. Although regurgitating a memorized passage seems mundane, there's something very meaningful about a room full of believers professing aloud their Christian beliefs.

There are two phrases that usually beg explanations. It's easy to read as it affirms the trinity of God the Father, the Son, and the Holy Spirit, his birth, his death under the reign of Pontius Pilate and then ... whoah...."descended to hell?" The original Creed states "descended to the dead." "Descended to hell" was the phrase later edited. Did Jesus go to hell after He died? Figuratively speaking, He was separated from God the Father during the three days in the tomb. Secondly, the holy catholic church is the universal Christian church. FYI- the Catholic Church was the first original Christian denomination.

Traditional church services are unpopular with Generation Z, but there's much to be learned while singing old hymns and reciting a creed. It's not as humdrum as assumed.

[12]The Apostles Creed. *Trinity Hymnal*, Great Commission Publications, Inc., 1990, 845.

Take5forHIM

APRIL 14

"For this reason, I kneel before the Father, from whom every family in heaven and on earth derives its name. I pray that out of His glorious riches He may strengthen you with power through His Spirit in your inner being, so that Christ may dwell in your hearts through faith. And I pray that you, being rooted and established in love, may have power, together with all the Lord's holy people, to grasp how wide and long and high and deep is the love of Christ, and to know this love that surpasses knowledge— that you may be filled to the measure of all the fullness of God.

Now to Him who is able to do immeasurably more than all we ask or imagine, according to His power that is at work within us, to Him be glory in the church and in Christ Jesus throughout all generations, forever and ever! Amen." (Ephesians 3:14-21 NIV)

Our human minds have no comprehension of how wide, how long, how high and deep God's love is for us. We take it for granted. Breathe in the below verses because nothing can separate us from the love of Jesus.

Stop. Read Romans 8:31-39.

When downcast, let these verses be an anthem. Repeat after me, "NOTHING CAN SEPARATE ME FROM THE LOCATE OF CHRIST."

Take5forHIM

APRIL 15

Early Christians were persecuted for their new faith, including Jews. Daggers were thrown their way by family and the strong religious community. The author of the Book of Hebrews exalts the Son of God and encourages fellow new believers to press on in their new-found freedom of Christianity.

The Jews held high esteem for the high priest chosen by men. They respected him as their mediator to God through prayer and sacrificial offerings. Innocent animals were brought to the high priest as an offering to be sacrificed for their guilt or sins. Modernity is far extreme from the ideals of Bible times, so their religious system is extrinsic. It's perverse for our sterile mindsets to visualize a man carrying a sweet lamb or calf into the temple to be slaughtered and burned. Jesus not only died as the final sacrifice, but He also became the high priest. Read the below verses.

"For every high priest chosen from among men is appointed to act on behalf of men in relation to God, to offer gifts and sacrifices for sins. He can deal gently with the ignorant and wayward, since he himself is best with weakness. Because of this, he is obligated to offer sacrifice for his own sins just as he does for those of the people. And no one takes this honor for himself, but only when called by God, just as Aaron was (Moses' brother who was appointed as the first temple's high priest). So also Christ did not exalt himself to be made a high priest, but was appointed by him who said to him, 'You are my Son, today I have begotten you'; as he says also in another place, 'You are a priest forever, after the order of Melchizedek." (Hebrews 5:1-6 ESV)

"And every priest stands daily ministering and offering time after time the same sacrifices, which can never take away sins; but He, having offered one sacrifice for sins for all time, sat down at the right hand of God." (Hebrews 10:11-12 NAS)

"Therefore, brothers, since we have confidence to enter the holy places by the blood of Jesus, by the new and living way that he opened for us through the curtain, that is, through his flesh, and since we have a great priest over the house of God, let us draw near with a true heart in full assurance of faith, with our hearts sprinkled clean from an evil conscience and our bodies washed in pure water. Let us hold fast the confession of our hope without wavering, for He who promised is faithful. And let us consider how to stir up one another to love and good works, not neglecting to meet together, as is the habit of some, but encouraging one another, and all the more as you see the Day drawing near." (Hebrews 10:19-25 ESV)

Take5forHIM

APRIL 16
No Excuses

Girls, Girls, Girls, monthly hormones are not an excuse to be rude, unkind or sassy with friends and family. Everybody has days when we feel rotten or a little down, but don't treat the ones closest to you like dirt because of it. It's better to tame the tongue and not say a word than to say something regretful. There's a right way and a wrong way to say everything. Sometimes saying the same thing in a softer tone of voice makes all the difference. Read John 15: 1-11. Verse 11 ends with, *"These things I have spoken to you that my joy may be in you, and that your joy may be full."*

APRIL 17

Do you suffer from wonderlust? Not wanderlust as in the desire to travel and explore, BUT WONDERLUST- WONDERING IF THE NEXT STEP IS GOING TO BE BETTER THAN WHAT YOU'RE LIVING RIGHT NOW. Quite a few girls can't enjoy the life they're living because they're constantly thinking if they could just get to be a teenager, to drive, to go to Prom, to senior year, to college, to a sorority, find Prince Charming, to college graduation- then, life will be better. Don't confuse this with having dreams and goals because we need to reach to our highest potential, and believe the best is yet to come. Or, simply discontentment- thinking the next stage is going to be better than RIGHT NOW.

Don't miss opportunities—aspire for more—DREAM BIG—Work hard for the POT OF GOLD AT THE END OF THE RAINBOW—Take risks---Believe you're going to make a difference---"I'm going to save the world" mentality---Be ambitious---Don't settle for less---TAKE LEAPS OF FAITH---Get out of your comfort zone---YOU can do anything through Christ who strengthens YOU- BUT, enjoy TODAY's moments!

"Give thanks in all circumstances;
for this is the will of God in Christ Jesus for you."
(1 Thessalonians 5:18 ESV)

"Therefore do not be anxious, saying, 'What shall we eat?'
or 'What shall we drink?' or 'What shall we wear?'
For the Gentiles seek after all these things,
and your heavenly Father knows that you need them all.
But seek first the kingdom of God and his righteousness,
and all these things will be added to you.
Therefore, do not be anxious about tomorrow,
for tomorrow will be anxious for itself.
Sufficient for the day is its own trouble."
(Matt 6:31-34 ESV)

"The heart of man plans his way,
but the Lord establishes his steps."
(Proverbs 16:9 ESV)

Take5forHIM

APRIL 18

It's easy to play favorites. Eyes are visually drawn to beautiful people. It's our first impression. The opposite is also true. We are guilty of being prejudice against not so attractive or people unlike us.

Read James 2. It's convicting to read about the sin of showing partiality. It happens with teachers in the classroom, the workplace, and so many areas of life. Read and ponder James 2: 1-13 as the problem is addressed. Do you play favorites based on someone's appearance, wealth, status? If anything, we should give extra attention to the oppressed and lowly. Jesus did.

APRIL 19

Girls' friendships can be an up and down battle. Hate to say it, but girls are like cats-stay to themselves, hide under a bed, cuddle, or have a cat scratch fight. I'm a girl, and all of the above. Cat-like behavior is the culprit as to why many freshman friendships don't make it to senior year. Therefore, all girls need at least one guy friend for calming balance. Guys are laid back and chill. They'll listen because they're removed from the drama. If you have a guy friend who loves the drama, ditch'em 'cause he's ruining my point!

The positives are:
-Most guys let anything they hear slide off their back.
-Get a guy's perspective.
-Freedom to be yourself without fear of rejection.
-Guys don't get mad easily in a girl-boy friendship.
- Having a guy friend builds a comfort level with the opposite sex .
-Fun

Problem: Sometimes girls think the best scenario is to first be friends and then start dating. There are pros and cons, and it really depends. The big con? Most likely you'll break up and then you'll mourn the loss because the friendship will never, ever be the same. Once romance enters the picture, dynamics change, and you can't revert. The old adage, "Let's just be friends" is a tale because romance changes everything.

Advice: If you have a best friend who is a guy friend, don't let the "boy" friend interfere with your boyfriend. A boyfriend doesn't want competition. Jealousy ferments when you talk a lot about the friend, share dating details, hang out, and chat with him more than your BF. Share time with a multitude of friends, all of which will be a non-threat to your dating relationship.

Like girl friendships, seek a friend you can trust with deep dark secrets, provide advice, mutual respect, and clear boundaries. Find a guy who can be a good side by side friend- meaning there's absolutely no love interest. Look to him as a brother figure and use extreme caution if your heart starts fluttering.

"Therefore, as God's chosen people, holy and dearly loved,
clothe yourselves with compassion, kindness, humility, gentleness and patience.
Bear with each other and forgive one another if any of you has a grievance
against someone. Forgive as the Lord forgave you. And over all these virtues
put on love, which binds them all together in perfect unity."
(Colossians 3:12-14 NIV)

Take5forHIM

APRIL 20

Ever heard the phrase talking out of two sides of the mouth?

One evening at the dinner table, I was telling my family about running into a former co-worker in the Post Office parking lot that afternoon. She yacked for 30 minutes about office drama while I stood neutral with pursed lips. I told them I was glad not to no longer be working in that office environment.

Next conversation. Mom started wagging her tongue about someone and then another and then another until my sons left the table abruptly. I looked at my husband and said, "I blew it. What a terrible witness." I shut my mouth in silence, convicted of all I just said. I apologized and made it clear I had sinned, and it was wrong even if I justified my words with a humorous story. Sin is sin. Wrong is wrong. Read James 3- all of it!

Key phrases: "The tongue is a fire!" "It pollutes the whole body, sets the course of life on fire, and is set on fire by hell." "It is a restless evil, full of deadly poison." (HCSB)

APRIL 21

Easter's Over, Now What?

The climax of a pastor's big rah-rah message at the Easter Service about Jesus' resurrection lights us up- kinda like a one-day youth retreat. We're on a Jesus high in the church service and then……

Monday,
Tuesday,
and Wednesday come.
And then another week.

What you felt on Easter Sunday may be long gone. The chocolate bunny was devoured within days and thoughts of Jesus' resurrection……Hmmmm……not so much. You might not think about it again until the next church retreat. And if you miss the retreat, there's always next year for that "feel good time" to thumb through Matthew, Mark, Luke & John to read each writer's account of Holy Week.

How do you keep the jubilation? FOR THAT MATTER, how do you know the story is true, believing something that happened over 2,000 years ago? You're basing beliefs off what you've read in the Bible and what you've been taught [either from your parents or the church].

How do you shake doubts of Christianity?

First look at the disciples. They walked daily evangelistic paths and witnessed miracles yet when Mary ran to them with the empty tomb news, they did not believe. *("And when they heard that He was alive, and had been seen by her, they refused to believe it." Mark 16:11 NAS)* They believed once they had a face to face encounter. *("When therefore it was evening on that day, the first day of the week, and when the doors were shut where the disciples were, for fear of the Jews, Jesus came and stood in their midst, and said to them, 'Peace be with you.' And when He had said this, He showed them both His hands and His side. The disciples therefore rejoiced when they saw the Lord." John 20:19-20 NAS)* Thomas gets the bad rap of Doubting Thomas, but the others did not believe when they were first told either. Poor Thomas simply said he would not believe until he saw the mark of the nails and put his hand into His side. He had eight days to wait before the Lord Jesus appeared to him [with the other disciples]. Once Thomas saw and touched, he said, *"My Lord and My God." Jesus* replied, *"Blessed are they who did not see, and yet believed." (John 20:29 NAS)*

How could the twelve disciples not surrender their trust in Him? Judas betrayed Him by accepting silver from the soldiers in return for Jesus' location, and Peter denied Him out of embarrassment to be known as a Christ follower due to the dissention about "this Jesus." And, the men weren't convinced He rose from the grave until they saw Him with their own eyes.

So how can we believe what we have not seen?

Paul, the most influential evangelist in the Bible was not one of the disciples. He wrangled, rebelled, and resisted the Gospel. When Jesus revealed Himself (Acts 9:17-18), he was transformed. He was imprisoned, beaten, and eventually died for the cause of spreading the best news he'd ever heard. He believed without hearing a podcast or touching the nail driven scars.

The choice is to believe [or not believe] without seeing. I first believed because I grew up in a Christian home. Eventually I adopted it as my own faith. My prayer life has deepened to the extent that I'm praying for things I've never prayed before. God also places people on my heart and won't let me shake them outta my head. More than once, I've randomly run into someone after a strong bout of prayer. Striking up conversation, I realize why God put them on my heart. He wanted me to pray and disciple them. I've even had someone in mind and received a random prayer request text or a phone call for needed advice, for example. That's God- not coincidences.

The point is to make Jesus real in your life. Read THE WORD, pray deep prayers for wisdom, compassion, love for others, healing, and be the light on His behalf. Take ownership of your faith instead of practicing religion on the holidays. Like Paul, you'll be on fire for the Lord as the scales fall off your eyes knowing He alone is THE WAY, THE TRUTH, AND THE LIFE (John 14:6).

He is risen. He has risen indeed. Hallelujah! What a Savior!

(Read all of Acts 9 for an amazing conversion story and the beginning of Paul's ministry.)

APRIL 22

God's new covenant with His people was prophesied by Jeremiah in the Old Testament.

"Look the days are coming"- this is the Lord's declaration- 'when I will make a new covenant with the house of Israel and with the house of Judah. This one will not be like the covenant I made with their ancestors on the day I took them by the hand to lead them out of the land of Egypt- my covenant that they broke even though I am their master'- the Lord's declaration. 'Instead, this is the covenant I will make with the house of Israel after those days'- the Lord's declaration. 'I will put my teaching within them and write it on their hearts. I will be their God, and they will be my people. No longer will one teach his neighbor or his brother, saying, 'Know the Lord, for they will all know me, from the least to the greatest of them'- this is the Lord's declaration. 'For I will forgive their iniquity and never again remember their sin.'" (Jeremiah 31:31-34 CSB)

God's original covenant with His people was not the problem; the people were the problem. They turned their backs on Him and broke their commitment to follow Him. The above text is prophesying the new covenant that salvation thru faith in Jesus Christ would bring. We are the new covenant people. Hallelujah!

Take5forHIM

APRIL 23

Lord, I cover this reader in prayer today. Holy Spirit, run through her veins to work in and through her. Permeate her soul with Your spirit. May she be overwhelmed, hungering to know the Author of Life. Give her the desire to read Your Word more; pray often; depend on You for everything; choose You as her first love; and tell others how You give daily purpose.

Let her life reflect You from every viewpoint. I pray she will not conform to secular society but will be transformed into Your likeness. Surround her with Christian friends and may they be the light in the halls of campus, on the job, and wherever they go. I pray for academic success throughout the day of quizzes and tests. Tug her heart to give You a little time today, and may those moments be refreshing as she tackles a hectic schedule.

Give her a clean heart, mind, and mouth. I pray she will make good choices which will honor Your name. I pray for boldness to stand up for what is right in a society that is slipping away from You. Permeate her soul to become the godly woman You designed. In Christ's holy name. Amen.

APRIL 24

What's your weakness? Mine is decorating. I'd rather buy a lamp, pillows, or another home item than a piece of clothing. I love magazines and home decorating TV shows. I enjoy shopping estate sales and re-painting old furniture. It's a hobby and weakness. It's a good thing God didn't give wealth because I struggle with materialism. It's temporal happiness, so I keep the right perspective, re-focus, and turn my eyes back on the eternal.

We'll always struggle living in the flesh and world. There's nothing wrong with enjoying the things of this world as long as we keep priorities in line.

"Among them we too all formerly lived in the lusts of our flesh, indulging the desires of the flesh and of the mind, and were by nature children of wrath, even as of the rest. But God being rich in mercy, because of His great love with which He loved us, even when we were dead in our transgressions, made us alive together with Christ (by grace you have been saved), and raised us up with Him, and seated us with Him in the heavenly places, in Christ Jesus, in order that in the ages to come He might show the surpassing riches of His grace in kindness toward us in Christ Jesus." (Ephesians 2:3-7 NAS)

APRIL 25

*"How happy is the man who does not follow the advice of the wicked
or take the path of sinners or join a group of mockers! Instead,
his delight is in the Lord's instruction, and he meditates on it day and night.
He is like a tree planted beside streams of water that bears its fruit
in season and whose leaf does not wither."*
(Psalm 1:1-3 HCSB)

*"Blessed is the man who trusts in the Lord and whose trust is the Lord.
For he will be like a tree planted by the water, that extends its roots by a
stream and will not fear when the heat comes; but its leaves will be green,
and it will not be anxious in a year of drought nor cease to yield fruit."*
(Jeremiah 17:7-8 NAS)

Happiness is a life ambition. Parents adore smiles on their kids' faces throughout the growing years into a happy adulthood. You, in turn, desire it more than they can ever imagine. However, happiness cannot be achieved in circumstances, meeting a career goal, financial wealth, or by finding Mr. Wonderful. Happiness is brief, and at the end of life is a compilation of momentous memories. The text from Psalm 1 describes a lifestyle of happiness that's not short lived.

Trees planted along waterfronts don't depend on an irrigation system to thrive. Their roots are fed underground from water that slowly seeps upward from the body of water. The tree remains watered in droughts, but vegetation that's planted further from the waterfront, receive less and less moisture. Their leaves yellow and dry out. As Verse 3 suggests, happiness is found when our roots are grounded in the Lord for guidance and nourishment. In droughts, the Lord remains faithful for sustenance. We'll bear fruit and delight in the Lord in all seasons. This is the long-term happiness of joy-filled vitality.

Take5forHIM

APRIL 26

Trust is something built in drops but lost in buckets.

Friendships dissolve over trust issues. Trust is lost in marriages, friendships, and co-working relationships because sinners wag our tongues far too often. The sworn secret a friend shares or the juicy news is just too good to keep to ourselves. The consequences and lies to cover up the violation of trust are not worth the turmoil which dissolves ties. So, why do you put so much faith in trusting someone not to rattle off your business? Have you not done the same? Are you perfect? No. So, the moral of the story is to be careful who/what info you share.

"Even my close friend in whom I trusted, who ate my bread,
has lifted up his heel against me."
(Psalm 41:9 NAS)

"It is better to take refuge in the Lord than to trust in man."
(Psalm 118:8 ESV)

"A contrary person spreads conflict,
and a gossip separates close friends."
(Proverbs 16:28 CSB)

APRIL 27

We do not serve three gods. We serve the Triune God- three in one; God the Father, God the Son, and God the Holy Spirit. Questions like "who to address in prayers?" are confusing. Here's a stab at explaining the Trinity. Keep in mind, each person of the Trinity has certain characteristics but all three complement each other for one purpose.

God is the Creator who has always been and always will be. Where did He come from if He's always existed? That's unexplainable and will always be a mystery because there was no point of beginning in time. He created Heaven, Earth, the stars, the other planets, galaxies, and every person who has ever lived. He's the Father.

God sent His Son from Heaven as a baby to live and breathe among us, to teach, and to end the need for sacrificing animals as an expression of repentance. Jesus was the perfect lamb slain as an atonement for our sins. His resurrection is a picture of serving a living God. The Bible says He sits at the right hand of God the Father [in Heaven].

The Holy Spirit is God's spirit indwelling in us. The Spirit was a gift when Jesus was resurrected and ascended to Heaven.

Who to direct prayers? The most important point is to pray. Don't get hung up on whether to pray, "Dear God," "Dear Lord Jesus," or "Holy Spirit..." Savor the fellowship of knowing you can come to Him with all requests, praises, and pleas because He's always ready and waiting. In general, God is Father who reigns over all; Jesus is our intervener; the Holy Spirit is the one who moves and stirs hearts to change.

Examples of prayer:
"Dear God, thank you for your faithfulness. You are majestic and holy and just. I pray for....."

"Dear Jesus, I pray for Grandma Jones' heart surgery. I pray for healing and recovery. Strengthen her in the days ahead. Holy Spirit, work in her spiritual heart condition, too. Soften her heart to know You through this time of uncertainty as to whether she'll survive major surgery. I pray Holy Spirit that I will have an opportunity to share the gospel and pray with her. Speak through me. Jesus, please don't let her die without knowing You."

"that your faith should not rest on the wisdom of men, but on the power of God. Yet we do speak wisdom among those who are mature; a wisdom, however, not of this age, nor of the rulers of this age, who are passing away; but we speak God's wisdom in a mystery, the hidden wisdom, which God predestined before the ages to our glory;

Take5forHIM

the wisdom which none of the rulers of this age has understood; for if they had understood it, they would not have crucified the Lord of glory; but just as it is written, 'Things which eye has not seen and ear has not heart, and which have not entered the heart of man, all that God has prepared for those who love Him. For to us God revealed them through the Spirit; for the Spirit searches all things, even the depths of God...But a natural man does not accept the things of the Spirit of God; for they are foolishness to him, and he cannot understand them, because they are spiritually appraised." (1 Corinthians 2:5-10, 14 NAS)

Also read: Matthew 28:19; John 10:30; John 14:26.

Take5forHIM

APRIL 28

Switching channels to guy advice......

What's your opinion if a friend welcomed back her boyfriend after he cheated? Maybe he was "innocently" talking online to a girl in another state. Maybe he was messaging with a cheerleader at another high school. Maybe he had sex with an old girlfriend. Maybe he got drunk, hooked up with a random girl, and didn't "know what he was doing until it was too late." Maybe this wasn't the first time. Maybe it's happened once, twice, or times she doesn't know about. Whatever the excuse, would you support a friend's decision to stay together with her boyfriend? Answer?

Advice: She's a fool to continue dating a guy who doesn't care enough about her to be allegiant. If a guy cheats once, he shouldn't be given a second chance. The trust was zapped, and there's a good chance it will happen again.

Same goes for you. You deserve better, and cheating is a sore point of an unstable relationship.

> *"The one who lives with integrity lives securely,*
> *but whoever perverts his ways will be found out."*
> *(Proverbs 10:9 CSB)*

Take5forHIM

APRIL 29
Cancer Sucks!

Recently I spent a day taking a friend to cancer treatment. As I sat in the waiting room, it was humbling to see men and women wearing hats and scarves to cover bald heads. So tired and weary, one lady was even curled up in the chair napping. There was a cluster who must have frequent same time appointments. They were empathetic friends as they conversed about oncology appointments, side effects, and next steps. A part of me felt guilty as I sat for a mere 30 minutes looking at a decorating magazine, visualizing a bedroom paint color, and flipping pages of back porch ideas for a home project. I'm healthy with a long "to do" list for the day/week while my friend, the patients, and families seek a medical breakthrough to cure the poisonous disease that's ravaging their bodies. Life has come to a screeching halt, and nothing is more important. The desperation hit me as I drove through a terrible storm with the windshield wipers at full speed. At times I couldn't see the highway lines, but by golly she wasn't going to miss the recommended daily radiation that could extend or save her life. We were on a mission!

I wouldn't trade the day with the friend who has meant more to me than I could ever give to our friendship. She's been a rock over the years as she raised rambunctious children who are now grown adults. Over the years she encouraged me with life experiences of sticking through hard child rearing and being a prayer warrior wife and mother. Her testimonies of hard-core prayer [for her kids] inspired me to kneel at my kids' empty bedsides to pray in dark times in a way I never had before. Her once vigorous lifestyle of running and hiking is in the past. Her eyes unframed with eyelashes, slow moving steps, and weak body is too tired to carry on the same vigorous conversations. Her outlook is realistic, and it feels like empty words to say, "Hang on, God's holding you." Cancer sucks, so the only response is to listen, love, reminisce, and pray intense prayers for healing. It's hard to watch the suffering, and deep-down wonder if the end is near. God wants us to pour out prayers for the sick and depend on Him to do the rest. Never give up; pray mighty, bold, never ceasing, unrealistic prayers. While God may not heal the cancer, He has a glorious life in Heaven [for the Christian] when they step out of this world into the next. On that day while we'll weep the loss on earth, that diseased body will be renewed. The seeds and legacy of the Christian's life work will be accomplished, and then we'll naturally rejoice that God has called His child home.

People ask why God allows sickness and suffering. Jesus said, "In this life there will be trouble." We live in a broken world with sin, hurts, pain, and trials which all started when Adam and Eve ate the forbidden fruit. There will never be peace nor paradise on earth, but having a strong faith rooted in the Lord provides a degree of peace and comfort in out of control torment. His living word becomes a thread of hope when there's a plot twist in life.

"Rejoice always, pray without ceasing, give thanks in all circumstances;
for this is the will for you in Christ Jesus."
(1 Thessalonians 5: 16-18 NAS)

Jesus said, "I have told you these things, so that in me you may have peace.
In this world you will have trouble. But take heart! I have overcome the world."
(John 16: 33 NIV)

"He will wipe every tear from their eyes. There will be no more death
or mourning or crying or pain, for the old order of things has passed away."
Revelation 21:4 NIV)

"Brothers and sisters, we do not want you to be uninformed about those
who sleep in death, so that you do not grieve like the
rest of mankind, who have no hope."
(1 Thessalonians 4: 13 NIV)

"Haven't I commanded you; be strong and courageous?
Do not be afraid or discouraged, for the Lord your God is
With you wherever you go."
(Joshua 1:9 CSB)

APRIL 30

Jesus' last words were, "It is finished." Interpretation? After generations of Jews who repented of their sins by sacrificing animals, Jesus paid the last sacrifice by dying a horrific death on the cross. Our sins were paid by His blood, and the work of redemption was finished. Jesus, The Author of Salvation.

"After this, Jesus, knowing that all was now finished,
said (to fulfill the Scripture), 'I thirst.' A jar full of sour wine stood there,
so they put a sponge full of the sour wine on a hyssop branch
and held it to his mouth. When Jesus had received the sour wine,
he said, 'It is finished," and bowed his head and gave up his spirit."
(John 19:28-30 ESV)

MAY

"I give all the glory to God. It's kind of a win-win situation. The glory goes up to Him, and all the blessings fall down to me."

-Gabby Douglas after winning the Gold, Women's All-Around Gymnast

Take5forHIM

MAY 1

Stressed out about the final push of the school year? Drowning in textbooks, finals, and projects? Don't let academics consume you, find peace by searching for comforting verses to reschedule priorities.

"Out of my distress I called on the Lord; the Lord answered me and set me free."
(Psalm 118:5 ESV)

"Cast your burden on the Lord, and he will sustain you,
He will never allow the righteous to be shaken."
(Psalm 55:22 CSB)

Written thousands of years ago, but our God is the same God who brings comfort and calming words to weary and stressed lives.

Take5forHIM

MAY 2

"Therefore, since we also have such a large cloud of witnesses surrounding us, let us lay aside every weight and the sin that so easily ensnares us. Let us run with endurance the race that lies before us, keeping our eyes on Jesus, the source and perfecter of our faith, who for the joy that lay before Him endured a cross and despised the shame and has sat down at the right hand of God's throne." (Hebrews 12:1-2 HCSB)

A runner girl? This passage is for the race runners out there who run hearts (and legs) out to reach the finish line. Instead of a big banner and a time keeper clicking race times, picture Jesus standing at the finish line of heaven when you enter His presence. Keep your eyes on Jesus in the race of life.

"I have fought the good fight, I have finished the race, I have kept the faith."
(2 Timothy 4:7 CSB)

"But those who wait on the Lord shall renew their strength;
they shall mount up with wings like eagles; they shall run and not be weary,
they shall walk and not faint."
(Isaiah 40:31 NKJV)

Take5forHIM

MAY 3

My Daddy warned many times not to argue with anyone about politics or religion. "If you do, you'll either lose a friend or not make a new one." Although his gentle, non-confrontational nature steers from touchy conversations, there are times when it's fitting to defend beliefs. Many avoid the topic of religion fearing to say the wrong thing (being a poor representative).

It's better to pre-determine how to respond to tough questions and lines such as: "How do you know God is real when you cannot see or hear Him?" "Why did Jesus die on the cross? How do you know he rose from the dead?" "Jesus was a good man, but why do you think he was the Messiah?" "I don't have a problem with Jesus, but I'm sore with the church. They hurt me a long time ago, so I'm never steppin' foot in one again." "The Bible says _____ (and they rattle off garbage that you know isn't true, but you don't have an answer)" "Every time you see a red cardinal, that's a deceased loved one letting you know they're OK."

Pray if the situation arises that the Holy Spirit will speak through your mouth. More importantly, don't be defensive but speak in a kind tone of voice. Don't be pompous or self-righteous but speak out of love. Read 1 Corinthians 13:1-3.

"Who then will harm you if you are devoted to what is good? But even if you should suffer for righteousness, you are blessed. Do not fear what they fear or be intimidated, but in your hearts regard Christ the Lord as holy, ready at any time to give a defense to anyone who asks you for a reason for the hope that is in you. Yet, do this with gentleness and respect, keeping a clear conscience, so that when you are accused, those who disparage your good conduct in Christ will be put to shame. For it is better to suffer for doing good, if that should be God's will, than for doing evil." (1 Peter 3:13-17 CSB)

MAY 4

Butting heads with Mom? At your age, it can be a daily occurrence. I've been on both ends, as the daughter and as the mom. It stinks because neither want tension, but it's there.

Problem: It takes two to make a great relationship, and a lot of daughters push mothers out of their lives between 14-22 years old. The daughters who once were "Mommy's Little Girl" now want to do anything but bake cookies together. Female hormones under one roof is like two rams butting heads as a daughter seeks independence. And, many moms have a difficult time letting go, so WWIII erupts from many corners such as:

-Mothers have flashbacks of their own mistakes and don't want the same for their daughter.

-Mama's little girl growing up with her own plans is hard because up until now she's arranged the play dates. Mama Bear reacts with a tight grip.

-Girls become busy with after school activities, jobs, and friends. Quantity and quality time are limited.

-If you accidentally slip dirty details about a classmate and then months later say you're going out with X.....of course, Mom is going to flip! She only knows what you've told her, so her opinion is distorted until she hears positive info to approve the new friend is worthy to hang out with HER PERFECT CHILD. This, by all means, does not mean you should be hush mouth, but beware that what you share may bite back.

-Personality clashes! Heads butt when the daughter is not a mini-mom clone.

-Disagreements on clothing purchases!

-SOME girls are guilty of wanting mom to supply the cash flow yet downright hateful when it comes to carrying a conversation. "I'll be sweet when I want something." This begins the progression of buying love (or Mom trying to be her daughter's BFF) which is totally unhealthy. Moms become the debit card thus resent financial abuse with no reciprocation of appreciation or respect.

-Then there's the over-protective Mom who worries incessantly. She wants her daughter to call as soon as she gets to Point B (or phone tracks), ask permission for every little thing, and is obsessed with the daughter's world. The result is a daughter who sneaks, lies, and rebels because she feels smothered.

Moms have good intentions! Discipline and guidance are love actions, but a rebelling teenage girl doesn't appreciate anything her mom says right now.

If these scenarios are commonplace....

TAKE ACTION TO BREAK THE VICIOUS CYCLE. She wants to enjoy being your mom, so don't make home HELL with on-going hissy fits. Tell Mom that you want a healthy relationship, and it's going to take both of you. BE HONEST. Let her know you need space to grow. You need guidance to make good choices but need to figure out some things on your own even if mistakes are made along the way. COMMUNICATE. Keep the communication ongoing. Make compromises on boundaries and curfews and stick to your end of the deal. In other words, she's the mother but you may BE THE ONE TO TAKE ACTION to eradicate strife. Your mother may not have taught about God nor been a good example. Regardless of your upbringing, family dynamics, or the conflicts between you- set the example for change. It could take years to build a robust relationship, but your mother will be thrilled beyond words to witness the maturity and sincerity.

You are given one mom. HONOR HER with kind words, actions, and LOVE. Do whatever it takes to get it right because your spirits will be full of dissension until there's a positive turn-around.

*"And be kind and compassionate to one another, forgiving one another,
just as God also forgave you in Christ."
(Ephesians 4:32 HCSB)*

*"Foolishness is tangled up in the heart of a youth,
the rod of discipline will drive it away from him."
(Proverbs 22:15 HCSB)*

*"There are those who curse their fathers and do not bless their mothers."
(Proverbs 30:11 NIV)*

*"May your father and mother rejoice;
may she who gave you birth be joyful!"
(Proverbs 23:25 NIV)*

*"...Her children rise up and call her blessed...."
(Proverbs 31:28 NKJV)*

*"The rod and rebuke give wisdom, but a child left
to himself brings shame to his mother."
(Proverbs 29: 15 NKJV)*

Take5forHIM

MAY 5

Today is a teaser for a four-day study on Revelation. Read the below powerful passages, and maybe it'll peak an interest.

"Holy, Holy, Holy is the Lord God, the Almighty,
who was and is and is to come!"
(Revelation 4:8 ESV)

"Worthy are you, our Lord and our God, to receive glory and honor and power,
for you created all things, and by your will they existed and were created."
(Revelation 4:11 ESV)

"Behold, he is coming with the clouds, and every eye will see him,
even those who pierced Him, and all the tribes of the earth will wait
on account of him. Even so. Amen. 'I am the Alpha and the Omega,'
says the Lord God, who is and who was and who is to come, the Almighty.'"
(Revelation 1:7 ESV)

Last Chapter..."Look! I am coming quickly, and My reward is with Me
to repay each person according to what he has done. I am the Alpha and Omega,
the First and the Last, the Beginning and the End.'"
(Revelation 22:12-13 HCSB)

See a pattern?

MAY 6

The last few lines of the Bible.

"'I, Jesus, have sent My angel to testify to you these things in the churches. I am the Root of the Offspring of David, the Bright Morning Star.'

And the Spirit and the bride say, 'Come!' And let him who hears say, 'Come!' And let him who thirsts come. Whoever desires, let him take the water of life freely.

For I testify to everyone who hears the words of the prophecy of this book: If anyone adds to these things, God will add to him the plagues that are written in this book; and if anyone takes away from the words of the book of this prophecy, God shall take away his part from the Book of Life, from the holy city, and from the things which are written in this book.

He who testifies to these things says, 'Surely I am coming quickly.'
Amen! Even so, come, Lord Jesus!
The grace of our Lord Jesus be with you all. Amen."
(Revelation 22:16-21 NKJV)

People detour Revelation because it's scary, mysterious, and there are a lot of unknown symbolisms in John's visions while he was imprisoned on an island called Patmos. I'm not a scholar on the Book of Revelation, but it's utterly engrossing as it reveals the second coming of Jesus. The splendor of Jesus' return and the paradise of the new earth for believers throughout generations to live forever in perfect harmony without sorrow, pain, stress, and worry of this current life. We'll be worshipping forever in unity with our Creator who created a perfect world from the beginning until the moment it was blemished with sin.

Don't suffer Revelation phobia. Read, research, and sign up for a Revelation Bible Study when you come across one.

Take5forHIM

MAY 7

Day three on Revelation is more info on John's visions and writing the book.

"The revelation of Jesus Christ that God gave Him to show His slaves what must quickly take place. He sent it and signified it through His angel to His slave John, who testified to God's word and to the testimony about Jesus Christ, in all he saw. The one who reads this is blessed, and those who hear the words of this prophecy and keep what is written in it are blessed, because the time is near!" (Revelation 1:1-3 HCSB)

John deduced Jesus' return was imminent. Over two thousand years later, we're still in anticipation. *"Look! He is coming with the clouds, and every eye will see Him, including those who pierced Him. And all the families of the earth will mourn over Him." (Revelation 1:7 HCSB)* Commentaries convey this verse is taken from Daniel 7:13 and Zechariah 12:10. Scholars also assert the term mourn is an understood reference of those whom it is too late to be saved.

"I, John, your brother and partner in the tribulation, kingdom, and endurance that are in Jesus, was on the island called Patmos because of God's word and the testimony about Jesus. I was in the Spirit on the Lord's day, and I heard a loud voice behind me like a trumpet saying, 'Write on a scroll what you see and send it to the seven churches: Ephesus, Smyrna, Pergamum, Thyatira, Saris, Philadelphia, and Laodicea. I turned to see whose voice it was that spoke to me. When I turned I saw seven gold lampstands, and among the lampstands was One like the Son of Man, dressed in a long robe and with a gold sash wrapped around His chest. His head and hair were white like wool- white as snow- and His eyes like a fiery flame. His feet were like fine bronze as it is fired in a furnace, and His voice like the sound of cascading water. He had seven stars in His right hand; a sharp double-edged sword came from His mouth, and His face was shining like the sun at midday.

When I saw Him, I fell at His feet like a dead man. He laid His right hand on me and said, 'Don't be afraid! I am the First and the Last, and the Living One. I was dead, but look- I am alive forever and ever, and I hold the keys of death and Hades. Therefore write what you have seen, what is, and what will take place after this. The secret of the seven stars you saw in My right hand and of the seven golden lampstands is this: the seven stars are the angels of the seven churches, and the seven lampstands are the seven churches.'" (Revelation 1:9-20 HCSB)

It's heavy, and that's why many avoid preaching or investigation studies. Do not fear Revelation, but dive in and study what's prophesied to come. Be ready because He's coming, but God's Word says not even the angels know the time (Mark 13:32).

Take5forHIM

MAY 8

Day four on Revelation is what some title as the scene of heaven. As mentioned in the first two days of writing on Revelation, the following passage is unlike any description we can conceptualize. It exalts the holy God the way we will see in heaven. Our earthly beings will not gauge how great our God is until we see Jesus face to face and are in the presence of God Himself.

"After this I looked, and there in heaven was an open door. The first voice that I had heard speaking to me like a trumpet said, 'Come up here, and I will show you what must take place after this.'

Immediately I was in the Spirit, and a throne was set there in heaven. One was seated on the throne, and the One seated looked like jasper and carnelian stone. A rainbow that looked like an emerald surrounded the throne. Around that throne were 24 thrones, and on the thrones sat 24 elders dressed in white clothes, with gold crowns on their heads. Flashes of lightning and rumblings of thunder came from the throne. Seven fiery torches were burning before the throne, which are the seven spirits of God. Something like a sea of glass, similar to crystal, was also before the throne. Four living creatures covered with eyes in front and in back were in the middle and around the throne. The first living creature was like a lion; the second living creature was like a calf; the third living creature had a face like a man; and the fourth living creature was like a flying eagle. Each of the four living creatures has six wings; they were covered with eyes around and inside. Day and night they never stop, saying:

'Holy, holy, holy, Lord God, the Almighty, who was, who is, and who is coming.'

Whenever the living creatures give glory, honors, and thanks to the One seated on the throne, the One who lives forever and ever, the 24 elders fall down before the One seated on the throne, worship the One who lives forever and ever, cast their crowns before the throne, and say: 'Our Lord and God, you are worthy to receive glory and honor and power, because You have created all things, and because of Your will they exist and were created." (Revelation 4 HCSB)

There was no copying and pasting this passage. It was typed word for word so that the magnitude could be consumed. WOW!

Take5forHIM

MAY 9

Heavenly Father,

After four days of studying Revelation, we come before You speechless. The images in Revelation are mind boggling but speak of how divine and almighty You truly are. Thank you for the details of Your Word. There's so much that our little brains cannot wrap around when it comes to what's ahead. The symbolisms and the visions are bewildering, but powerful and encouraging at the same time. Thank you for providing a vivid glimpse that's unimaginable. May these young women be lit with excitement for the journey to eternity. May we be ready to meet you in Heaven by death or when You sound the trumpet at the Rapture. Until then, speak to their souls to raise them up as a generation hungry to know You more. In Christ's holy name, Amen.

MAY 10

Read John 21:1-19. Verse 17- *"He said to him the third time, 'Simon, son of John, do you love me more than these?' Peter was grieved because He said to him the third time, 'Do you love me?" And he said to Him, 'Yes, Lord, you know that I love you.' 'Jesus said to him, 'Feed my lambs.'" (John 21: 17 ESV)*

We're serving in the ministry whether full-time pastors or lay people. Ministry is hard. It's messy, and it can be downright unpleasant. There are times when I've personally felt like throwing in the towel, but God scoops me back up with a second wind. Whether it's lost family members, a cold-hearted neighbor, or little children- it's worth the dirtiness to invest in a few who need to see Jesus. He refreshes the spirit to keep it up.

MAY 11

Wretched. My South Georgia hometown was struck with two devastating tornadoes within a few months. The tornadoes battered some of the city's most historic, picturesque neighborhoods, and plowed down a plantation. Huge pines were uprooted. One-hundred and fifty+ year-old oak trees were left standing with wispy strands of moss, limbs from other trees blown and wedged in between branches, barren of leaves, and stripped of bark in patchy spots. Totally disfigured, they've lost their beautiful shape and appear in despair.

Like the trees, we get struck by unexpected storms. From one moment to the next, life can change. Tragedy can hit. We're not prepared nor will we ever be armed & ready for the storms of life. They happen, and it's a time of trusting God to heal and provide strength that we didn't know existed inside. It's a faith building time to trust God to turn gloomy heartache to peace. This is sometimes called being pruned with the visual imagery of trimming a bush's dead or overgrown branches in order for new growth (or fruit) to sprout. It's good for the bushes, and it's good for us (in a weird way). I wish none of us had to endure pain. It's heart wrenching and hard to gasp for air when it strikes. In the moment, it's hard to see how anything good can possibly come from it, but we fall on our knees knowing there's no other choice than to turn to God. Even name only Christians and non-believers turn to God during trials. In sorrow, people grab a Bible out of a drawer and blow the dust off, scrambling for verses to somehow ease the misery. Strength transpires from prayer and His Word, and being firmly faith grounded prior to the storm makes a difference how one reacts. He alone will provide hope and pull one through, bringing joy and immeasurable beauty.

Back to the oak trees...... The SOWEGA (Southwest Georgia) trees loom dead, but they are not. A quick glance while driving by, they appear unsightly until you zoom in on tiny new leaves sprouting. Unless stricken with disease, oak tree roots are grounded deep and expansive in the soil.

The SOWEGA trees will take on new shape and become full and bushy again. They will rise from the damage. Despite the storm damage, they will be stately, gorgeous, & strong again. It will take time because nothing comes quickly. The same is true for those grounded in Christ during trials and suffering.

"For whatever things were written before were written for our learning,
that we through the patience and comfort of the Scriptures might have hope."
(Romans 15:4 NKJV)

Additional reading: 2 Thessalonians 3:16; Psalm 147:3; 2 Corinthians 4:8-9.
Take5forHIM

MAY 12

"Iron sharpens iron, so one man sharpens another."
(Proverbs 27:17 NAS)

Visualize a blacksmith rubbing two pieces of iron together to sharpen and smooth the edges. There's so much visual imagery in the ancient writings of the Bible.

We need each other in our walk to encourage and build up one another. We're the light to a friend on a cloudy day. We cheer them on in their races. We're there for celebration hugs and in sorrow. We're there for a prayer and the right verse at the right moment. If persecuted, we defend them. Iron sharpens iron.

MAY 13

A group discussion began with the question, "Think of someone who is prideful. Describe his or her characteristics which expose pride." Two guys gave each other "the look" and "the nod." One grinned and said, "We're thinking of the same person." As they described this person, there were no positives. One guy even said this person doesn't have many friends except people who are just like him. Both agreed he's not high on their list nor do they enjoy his presence. Funny thing is, I figured out exactly who it was without the boy's name ever being mentioned because the bad pride is a character flaw that comes up in many conversations regarding him.

Live humbly. Take an occasional self-examination. Do you *appear prideful or humble? Is your heart prideful or humble?* More of HIM- Less of ME!

Take a few minutes to look up the following passages. Philippians 2:3; Jeremiah 9:23; Galatians 6:4; Isaiah 2:12; James 4:6; Proverbs 11:2.

"Clothe yourselves in humility"
(1 Peter 5:5 CSB)

MAY 14

Admit it. There's a tiny grain that seeks popularity. You envy those viewed as popular. They receive social media attention, beautiful picture posts with beautiful people, hangin' with a variety of people, and just seem to have it all.

You want that. You want to be noticed, talked about, viewed that way- thousands of followers and "likes." You want the most cheers on the playing field or auditorium. You want the most votes to win. You want to be invited to so many gatherings but cannot be two places at once. You don't ever want to be home because it would not be good for your reputation. You don't want to miss out on being at a party because you don't want to be left out. You don't want to go to the party and not drink (smoke weed or vape) because you don't want to be scorned that you're boring/not cool/unsocial, so you give in. Then, you've arrived.

Yay, you're cool. You party. You drink. You're the life of the party. You have a boyfriend who is Mr. Popular, too. They want you in their pictures and posts. Everyone knows you party and have multiple friend groups.

Yay for you! This is the life you wanted, right? Is it really so great?

"For what does it profit a man if he gains the whole world
and loses or forfeits himself?"
(Luke 9:25 ESV)

"Be sober-minded; be watchful. Your adversary the devil prowls
around like a roaring lion, seeking someone to devour."
(1 Peter 5:8 ESV)

"If the world hates you, know that it has hated me before it hated you. If you were of the world, the world would love you as its own; but because you are not of the world, but I chose you out of this world, therefore the world hates you. Remember the word that I said to you: 'A servant is not greater than his master.' If they persecuted me, they will also persecute you. If they kept my word, they will also keep yours. But all these things they will do to you on account of my name, because they do not know him who sent me. If I had not come and spoken to them, they would not have been guilty of sin, but now they have no excuse for their sin..." (John 15:18-25 ESV)

Take5forHIM

MAY 15

As I was pulling weeds in the yard one day I couldn't help but think how great the lawn looks from the street. It's got curb appeal for those who walk by and see the lush freshly cut green grass, shrubs, and edged driveway. It looks fab until you walk into the yard and look down. There's an assortment of weeds mixed in the grass and always a thorny weed vine, some call devil's tails, making its way out of a bush.

Those devil's tails are evil! Their sweet potato-like roots grow deep in the soil and sometimes hard to reach because they love to form in the roots of bushes. Snipping is a temporary fix because it always grows back, so it takes muscles and a shovel to yank that darn root ball.

Then there's another weed that's easily pulled up. I couldn't figure out how they kept spreading when they're pricked weekly until I inspected the itty-bitty seeds underneath. They must also be plucked by the roots and carefully tossed in a bucket to prevent seeds from falling back onto the soil. There are so many sprout varieties that could be analyzed!

At a distance, it's picture perfect. The first glance is deceiving. Upon inspection, it's assorted greens. The professional landscaper's easy solution is to squash the weeds with poisonous sprays, but it's harmful for the environment and a lazy fix. All the ugly stuff must be pulled by the roots, discarded or they'll resurface. You know where this is going, right?

The Bible compares us to sheep, but our natures are also equivalent to weeds. All looks good at a distance, but there's a crop of weeds upon a closer look. Not pretty green plants- weeds. Some of our weeds are easily cured when we're reprimanded for bad behavior and some are challenging to rid because they're widespread and deep. There's one thing for sure, though, they must be grabbed by the root and disposed.

The prettiest yards still have a few weeds. How's your lawn?

> "The heart is more deceitful than all else and is desperately sick;
> Who can understand it?"
> (Jeremiah 17:9 NAS)

Romans is an excellent book to explore the conflicts of the flesh, and the reliance on Christ to combat the weeds.

Take5forHIM

MAY 16

"This is the verdict: Light has come into the world, but people loved darkness instead of light because their deeds were evil. Everyone who does evil hates the light and will not come into the light for fear that their deeds will be exposed. But whoever lives by the truth comes into the light, so that it may be seen plainly that what they have done has been done in the sight of God."
(John 3:19-21 NIV)

John 3:16 and the above text are the result of a heart-to-heart evangelistic conversation Jesus had with a Jewish leader named Nicodemus. He came to visit Jesus one evening obviously very curious to know more about Him. He recognized Jesus as "Rabbi" (a teacher sent from God) with questions at the beginning of John 3 about what it means to be born again.

Jesus laid it out in terms Nicodemus could relate. Even though John 3:19 begins with, "THIS IS THE VERDICT (or judgment)," Jesus didn't point any fingers but spoke of living in the light versus the darkness. This is how Jesus modeled how to share the truth of who He is to non-believers. Speak in gentleness and not a self-righteous demeanor. Show Jesus through words and actions. In other words, walk the talk. That's when others see HIM living in you and become more curious about the faith.

Read John 3:16-18.

Nicodemus is later mentioned in his official role as a member of the Sanhedrin as they considered what to do about Jesus. Nicodemus had the opinion that Jesus should not be dismissed or condemned until they heard from Him personally: *"Does our law condemn a man without first hearing him to find out what he has been doing?"(John 7:51 NIV)* However, the rest of the Council rudely dismissed Nicodemus's comment. It was later mentioned in the burial of Jesus that he brought seventy-five pounds of spices to help Joseph of Arimathea in the burial preparation of Jesus' body.

Do you think he rejected or believed Jesus was the Son of God?

Take5forHIM

MAY 17

"If we confess our sins, He is faithful and righteous
to forgive us our sins and to cleanse us from all unrighteousness.
If we say, 'We don't have any sin, we make Him a liar,
and His word is not in us."
(1 John 1:9 NAS)

Miserably, sin is a part of our human lives, but we never like to admit it. Sin is really a four-letter word. Even from the pulpit, words like brokenness, weakness, hang-ups, and failures are used because it's shameful. Nobody likes to hear or think "sin." It's grotesque and reveals a side of us we don't want unveiled.

Recognizing we've sinned and confessing it to our Lord is humbling. When we fall on our knees pouring out fault, we stand up refreshed and cleansed. Verbal admission pleases Him, the One who created you for His glory.

MAY 18

The short five chapters of James can be read in less than an hour although the Book is so rich and full.

Did you know?

James was the half-brother of Jesus. Mary and Joseph were his parents, but he's the half-brother because Jesus' father is God.

It's an opinion, but James' tone is similar to Jesus, who must've inevitably been influenced by Jesus' demeanor, young wisdom, and teachings. Do you wonder if it was public knowledge that Jesus was the Son of God or a suppressed family secret?

The Bible and the people in it will come alive if you'll take the time to plunge, read, think, and daydream.

MAY 19

<u>Serenity Prayer</u>
God grant me the serenity
to accept the things I cannot change;
courage to change the things I can;
and wisdom to know the difference.

Living one day at a time;
enjoying one moment at a time;
accepting hardships as the pathway to peace;
taking, as He did, this sinful world
as it is, not as I would have it;
trusting that He will make all things right
if I surrender to His Will;
that I may be reasonably happy in this life
and supremely happy with Him
forever in the next.
Amen.[13]
Reinhold Niebuhr (1934)

Life brings harsh blows, many which are complex because others are involved, OR, God is working in a way that you may not like. As long as you're praying and giving it to Him, believe He's working for the best for all involved even if it appears unfavorable. Does that make sense? It may not because you could be praying yet the situation is WORSE. It may seem like it'll never improve. Pointless. Discouraging. Draining. Stressful. Numb. Blah. A downward spiral.

It's easy to turn away from God because it feels like He's working against you, and prayers are being ignored. "If God is so good, then why....?" Don't give up on God because He hasn't given up on you [nor will He ever]. He is always pursuing You. Always yearning for You to come back to Him. Always jealous to spend time with you (Exodus 34:14). Always there.

The Serenity Prayer is a common, simple prayer reminder. What is serenity? Being calm, peaceful and untroubled.

Sooooooo......In all crises, turn your eyes to Jesus. He wants a relationship—not a selfish, desperate plea. Constant fellowship with Christ will change your panorama and bring serenity as you walk barefoot on roads of broken glass.

Take5forHIM

"For my thoughts are not your thoughts,
neither are your ways my ways," declares the LORD."
(Isaiah 55:8 NAS)

"Don't worry about anything, but in everything, through prayer and
petition with thanksgiving, let your requests be made known to God.
And the peace of God which surpasses every thought,
will guard your hearts and minds with Christ Jesus."
(Philippians 4: 6-7 HCSB)

Romans 8:28 is naturally an appropriate verse, but it's one of the most over-used and misinterpreted verses rolling off tongues. Our definition of good and God's may not be equivalent.

[13]Niebuhr, Reinhold (1934). *Wikipedia.* 2018. www.wikipedia.org/wiki/Serenity_Prayer.

MAY 20

A ten-year old girl caught my eye at a Sunday morning worship service. For every song, she stretched out her arms, sang wholeheartedly, and lifted her eyes to heaven. Parents with arms by their sides, this little one was praising her Lord and not copying Mom and Dad.

Children are so open to loving Jesus. When middle school and high school hits, things start changing. Suddenly the pressure to conform to secular society takes effect. Infatuations with Baby Jesus as a small child gradually creeps away. When we care what the world thinks, the childlike faith slips and then it appears as if it was a phase instead of a lifestyle.

If you've lost that radical passion, close your eyes, and meditate on Baby Jesus. His character. Daydream about Jesus. Imagine what He looks like, His miracles, His goodness, the scars on His hands and feet. Be childlike!

"Let the little children come to me and do not hinder them,
for to such belongs the kingdom of God."
(Matthew 19:14 NKJV)

MAY 21

Did you grow up being read Bible stories nightly by a parent or being taught in a Sunday School class? If not, you're missing out on stunning stories. It's a memorandum that God uses ordinary people [like us] for big purposes?

Get your hand on a childhood Bible story book. Read the stories and then the original story written in the Bible. Stories like: David & Goliath, Daniel in the Lion's Den, Hannah and baby Samuel, the angel's conversation with the boy Samuel, Abraham and Sarah's faith, story of Isaac, Queen Esther, Ruth and Boaz, the talking donkey...

Many of these stories will be read in Take5forHIM during the year but get familiar on your own.

MAY 22

"For you have not received a spirit of slavery leading to fear again,
but you have received a spirit of adoption as sons (and daughters!)
by which we cry out, 'Abba, Father!'"
(Romans 8:15 NAS)

Also Read Romans 8:23, Galatians 4:15, and Ephesians 1:5.

There's an incredible family who vacationed in Turkey while there was a fatal earthquake which killed their four small children. A year later, the grieving couple adopted four children from Kazakhstan because they could not bear to leave with just one because all four needed a good home. The kids grew to be fabulous teenagers who are grounded, happy, loved, and well rounded. There's a chance they would have never been adopted or ended up in a bad home. They were saved, given hope, and a better life than ever imagined. Adoption is a beautiful example of how God takes us, loves unconditionally, gives hope, and a purpose. We are His adopted daughters!

MAY 23

"Moses then said to the Israelites: 'Look, the Lord has appointed by name Bezalel son of Uri, son of Hur, of the tribe of Judah. He has filled him with God's spirit, with wisdom, understanding, and ability in every kind of craft to design artistic works of gold, silver, and bronze, to cut gemstones for mounting and carve wood for work in every kind of artistic craft. He has also given both him and Oholiab son of Ahisamach, of the tribe of Dan, the ability to teach others. He has filled them with skill to do all the work of a gem cutter; a designer; an embroiderer in blue, purple, and scarlet yarn and fine linen; and a weaver. They can do every kind of craft and design artistic designs. Bezalel, Oholiab, and all the skilled people are to work based on everything the Lord has commanded. The Lord has given them wisdom and understanding to know how to do all the work of constructing the sanctuary.

So Moses summoned Bezalel, Oholiab, and every skilled person in whose heart the Lord had placed wisdom, everyone whose heart moved him, to come to the work and do it. They took from Moses' presence all the contributions that the Israelites had brought for the task of making the sanctuary. Meanwhile, the people continued to bring freewill offerings morning after morning.

Then all the craftsmen who were doing all the work for the sanctuary came one by one from the work they were doing and said to Moses, 'The people are bringing more than is needed for the construction of the word the Lord commanded to be done.'

After Moses gave an order, they sent a proclamation throughout the camp, 'Let no man or woman make anything else as an offering for the sanctuary.' So the people stopped. The materials were sufficient for them to do all the work. There was more than enough." (Exodus 35:30 - 36:7 HCSB)

The history behind this rad story is that God had given Moses precise instructions to build the first tabernacle (or church) so that He could dwell with His people (Exodus 25:8). That's been His desire since Day One.

God provided the fabric measurements and every minor detail on how to construct the tents and courtyard of the tabernacle. B and O's claim to fame was that they were name appointed by God to do His handiwork, as well as "every skilled person in whose heart the Lord had placed wisdom, everyone whose heart moved Him, to come to the work and get it done." Imagine the elation to lead this project, and for the worker bees to sew and build. Think of a group of ladies who are given the task to decorate a church sanctuary with Christmas trees, wreaths, bows, gold ornaments, and lots of garland. The adrenaline is passionate in decorators' blood, and the tabernacle was the most honorable appointment ever.

Take5forHIM

But everyone had a piece in the project. Daily, the Israelites brought goods and whatever they had to give so that the finest could be artistically crafted for God's house of worship. This was a type of tithing because there wasn't a money establishment at the time. Their tithing was livestock and material items.

The placed buzzed to the extent that Moses said, "Stop giving! We have more than enough!" That's a fundraising chair's dream.

The Old Testament is full of engaging stories like this one. There's a stigma that the Old Testament. is a difficult to comprehend, but God's character is revealed in the Old Testament books. Read to gain an understanding of His faithfulness to the Jewish people; why Jesus died on the cross as the ultimate sacrifice for sins; and how we are His adopted children when we become Christ followers. It will be time well spent.

MAY 24

Here's a crash course of how the books of the Bible are set up which is not necessarily in chronological order as assumed.

Genesis- Beginning of time; Exodus, Leviticus, Numbers, Deuteronomy- primarily Moses' leadership, fleeing from Egyptian slavery, Ten Commandments, Laws, Passover and other festival instructions, setting up the temple, 40 years in the wilderness; Joshua- leading Israelites into the Promised Land and Joshua's leadership; Judges- the people needed direction to keep them in line, so God appointed judges which were military and civil rulers (not kings) to govern Israel. There were twelve during this era which was a tough time period for the Israelites because they were living an up and down roller coaster of faith; Ruth and 1st & 2nd Samuel- encouraging stories of the birth of Samuel thru King David; 1st & 2nd Kings- historical and descriptive evaluations of the kings' faithfulness and the divisiveness of the region with wars over land. The next seventeen books are the books of prophets. The first five books are called the Major Prophets: Isaiah, Jeremiah, Lamentations (written by Jeremiah about his lamenting over the destruction of Israel), Ezekiel, and Daniel. The next twelve are the Minor Prophets which has nothing to do with their importance or chronology, but the length of each book. The Minor Prophets (books) are: Hosea, Joel, Amos, Obadiah, Jonah, Micah, Nahum, Habakkuk, Zephaniah, Haggai, Zechariah, and Malachi. Psalms and Proverbs are in the middle of the Bible which are praises, thanksgiving, and words of wisdom. There are thirty-nine books in the Old Testament, many which are not listed in this summary.

From there, begins the New Testament. Matthew, Luke, and John are all written by the book names and give accounts of Jesus' birth, life, parables, miracles, death, and resurrection. Acts provides the rest of the story after Jesus' resurrection. It's the story of His appearing to the apostles, commissioning to tell all the world about Him, ascension to Heaven, and the early years of the church. The next set of books thru Jude are the letters, evangelism, and early ministry of Paul, Peter and others who traveled proclaiming the Good News of Jesus. Revelation is the last book of the Bible which is a vision given to the apostle John while he was imprisoned on the island called Patmos. The purpose was to unveil the spiritual state of the seven churches in Asia Minor which John knew and to reveal to John visions of Heaven, Christ's return, the final battle with Satan, and the eternal paradise of a new heaven and earth.

There are a total of sixty-six books in the Bible. The combined books merge a story of God's love for His people, judgment, punishment, discipline, salvation, and redemption.

Take5forHIM

MAY 25
Milestones- A Tribute to High School Seniors

Take a deep breath. The graduation milestone is a biggie. Teachers spent years preparing you for diploma day; their task is completed. Parents and mentors have guided, prayed, and loved. The ripe age of 18 and graduation doesn't end their investment, and the bounty may not be evident for years to come.

Read the book of Nehemiah: rebuilding Jerusalem's wall. Like graduation, the wall was not built in a day. It takes years to build something great. Nehemiah had a deep concern for the city, spent time earnestly praying, and developed a plan to rebuild the surrounding wall. He faced opposition from powerful men but was certain rebuilding the wall was God's calling. His story exemplifies how God works through one person's faithful prayers, diligence, leadership, and determination. Your parents have raised a beautiful young woman who is capable of grand accomplishments; and God's not finished. Like Nehemiah, you've reached a milestone. Yours marks the beginning of adulthood, but you'll still need guidance, love, and prayers.

Time flies, so enjoy the happiness of this occasion and look toward the next season. Don't be fretful about the future; the Lord will direct your path (See Philippians 4:6 and Proverbs 3:6). Regardless of how accomplished you are at 18 years old, you have not reached your prime. Keep your eyes, ears, and heart open because God may call you to "build a wall."

Give Him the glory for all He has done and all He will do.

"Train up a child in the way he should go.
Even when he is old he will not depart from it."
(Proverbs 22: 6 NAS)

"...the joy of the Lord is your strength."
(Nehemiah 8:10 ESV)

"You are the Lord, you alone. You have made heaven, the heaven of heavens,
with all their host, the earth and all that is on it, the seas and all that is in them;
and you preserve all of them; and the host of heaven worships you."
(Nehemiah 9:6 ESV)

Take5forHIM

MAY 26

Congratulations to anyone reaching a high-five accomplishment. Whether confident about the future or plans are a little iffy- put God first and trust HIS directions. There's no need to hyperventilate over the next season.

Jesus said, *"Therefore I tell you, do not worry about your life, what you will eat or drink; or about your body, what you will wear. Is not life more than food, and the body more than clothes? Look at the birds of the air; they do not sow or reap or store away in barns, and yet your heavenly Father feeds them. Are you not much more valuable than they? Can any one of you by worrying add a single hour to your life? And why do you worry about clothes? See how the flowers of the field grow. They do not labor or spin. Yet I tell you that not even Solomon in all his splendor was dressed like one of these. If that is how God clothes the grass of the field, which is here today and tomorrow is thrown into the fire, will he not much more clothe you- you of little faith? So do not worry, saying, 'What shall we eat?' or 'What shall we drink?' or 'What shall we wear?' For the pagans run after all these things, and your heavenly Father knows that you need them. But SEEK FIRST HIS KINGDOM AND HIS RIGHTEOUSNESS, AND ALL THESE THINGS WILL BE GIVEN TO YOU as well. Therefore, do not worry about tomorrow, for tomorrow will worry about itself. Each day has enough trouble of its own."* (Matthew 6:25-34 NIV)

MAY 27

What's the best definition of grace? Grace is a gift given only from God- a gift we don't deserve yet He gives freely to us anyway. He forgives us upon asking though our sins don't deserve it. He gushes grace even though we cannot forgive nor forget our sins at times. It seems unfathomable that He redeems us and rains His loving grace in the form of forgiveness. Our minds will never encompass such love to the extent that we feel like we should keep begging forgiveness, but it's unnecessary.

"Amazing Grace, how sweet the sound that saved a wretch like me. I once was lost but now I am found. Was blind but now I see."[14] Besides the Bible, nothing describes the beauty of grace like the hymn "Amazing Grace."

[14]Newton, John. "Amazing Grace!". *Trinity Hymnal*, Great Commission Publications, Inc., 1990, 460.

Take5forHIM

MAY 28

The story behind the writing of "Amazing Grace" resonates the author's thankfulness to a great God who saved him and opened his eyes to the redemption of a loving Savior.

John Newton lived in the mid-1700's. He was raised in the Catholic church but was far from a living the life of a religious man. As a young adult, he lived on the edge and had several close encounters with death which should've been a wake-up call, but he continued to fall back into sinful ways by rejecting Christianity. His reputation was one of the filthiest mouths in the Royal Navy and later in the Atlantic slave trade business. He mocked the ship's captain by writing obscene poems and songs which the crew would join in singing. The ship's captain was disgusted with the obscenity, so he punished John by letting him almost starve to death. Afterwards, he was chained like a slave and sent to work for a plantation, but his father rescued him after receiving a letter whining about the mistreatment [at the plantation].

In 1748, John was on a boat during a violent storm off the coast of Ireland in which he surprisingly cried out to God for mercy in fear of being tossed into the ocean. For hours the crew emptied water from the ship and expected to be capsized. He and another crew member even tied themselves to the ship's pump to prevent being thrown overboard. He asked the Lord to have mercy on them. He steered the boat for over eleven hours while he thought of what had come out of his mouth under dire straits. The tattered ship made landfall two weeks later. Newton's thought of God in the near-death experience caused him to examine Christianity after he had written God off as a myth and joked about Christians. He deliberated whether he was worthy of God's mercy. His conversion was a slow process as he studied the faith intensely.

His career in slave trading did not change, but he cleaned up the filthy language. His hardened heart was finally softened to Jesus and that's when he was convicted of the horrors of selling lives for slavery. A changed man, he protested slavery in England based on his own experience. He became sold out for Jesus and was touched that He would save a wretch like John Newton. He was blind, but his clouded eyes became crystal clear when Jesus showered grace and mercy on his life.[15]

Transformed from a life of sin, selfishness, profanity, and rebellion to a man who wrote the most loved hymn in the Christian world.

Powerful verses on the gift of grace: 2 Corinthians 12:9; Romans 11:6; Romans 6:14; Ephesians 2:8-9.

[15]Amazing Grace. *Wikipedia.* 2018. https://en.wikipedia.org/wiki/Amazing_Grace.

MAY 29

How do you define the end of this school year? What was the general life theme this year? Looking back, how did you see God in it? Did you allow Him in? Depending on when you began reading Take5forHIM, refer to August 29, nine months ago when asked what you want to accomplish, learn, or be the theme of the year. If you started the book on a different time table, think now about what defined this school year and what's a reasonable goal for a year from now.

Take5forHIM

MAY 30

Can't wait to break away from the reigns of home? Looking forward to doing what you want, whenever you want? Love it when Mom and Dad are out of town? Jealous of friends without a curfew?

There's danger in too much freedom. Think back to elementary school. Lunches were confined to classmates at one table, a fenced playground, tight rules on end of the day dismissal, and riding the bus home with a friend. Middle School: a wee bit more elbow room including changing classes and a locker. In high school, there's choice seating in the cafeteria, walk a preferred route to the next class, more curriculum choices, get home however you can hitch a ride, check yourself in/out in the attendance office. Post-high school: 100% INDEPENDENCE. The gradual baby steps to freedom is spaced out with age. It's a disaster to have too much independence before the ripeness of graduated maturity. There are safety issues to protect girls from physical harm, and a shelter to guard girls from growing up before it's time. Advice: be compliant. There's reason for bubble wrap. It's a necessary buffer.

"When I was a child, I spoke like a child, I thought like a child,
I reasoned like a child. When I became a man, I put aside childish things.
For now we see indistinctly, as in a mirror, but then face to face.
Now I know in part, but then I will know fully, as I am fully known."
(1 Corinthians 13:11-12 HSCB)

"Whoever heeds discipline shows the way to life,
but whoever ignores correction leads others astray."
(Proverbs 10:17 NIV)

Take5forHIM

MAY 31

Studying Moses provides a generous understanding of the Old Testament stories of God leading the Israelites, and the up and downhill crusades until Jesus died as the final sacrifice for the sins of the world. Many only visualize cartoon pictures of Moses holding up the stone tablets of the Ten Commandments, but he was a faithful man of God who had a face to face relationship with the Lord. Below is an excerpt of this special bond.

"The Lord spoke with Moses face to face, just as a man speaks with his friend. Then Moses would return to the camp, but his assistant, the young man Joshua son of Nun, would not leave the inside of the tent.

Moses said to the Lord, 'Look, You have told me, 'Lead this people up,' but You have not let me know whom You will send with me. You said, 'I know you by name, and you have also found favor in My sight.' Now if I have indeed found favor in Your sight, please teach me Your ways, and I will know You and find favor in Your sight. Now consider that this nation is Your people.'

Then He replied, 'My presence will go with you, and I will give you rest.'

'If Your presence does not go,' Moses responded to Him, 'don't make us go up from here. How ill it be known that I and Your people have found favor in Your sight unless You go with us? I and Your people will be distinguished by this from all the other people on the face of the earth.'

The Lord answered Moses, 'I will do this very thing you have asked, for you have found favor in My sight, and I know you by name.'

Then Moses said, 'Please, let me see Your glory.'

He said, 'I will cause all My goodness to pass in front of you, and I will proclaim the name Yahweh before you. I will be gracious to whom I will be gracious, and I will have compassion on whom I will have compassion.' But He answered, 'You cannot see My face, for no one can see Me and live.' The Lord said, 'Here is a place near Me. You are to stand on the rock, and when My glory passes by, I will put you in the crevice of the rock and cover you with My hand until I have passed by. Then I will take My hand away, and you will see My back, but My face will not be seen.'" (Exodus 33:11- 23 HCSB)

It reads like a conversation between best friends, although God drew the line of boundary- but He protected his eyes as He passed. Read about Moses in Exodus, Leviticus, Numbers, and Deuteronomy.

Take5forHIM

JUNE

"I love to think of nature as an unlimited broadcasting station, through which God speaks to us every hour, if we will only tune in."

-Booker T. Washington

Take5forHIM

JUNE 1

It's saddening that after all the years Moses spent leading the Israelites, God didn't grant the honor to usher them into the Promised Land. Moses was punished (Numbers 20:1-13) because he and brother Aaron did not give God the glory for bringing water from a rock (Also read Deuteronomy 32: 48-52). While it seems harsh, they were in the wrong. On the flip side, Moses was an old man. He was God's faithful servant, but it was appropriately time for new leadership. So, God called Joshua, a young whippersnapper who had shown influence.

Deuteronomy 34 is a stunning tribute to Moses.

"Then Moses went up from the plains of Moab to Mount Nebo, to the top of Pisgah, which faces Jericho, and the Lord showed him all the land: Gilead as far as Dan, all of Naphtali, the land of Ephraim and Manasseh, all the land of Judah as far as the Mediterranean Sa, the Negev, and the region from the Valley of Jericho, the City of Palms, as far as Zoar. The Lord then said to him, 'This is the land I promised Abraham, Isaac, and Jacob, I will give it to your descendants. I have let you see it with your own eyes, but you will not cross into it.'

So Moses the servant of the Lord died there in the land of Moab, as the Lord had said. He buried him in the valley in the land of Moab facing Beth-peor, and no one to this day knows where his grave is. Moses was 120 years old when he died; his eyes were not weak, and his vitality had not left him. The Israelites wept for Moses in the plains of Moab 30 days. Then the days of weeping and mourning for Moses came to an end.

Joshua son of Nun was filled with the spirit of wisdom because Moses had laid his hands on him. So the Israelites obeyed him and did as the Lord had commanded Moses. No prophet has risen again in Israel like Moses, whom the Lord knew face to face. He was unparalleled for all the signs and wonders the Lord sent him to do against the land of Egypt- to Pharaoh, to all his officials, and to all his land, and for all the mighty acts of power and terrifying deeds that Moses performed in the sight of all Israel." (Deuteronomy 34:1-8 HCSB)

Did you get misty eyed at the thought of Moses standing on a mountaintop, taking in the panoramic view as the Lord displayed the Promised Land as far as the eye could see? The Lord buried his faithful servant's earthly body, but he walked into the Land of Glory. He may have been punished from walking into the Promised Land, but God had a better homeland to share.

Take5forHIM

JUNE 2

After Moses passed away, Joshua became the new fearless leader. Canaan was the Promised Land the Lord intended for Abraham's descendants to thrive. The land was often described as flowing with milk and honey. By this time, the land was occupied by the Canaanites, Hittites, Hivites, Perizzites, Girgashites, Amorites, and the Jebusites.

Joshua had already checked out the land in Numbers 13 with eleven other spies sent by Moses. Now in charge, Joshua sent two spies to specifically check out Jericho. The men entered the house of Rahab, a prostitute in Jericho. This was perhaps a clever undercover locale. Who would have suspected anything, but you know what would be going on at a harlot's house? The king was suspicious of a takeover, so he sent a search team to capture them. She hid the men on the rooftop not to be found. When the king's men came looking for them, she lied and said they left before the city gate was closed for the night. She wholeheartedly believed the spies were God's men, the Israelites whom she had heard about. She put her faith in them to protect her parents and family from being harmed in the takeover.

"'Now then, please swear to me by the Lord that you will show kindness to my family, because I have shown kindness to you. Give me a sure sign that you will spare the lives of my father and mother, my brothers and sisters, and all who belong to them- and that you will save us from death.' 'Our lives for your lives!' the men assured her. 'If you don't tell what we are doing, we will treat you kindly and faithfully when the Lord gives us the land.' So she let them down by a rope through the window, for the house she lived in was part of the city wall.....Now the men had said to her, 'This oath you made us swear will not be binding on us unless, when we enter the land, you have tied this scarlet cord in the window through which you let us down, and unless you have brought your father and mother, your brothers and all your family into your house. If any of them go outside your house into the street, their blood will be on their own heads; we will not be responsible. As for those who are in your house with you, their blood will be on your head if a hand is laid on them. But if you tell what we are doing, we will be released from the oath you made us swear.' 'Agreed,' she replied. 'Let it be as you say.' So she sent them away, and they departed. And she tied the scarlet cord in the window." (Joshua 2:12-15, 17-21 NIV)

After the spies reported to Joshua, the people invaded and claimed the land God had promised. God indeed protected Rahab's family, and she was blessed with a son who was documented as one of Jesus' blood line ancestors. Yes, Rahab the Prostitute. The Bible always referred Rahab by her profession, but God reconstructs lives.

Take5forHIM

JUNE 3

Did you know God parted water twice for the Israelites to cross a body of water? The division of the Red Sea is riveting and featured in almost every Bible movie ever produced, but Joshua leading the Israelites across the Jordan River is scarcely known.

"And the Lord said to Joshua, 'This day I will begin to exalt you in the sight of all Israel, that they may know that, as I was with Moses, so I will be with you. You shall command the priests who bear the ark of the covenant, saying, 'When you have come to the edge of the water of the Jordan, you shall stand in the Jordan.' So Joshua said to the children of Israel, 'Come here, and hear the words of the Lord your God.' .....'And is shall come to pass, as soon as the soles of the feet of the priests who bear the ark of the Lord, the Lord of all the earth, shall rest in the waters of the Jordan, that the waters of the Jordan shall be cut off, the waters that come down from upstream, and they shall stand as a heap.' So it was, when the people set out from their camp to cross over the Jordan, with the priests bearing the ark of the covenant before the people, and as those who bore the ark came to the Jordan, and the feet of the priests who bore the ark dipped in the edge of the water (for the Jordan overflows all its banks during the whole time of harvest), that the waters which came down from upstream stood still, and rose in a heap very far away at Adam, the city that is beside Zaretan. So the waters that went down into the Sea of the Arabah, the Salt Sea, failed, and were cut off; and the people cross over opposite Jericho. Then the priests who bore the ark of the covenant of the Lord stood firm on dry ground in the midst of the Jordan; and all Israel crossed over on dry ground, until all the people had crossed completely over the Jordan." (Joshua 3:7-17 NKJV)

Then the Lord told Joshua to have one man from each of the twelve tribes carry a large stone [on their shoulders] from the Jordan to be a memorial to tell their children how the Lord cut off the flowing water of the River so that the children of Israel could walk on dry land to the Promised Land. You've gotta love how God was specific to pass on His miracles and traditions (such as Passover) on to future generations. Also, isn't it cool how the people are called CHILDREN OF ISRAEL which shows a Father's affection?

"On that day the Lord exalted Joshua in the sight of all Israel; and they feared him, as they feared Moses, all the days of his life."
(Joshua 4:14 NKJV)

Stay tuned for the next two days' messages leading up to the Battle of Jericho.

Take5forHIM

JUNE 4

Although the Israelites were slaves in Egypt, they ate. When Moses lead the Israelites out of Egypt into the wilderness, they moaned because they were hungry, so God provided manna which filled them up. Manna was white thin flakes that appeared on the ground every morning. It's described as white, like coriander seed, but tasted like wafers made with honey. They couldn't store it because it would spoil and infest with maggots. However, God made an exception on the sixth day of the week by providing twice more and said to bake or boil the manna to eat on the Sabbath Day. On Sabbath, there was none on the ground. They ate manna (and quail) for forty years until Joshua lead them to the border of the Promised Land.

"On the evening of the fourteenth day of the month, while camped at Gilgal on the plains of Jericho, the Israelites celebrated the Passover. The day after the Passover, that very day, they ate some of the produce of the land: unleavened bread and roasted grain. The manna stopped the day after they ate this food from the land; there was no longer any manner for the Israelites, but that year they ate the produce of Canaan." (Joshua 5:10-12 NIV)

This slight detail is casually written, but rich in lessons. Celebrating the Passover before they entered their new homeland was not a coincidence. Recall, Passover was celebrated the night before fleeing Egypt. Jesus was also crucified at Passover. These are deliverance stories and hopeful new beginnings for God's people.

There's not only a correlation of Passover, but an illustration of God's physical provisions. Most likely the wilderness was dry with infertile soil. Canaan's land wasn't literally flowing with milk and honey, but plenteous in livestock and rich soil. Holy Land travelers describe rich dirt and lush foliage.

The golden nugget is to comprehend that God provided food in the wilderness to the day He delivered them to their rightful homeland which was lavish in produce. Why worry about day-to-day expenses, college tuition, and the unforeseen? Don't for a minute think you're any different than the Israelites.

Take5forHIM

JUNE 5

As Joshua prepared 40,000 men to fight the Battle of Jericho, the first verse of Joshua 5 says the Amorites and Canaanites lost courage to fight the Israelites after they heard how the Lord dried up the Jordan River. No home field advantage.

The Lord told Joshua to march around the City of Jericho (surrounded by a stone wall) daily for six days along with the ark of the covenant. *"And seven priests shall bear seven trumpets and rams' horns before the ark. But the seventh day you shall march around the city seven times, and the priests shall blow the trumpets. It shall come to pass, when they make a long blast with the ram's horn, and when you hear the sound of the trumpet, that all the people shall shout with a great shout; then the wall of the city will fall down flat. And the people shall go up every man straight before him."* (Joshua 6:4-5 NKJV)

Joshua did exactly as the Lord said and told the men what to do for the next seven days. "You shall not shout or make any noise with your voice, nor shall a word proceed out of your mouth, until the day I say to you, 'Shout!' Then you shall shout." (Joshua 6:10 NKJV)

Take a few minutes to read thru verse 25, Joshua 6:11-25.

Pre-schoolers sing, "Joshua fought the Battle of Jericho and the walls came tumblin' down," as if it was an everyday occurrence. GIRLS, the silent marching of the 40,000 men surrounding the city's walls, then the vibration of the loud trumpets and shouting, caused the massive walls to crumble. The stone walls were estimated to be at least 13 feet high and very deep. Joshua didn't come up with this creative battle plan; God's masterful hand orchestrated the takeover.

Let's talk about Rahab. When the spies retreated, she knew these guys were different from the sorry men who were only interested in buying sexual satisfaction. She trusted them to save her family from the horror of death by war. Rahab had blind faith in the undercover work, and the Lord gave her a second chance as an adopted child of Israel. THE GOD OF SECOND CHANCES gave RAHAB THE PROSTITUTE a clean slate to live in the company of His Chosen People. Those living in despair, GET FIRED UP because our God is for you, not against you. If God is for us, who can be against us (Romans 8:31)?? He had a better life for Rahab, so why should anybody be convinced they're dog paddling in a pond of black tar. The next time Rahab's name is mentioned is in the lineage of the Jesus, but there's curiosity about the redemptive post-harlotry life in the land overflowing with milk and honey. What a testimony!

Take5forHIM

JUNE 6

As a mother of identical twin sons, I'm in awe. A fertilized egg splitting to produce two babies is a miracle. Genetically, they are identical and very similar, but they're not exactly the same. They have different voices, slightly different physiques, different hair, different walks, and totally different personalities; yet, they have common interests, similar talents, and they graduated with a .0002 difference in GPA! Their profiles are exactly the same. One is left-handed, the other is right-handed. One parts his hair on the left, the other the right. When wearing baseball caps, they are carbon copies of each other. Without caps, they are hmmmm... distinguishable. Mothers of multiples testify to God's brilliant ingenuity. There aren't two people with the same DNA makeup (not even identical twins who were split from a single fertilized egg). Our Creator has molded every person, who has ever lived, a little bit differently- even identicals! Thank God for our differences and that we're not robots who look, act, and think alike.

"We are the clay, and You are our potter; And all are the work of your hand."
(Isaiah 64:8 NIV)

"But even the hairs of your head are all numbered."
(Matthew 10:30 ESV)

"Your hands have made and fashioned me; give me understanding that I may learn your commandments. Those who fear you shall see me and rejoice, because I have hope in your word."
(Psalm 119:73-74 ESV)

Take5forHIM

JUNE 7

Ahhhhh, it's Summer! Time to take a break from academics. There's nothing like the leisure of sitting by a pool, vacations, and quality friend time. Even if you're filling days with a summer job, don't forget God in the day. This is not a time to rubberneck, but a few months with a little extra space not filled by tests and term papers. Make the best of it.

"How can a young person stay on the path of purity?
By living according to YOUR WORD."
(Psalm 119:9 NIV)

JUNE 8

This will be rated as one of the most unpopular messages, but I love you enough to speak the truth.

Ever heard the phrase, "Leave something to the imagination?" Boobs, skin, and fannies- way too much skin is exposed during summer months. Not that girls should wear grandma swimsuits, but there's a limit. Some refute that times have changed. We're living in America. God's standards in the Bible was a different era and culture. Hmm... As previously written on other topics, much is common sense and a personal decision, but here are a few verses to mull over.

"Like a gold ring in a pig's snout is a beautiful woman who shows no discretion."
(Proverbs 11:22 NIV)
OUCH!

"Or do you not know that your body is a temple of the Holy Spirit who is in you, whom you have from God, and that you are not your own? For you have been bought with a price; therefore, glorify God in your body."
(1 Corinthians 6:19-20 NAS)

"Likewise, also that women should adorn themselves in respectable apparel, with modesty and self-control, not with braided hair and gold or pearls or costly attire, but with what is proper for women who profess godliness- with good works."
(1 Timothy 2:9-10 ESV)

"'How degenerate is your heart!' says the Lord God,
'seeing you do all these things,
the deeds of a brazen harlot."
(Ezekiel 16:30 NKJV)

This is gonna ache even more. It's a huge turnoff to peers [and God] to post verses professing Jesus as Lord and then fall into the trap of looking just like the wicked world. Step back and review pictures. Evaluate what's in the closet. Does any article of clothing vaguely mimic a tramp? Is there anything you would not feel comfortable wearing while visiting Jesus? Do guys lust over your body due to clothing choices?

Ouch! Sorry, but somebody's gotta keep young women in line. It's important to know what God's Word says on all matters even when it's not what we want to hear.

Take5forHIM

JUNE 9

"And from everyone who has been given much shall much be required;
and to whom they entrusted much, of him they will ask all the more."
(Luke 12:48 NAS)

This commonly used verse applies to financial wealth and personal talents. If you're abundantly blessed financially, God may lay it on your heart to give more to your church or a mission field. If you have the gift of compassion, He may place those who need a shoulder to cry on and an ear to listen in your path. As Christians, we're called to go beyond the call of duty. Always ready and willing to serve.

June 10

"It's over." "My feelings have changed." "It's not working out." "I don't want a long-distance relationship." "I have feelings for someone else." "You've changed, and you're not the person you were when we first started dating." "Is there someone else?"

Nothing cuts deeper than a break-up. It's natural and part of growing up to experience the thrill of being special in the eyes of a guy, and vice versa. When the break-up happens, you wish you'd never had ooey-gooey feelings because the knife hurts. Tears flow as you recollect what seemed perfect. What went wrong? What could've kept the relationship alive? <Sigh> <Deep breath>

Nowadays nobody ever goes on casual one or two-night dates. It seems like teens make the biggest deal about "talking to someone" for a while and then "becoming official." It's ludicrous because a guy can't ask a girl to hang out without everyone (including the girl) thinking they're in a relationship. Cra-zy! My friends and I had lots of one-time dates with guy friends without any emotional attachments. It was light-hearted and the norm.

I had two serious boyfriends in high school. The first one totally broke my heart after one year, three months, and two days. Everything seemed great until he came back from a church ski trip. A few days later I knew something wasn't right, and then the slammer hit. I sobbed myself to sleep and woke up feeling like I'd been hit by a freight train. My mother drove me insane with questions and assumptions that his parents probably thought we were too serious for senior year. My dad teased (but it wasn't funny) with phrases like, "He's just a kid, there's probably a pretty girl in his Spanish class." On Monday, it was the chatter of the school although there was silence and distance between us. Within days, it was apparent there was a crush between him and a girl on the ski trip. How could his feelings switch from ME to HER? When two girls in Geometry said he broke up because he knew I wouldn't have sex with him, it really stung. True or not true, I never knew. Years later and happily married to someone else, these memories are vivid as if it happened yesterday. You never get over the feeling of rejection. You know what else? Her name pops up as a suggested social media friend. Years have passed, but there will always be a divider because she stole my boyfriend. And, that's why many adults discourage teen dating. Their own hurtful break-ups crop up unforgettable memories.

Break-up Advice: Smile upon the memories, but don't get bogged down because most likely he was not your forever boyfriend. Pray for the one God has designated to be your husband.

Take5forHIM

Write down the characteristics of the perfect guy. How does the ex match up? If not at all, be relieved it's over. The little romances along the way don't matter if you don't mind occasional heartsick perturbation. If he did match up, what are you to think? Pray because he may be for later when you've weeded through others and matured. It's possible. God brings hearts together whom He wants together- somehow, some way. Distance may divide at some point, but He will reunite if it's His will.

Breaking up is a slice in the heart, but when you pray towards the future it may progress the healing of a heart attack.

"When you pass through the waters, I will be with you;
and through the rivers, they will not overflow you.
When you walk through fire, you will not be scorched,
Nor will the flame burn you."
(Isaiah 43:2 NAS)

"He heals the broken-hearted and binds up their wounds."
(Psalm 147:3 NKJV)

"The Lord is near to those who have a broken heart,
and saves such as have a contrite spirit."
(Psalm 34:18 NKJV)

"May the Lord watch between you and me
when we are absent one from another."
(Genesis 31:49 NKJV)

JUNE 11

"But if we walk in the light as He Himself is in the light,
we have fellowship with one another,
and the blood of Jesus His Son cleanses us from all sin."
(1 John 1:7 HCSB)

"Then Jesus spoke to them again: 'I am the light of the world.
Anyone who follows Me will never walk in the darkness
but will have the light of life."
(John 8:12 HCSB)

Non-believers are living in darkness even though they aren't cognizant because it's all they've ever known. They're inquisitive when they see a Christian bubbling with light. "Why is she different?" You're a walking testimony.

Search for other scriptures on the contrasts of light and darkness.

JUNE 12

"For God loved the world in this way: He gave His one and Only Son,
so that everyone who believes in Him will not perish but have eternal life."
(John 3:16 HCSB)

One of the most well-known verses in the Bible. Tim Tebow wrote it on his hand. It's written on large signs at sporting events and spray painted on interstate bridges. It's assuring and evangelistic. The verses following are very specific about Jesus being the one and only way to eternal life in heaven.

"For God did not send His Son into the world that He might condemn the world, but that the world might be saved through Him. Anyone who believes in Him is not condemned, but anyone who does not believe in Him is already condemned because He has not believed in the name of the One and Only Son of God." (John 3:17-18 HCSB)

Take5forHIM

JUNE 13

Consider Paul's joy in the hub of pain. We'll experience different levels of physical and emotional distress in our life span. How will you cope when a dark cloud is hanging over? Will you hold on to joy? Until you walk in those shoes, an accurate reaction cannot be predicted. However, maintaining a moment by moment communion with Christ will be the best sustainer. Keep your focus on biblical truths such as:

"I will never leave you or forsake you", "I will uphold you with my righteous right hand", "He protects His flocks like a shepherd."

Finally, see Christ in the middle of the thunderstorm. We need Him regardless, but when we're suffering affliction, He's our ONLY hope. That's when it's you and HIM.

JUNE 14

1 Corinthians 13:4-8 is quoted at weddings, but it's referring to all types of love including God's extreme unconditional love for us- agape. Even better, are the prior verses leading up to The Love Chapter.

"Though I speak with the tongues of men and of angels, but have not love, I have become sounding brass or a clanging cymbal. And though I have the gift of prophesy, and understand all mysteries and all knowledge, and though I have all faith, so that I could move mountains, but have not love, I am nothing. And though I bestow all my goods to feed the poor, and though I give my body to be burned, but have not love, it profits me nothing." (1 Corinthians 13:1-3 NKJV)

No matter the depth of head theology, if we don't love with big hearts, NOTHING WE DO WILL MATTER. Without love, it's tantamount to volunteering for community service hours rather than serving.

JUNE 15

"Put on then, as God's chosen ones, holy and beloved, compassionate hearts, kindness, humility, meekness, and patience..."
(Colossians 3:12-14 ESV)

Sermons have been preached on these three verses but concentrate on verse 12-compassion. Do you have compassion for the sick, the afflicted, the deformed, the friendless, the broken hearted, the homeless, the unkind, the lonely, the less attractive? The list could go on and on. See yourself through another's eyes, and that's when humbleness kicks. Anyone could easily be in one of the categories listed. First, be grateful for your present circumstances and then compassionate to the stricken. Bless others with God's love on earth.

JUNE 16

Justifying a love interest by saying, "He's so cute and fun. He's a good guy for me to date for now. It's not like I'm going to marry him." As a Christian girl, it does matter. Your number one dating requirement should be boyfriend compatible to your faith. If he calls himself a Christian because he's not an atheist, family is a member of _____ Church, Great Grandfather was a pastor----he's not a Christian. What's the point because there's a divider. Brushing it off with, "He believes in God" or "He goes to church with me. I think he'll come around," doesn't get it. Does he love the Lord? Does he walk out his faith? Is he striving to deepen his faith?

WARNING: Don't get your heart interwoven with a guy you cannot share the most important thing in life. You'll start slipping away little by little until God gets tossed in the back seat. The high standard constricts choices to a few. And now for the worst news. If you think there will be thousands to choose from at a major university...nope! On scale, there will still be a small select group of great guys. However, God is faithful. With patience, He will draw you to an awesome, fun loving, like-minded boyfriend. While a Christian relationship doesn't guarantee total bliss, dating a non-believer is a wasteful compromise. You may boyfriend-less for a long time but better off.

JUNE 17

Father's Day is celebrated the third Sunday in June. Like Mother's Day, the day is set aside to honor Dad; give a gift; eat his favorite meal; and spend quality time together doing whatever he enjoys. In a perfect world, a Dad would be a strong but gentle man; loving and kind; look out for the best interests of family; financially provide; compassionate; protective; a fair disciplinarian; encouraging; supportive; a great communicator; and a man to be admired in all aspects. If this sums up your own Father, praise be to God! Count yourself blessed! However, we live in a broken world, and many girls long for a Dad with just one idealistic trait. Studies show that girls who have a poor Father/Daughter relationship (abused or neglected) are more likely to be promiscuous because they're yearning for what they haven't received at home. Misguided but true. Sadly, problems are later unraveled in counseling sessions as childhood and family dynamics define a person's emotional well-being.

A relationship is two-fold, and we're not responsible if a parent's behavior is not the image of excellence. Nobody's flawless, and it is unknown what effects the mesh of ancestors' genes (or childhood experience) had on a man who doesn't live up to top notch fatherhood. Hope comes from our Heavenly Father, Abba Father, who loves unconditionally. While incomparable to the day-to-day physical presence of an earthly Dad, God's not a Calculus tutor on a late Sunday Night or the one to walk his daughter down the aisle. But, He lovingly corrects (see below Hebrews 12:5-11), provides, gives wisdom (especially in Proverbs), and welcomes us back into His family if we stray away (Parable of the Prodigal Son- Luke 15:11-32).

If Father's Day isn't a merry celebration, spend time praying for your earthly Father. Give it to the Lord your God to work in accord. Be tenacious to resolve disagreements and moving in the direction of a healthy mutual affection. And remember, your Dad will never be perfect, but God is the author of perfection. He loves and knows you like no other.

"And call no man your father on earth,
for you have one Father, who is in heaven."
(Matthew 23:9 ESV)

"The Spirit you received does not make you slaves, so that you live in fear again;
rather, the Spirit you received brought about your adoption to sonship.
And by him we cry, 'Abba, Father.'"
(Romans 8:15 NIV)

Also read Hebrews 12:5-11; 2 Corinthians 1:3-4; Deuteronomy 8:5; John 1:12-13.

Take5forHIM

JUNE 18

"He said to them, 'But who do you say that I am?'"
(Mark 8:29 NKJV)

In general, folks don't mind talking about God, but when it comes to Jesus, there's scrutiny. If asked who is this Jesus who lived over 2,000 years ago, what would be the answer? Would you flounder for a rebuttal?

Your answer could be something like: "Jesus is God's only Son. He is the King of Kings, Prince of Peace, Alpha & Omega, 100% man/100% God, the only perfect one who ever lived. He died an excruciating death on the cross and walked out of the tomb three days later. He is who He said He is. He's my savior and Lord, and I believe I'll see His scarred hands and feet when I meet Him in Heaven." "I believe the Bible is the infallible word of God. Old Testament prophecies of His life were fulfilled. Jesus' teachings, death, and resurrection are in the Bible which I believe is the truth." "It's blind faith, but I believe He is the Son of God."

JUNE 19

*"Let us behave properly in the day, not in carousing and drunkenness,
not in sexual promiscuity and sensuality, not in strife and jealousy.
But put on the Lord Jesus Christ,
and make no provision for the flesh in regard to its lusts."*
(Romans 13:13-14 NAS)

Is this a huge request? For some, living a life without indulging in alcohol, sexual promiscuity, or arguing is a huge deal. It's striking that Paul lumped these particular sins together, but they can actually all occur as a result of another. Such as, sexual sin can result when someone is drunk (a good reason to avoid it!). Also, volatile arguments break out in drunkenness because emotions are elevated with alcohol.

Feed your souls with Jesus. Only He can satisfy your desires and give you a life of joy and contentment.

Take5forHIM

JUNE 20

Conflict happens even in Christian rapport. Human imperfection and communications get distorted. Words are misinterpreted, hurt feelings emerge, and he said/she said fabrications fly. A relationship can sink southward quickly, and it usually takes more than kissing a boo-boo to heal deep scratches.

First, guard your heart against bitterness. Don't let your heart calcify. Pray for choice words of wisdom! Pray for the Holy Spirit to move in the hearts of all involved. Then, take a step towards settlement by talking through it with your friend(s). Somebody needs to take the first step. Why not you?

"The peacemakers are blessed for they will be called sons (or daughters) of God."
(Matthew 5:9 HCSB)

"And whenever you stand praying, if you have anything against anyone,
forgive him, so that the Father in heaven will also forgive you your wrongdoing."
(Mark 11:25 HCSB)

Also read Luke 6:31; Matthew 5:22.

Take5forHIM

JUNE 21
HELP WANTED: Work Ethic of Ants

From riches to rags, a man in his late 60s left his second wife because he wanted to be free. His wife of 36 years was retired and financially successful. He hit the road a few days after they moved into a newly built home. He was awarded six figures from their divorce settlement. He bought a convertible, mobile home, and spent money freely. Within a few years, he sold the car to pay a debtor and lost his mobile home to pay another debt. Credit card bills escalated as his only way to survive.

Since the divorce, he's been scammed by multiple "get rich quick" artists- including foreigners calling promising big bucks. He cannot live on his sole income of a social security check. He buys one pre-paid cell phone after another to out-run debtors.

He was evicted from his apartment after missing two rent payments. He took what belongings he could fit in his car and left the rest on the curb for takers. Homeless, he lived at a shelter until a woman in his church offered a room to rent. He lives like a hermit with very little contact with anyone except his out of town sons.

Every scam "is THE ONE"- the miracle from God. He's a Christian man who hasn't learned from mistakes and unwilling to work for food. The last report had him hanging by a thread in hopes to inherit millions from a deceased, unknown millionaire in the Netherlands. He received a letter from a lady claiming an angel handed her the info with Mr. ____ as the heir of his estate. He returned personal information via mail and was told to wait for the check. He checked his mailbox daily, but never received a check. When scolded that this was a hoax, he had a pitiful look of disbelief. *He said, "Buuuuutttt, an* angel *told this woman.....and, and, AND why would they go through all of this trouble to get in touch with me.....theeeeeere's nothing in it for them...."* He's holding on to a get rich quick miracle. God's Word is full of hardworkers throughout the Bible- even hardworking ants. A lot can be learned about work ethic from those tiny little insects who carry crumbs on their backs and move dirt to build anthills.

"Go to the ant, O sluggard, observe her ways and be wise. Which, having no chief, officer or ruler, prepares her food in the summer, and gathers her provision in the harvest. How long will you lie down, sluggard? When will you arise from your sleep? A little sleep, a little slumber, a little folding of the hands to rest- and your poverty will come in like a vagabond, and your need like an armed man."
(Proverbs 6:6-11 NAS)

Go deeper with Proverbs 30:24-25; Colossians 3:23-25; Matthew 25:14-30, "The Parable of the Talents", an excellent lesson about and being a good steward of hardworking cash.

Take5forHIM

JUNE 22

Are you itchin' to know the future? Right now, are you anxious if you'll get accepted to your first choice college? Have jitters if you'll get into med school or even what career to choose? What about who you'll marry? Where you'll live? Is the future budding or grim?

You can set goals and make plans, but most likely the future will not unfold exactly the way imagined. God holds your future in His hands, and it will play out exactly the way He has planned. He knows best even when it doesn't look so hot from your rose colored glasses.

> *"Can any of you add a cubit to his height by worrying?*
> *If then you're not able to do even a little thing, why worry about the rest?"*
> *(Luke 12:25-26 HCSB)*

JUNE 23

Is there someone you need to make peace- a friend or family member? If someone has wronged you, I encourage you to be the peacemaker. Forgive and put it behind. If you have soured a relationship, have courage to own up to your fault by saying, "I'm sorry, I sinned against you. Will you forgive me?"

What's holding you back? Is it rejection, fear, the possibility of saying the wrong thing or being cussed out?

It's doubtful that the person would react negatively when you come apologetically. You may never regain the same relationship as before the conflict, but the ice will be broken, and Christian character will sparkle.

"Do not repay anyone evil for evil. Try to do what is honorable in everyone's eyes. If possible, on your part, live at peace with everyone. Friends, do not avenge yourselves; instead, leave room for His wrath. For it is written, 'Vengeance belongs to Me; I will repay,' says the Lord. But 'If your enemy is hungry, feed him. If he is thirsty, give him something to drink. For in so doing you will be heaping fiery coals on his head.' Do not be conquered by evil, but conquer evil with good." (Romans 12:17-21 HCSB)

JUNE 24

Wouldn't it be great if we could audibly hear God's voice? Frequently a notion or constant recurring thoughts are His voice. As you become stronger in tune with God, you'll have those prods more often. We're inundated with the sounds of music, TV, social media obsessions, and busyness. Be quiet so you can hear that small whisper.

Read Elijah's encounter with God (1 Kings 19) and be roused for quiet moments to hear God's voice.

"And after the fire there was a voice, a soft whisper. When Elijah heard it, he wrapped his face in his mantle and went out and stood at the entrance of the cave. Suddenly, a voice came to him and said, 'What are you doing here, Elijah?'"
(1 Kings 19:12-13 HCSB)

"Be still and know that I am God!"
(Psalm 46:10 NKJV)

As kids, we sang, "Jesus loves the little children, all the children of the world, red and yellow, black and white, they are precious in His sight, Jesus loves the little children of the world." Growing up in the deep south, I've witnessed progress in breaking the chains of racism, but we've got a long way to go. Watching news channels, nobody can deny there's a problem. It's got to stop. Slight remarks about another's skin color should send shivers down our spines. And, a Christian should be ashamed to allow a person's skin color (nationality, religion, or sexual orientation) to stand in the way of getting to know the person living inside.

There are plenty of racial slurs beyond black and white, but here are a few ghastly stories concerning prejudices in today's society.

There was a beautiful white girl who quietly dated an African American during high school. Her parents strongly disapproved, so the couple took extreme measures on Prom Night to make the evening work without her parents' knowledge. She finally confronted her parents after dating through college without her family having an inkling. It was tough, but when they realized the strength of the relationship, mutual respect, kindness, and how well he treated their daughter, the scenario made a positive turn. Her parents abolished the color barrier when they married after graduation.

An elderly man spewed baloney about the atrocity of interracial relationships. He justified the position by spouting that the Bible says not to marry outside tribes. Number 1: God didn't want the Israelites to marry outside the Israelite tribes because many were heathens who served false gods. Number 2: Man looks at the outward appearance, God looks at the heart. If a girl asks for an opinion about dating a certain nationality, suggest studying the cultural differences which could cause long term interference. Simply stated, an evaluation of family origin is a good practice before entering _any and all_ dating relationships.

Accusations that the country's high crime rate can be blamed on a certain group of people. Hogwash!

Whispering snide, ignorant, off color heinous comments are common- even in this millennial.

The story of the Tower of Babylon (Genesis 11:1-9) is the story theologians refer as to when distinctive languages were formed. How different skin pigments evolved is an unknown mystery, but God was inventive as He placed defining skin and facial features, as well as languages across the globe. We're all beautiful in His sight.

CHALLENGE: If you sit next to a girl in Calc 3 class who wears a long dress and a painted dot on her forehead, cross the line. Make eye contact, a bright smile, and say, "Hello." Don't dodge someone who's different. Show kindness. Love all people. Be the generation that changes the cold-hearted sin of prejudice. Heaven is packed with all walks of global life who committed their lives to the same God of Creation. True peace will be found in Heaven when we're worshipping with all colors in adoration of Our Father. Why wait for Heaven? Let there be peace on earth.

Read Genesis 11:1-9 and the Book of James.

JUNE 26

"Then Jesus said to His disciples, 'If anyone wants to come after Me,
let him deny himself, and take up his cross and follow Me.
For whoever wishes to save his life shall lose it,
but whoever loses his life for My sake shall find it.'"
(Matthew 16:24-25 NAS)

Ever read a verse twice? Verses such as verse 25 are common from Jesus' spoken passages when he flips an extreme to get a point across. This passage describes what it's like to make a 180-degree surrender to Christ. There's freedom in the abandoned life, but difficult because we want to be driving the car.

Write anxieties, burdens, worries, and fears on a sheet of paper. Fall on your knees in humility. Give it all to Him, tear the sheet in a hundred tiny pieces, and then throw it in a fireplace. Watch it burn to ashes as you get rid of it. You'll sniffle and weep, but there's freedom when you can physically rip it up. Walk away from the fire and follow HIM.

JUNE 27
Amazima

In 2006, Katie Davis was a senior in high school when she took a three-week mission trip during Christmas Break to Uganda. Her heart was drawn to the children and knew she was being called back. Family and friends assumed she'd come down from the mission trip high eventually, but she was adamant God was calling her to serve. Her parents warmed up a little to the idea by allowing her to take a gap year before college. Her Dad protectively traveled to Uganda with Katie hoping she would return home with him after a week-long stay, but he couldn't convince Katie to hop on the plane. The thought of leaving her in dirty living conditions and a country rampant with disease was difficult, but he put his trust in God and saw the light in her eyes.

She immediately fulfilled a need by teaching kindergarten at an orphanage. She quickly realized many of the kids were at the orphanage because their families could not feed or educate them, so she started Amazima Ministries (in Ugandan language means "truth"). Amazima accepts monetary donations which for a small cost educates and feeds the children, providing and education and hope for a better life when they grow up. The children attend school during the day and go home to their families at night [instead of the orphanage].

Katie could have lived the normal American progression of an 18-year girl by entering college, but instead fell in love with life in an unairconditioned third world country. Instead of falling asleep exhausted from the academic stress and resume building, her head hits the pillow after a packed day of physical and emotional extremes. She's witnessed miracles and death, joy and pain, and she wouldn't have it any other way. By age twenty-two, she became a single mom by adopting thirteen girls. She was/is a teacher, nurse, accepted, and loved by the Ugandans.

Katie's made Uganda home for over ten years. She married a nearby missionary who was coincidentally also raised in Tennessee. They have thirteen adopted daughters, and a biological son of their own. Trips to the U.S. are short and usually combined with fundraising and speaking engagements. Katie's journey can be read in two books she's published which are brimming with inspiring quotes of a deep love for Jesus and the Ugandan people, specifically the kids. Both books exhibit an epic testimony so distant to our thinking that it cannot be put down until the very last word is read.

This is a five-minute peek of Katie Davis Majors and Amazima Ministries. It's a privilege to give 10% of book sale profits to this incredible ministry. Research and watch a few interviews of Katie online. Be moved.

Take5forHIM

"I am the true vine, and my Father is the vineyard keeper. Every branch in me that does not produce fruit He removes, and He prunes every branch that produces fruit so that it will produce more fruit. You are already clean because of the word I have spoken to you. Remain in Me, and I in you. Just as a branch is unable to produce fruit by itself unless it remains on the vine, so neither can you unless you remain in me. I am the vine; you are the branches. The one who remains in Me and I in him produces much fruit, because you can do nothing without Me." (John 15:1-27 HCSB)

"For we know that if the earthly tent which is our house is torn down, we have a building from God, a house not made with hands, eternal in the heavens. For indeed in this house we groan, longing to be clothed with our dwelling from heaven; inasmuch as we, having put it on, shall not be found naked. For indeed while we are still in this tent, we groan, being burdened because we do not want to be unclothed, in order that what is mortal may be swallowed up by life. Now He who has prepared us for this very purpose is God, who gave to us the Spirit as a pledge." (2 Corinthians 5:1-21 NAS)

*"Don't let anyone look down on you because you are young,
but set an example for the believers in speech, in conduct,
in love, in faith and in purity. "
(1 Timothy 4:12 NIV)*

*"Remember those who led you, who spoke the word of God to you;
and considering the result of their conduct, imitate their faith."
(Hebrews 13:7 NAS)*

Take5forHIM

JUNE 28
Sleep Tight, Dream Bright

Sleeping on a sofa or multiple family members piling in a bed together is hard to imagine if you've always had your own place to catch zzzzz's. A huge population has no idea what it's like to stretch out in the comfort of their own sleeping space. Ginger Davis is a godly woman on a mission to provide a bed to every child in her corner of the world. Ginger and her friend Diane Freeman first heard of a similar organization and got involved right away. A Bed 4 Me is a spin-off with their own personalized loving touch to be the hands and feet of Jesus although the non-profit isn't stamped as a religious organization. Ginger, Diane, and a slew of volunteers host successful fundraisers and receive donations to meet the needs in a Florida county.

By word of mouth and social service agencies, kids are referred to A Bed 4 Me. The organization purchases twin beds at wholesale cost from a local mattress store. Volunteers buy a child's dream bedding which may be super heroes, princesses, favorite colors, you name it. Delivery days are fun when volunteers arrive to meet the family. It's a bed building party as kids pitch in to put their bed together and dress it up with happy new bedding. Kids beam with excitement as they are given a gift many have wished for, but the parents could not afford to purchase. The upbeat jubilation of mostly female volunteers and the children is a sight to behold. Snapshots capture jack-o-lantern smiles of gratefulness for the precious gift of a comfy, cozy bed. Volunteers seal their time together by giving each child a sweet bedtime storybook by a Christian author.

Ginger Davis found her niche and didn't hold back on the passion which has turned into a lot of hours/week guest speaking and working for the cause. Social media posts are cheerful about a day's deliveries with catchy phrases like "Sleep Tight, Dream Bright." Statistics emphasize the positive effects of quality sleep on academics and lifestyle. The organization is giving hope for brighter futures and planting the seeds of the gospel with pre-school thru high school kids.

It's an honor to award 10% of Take5forHIM book sale profits to A Bed 4 Me Foundation.

Lord Jesus, may Your hand be on every girl and boy who receives a brand new bed of their own. This gift will make a difference, so we pray the children will lie in bed for years to come remembering the joyful ladies who touched their lives in the hour they spent together. Give hope for a better future. We're praying for curiosity about this great God they read about in the bedtime story. After reading the book, we pray they'll come to know You as their Lord and Savior. From there, give them a hunger for more in the Bible. May they never get enough of You. Our desire is that they spend time praying and thinking in their space. Thank you for this ministry and the way it subtly shares Your love with families on the Gulf Coast. Amen.

"And how can they preach unless they are sent? As it is written,
'How beautiful are the feet of those who announce the gospel of good things!"
(Romans 10:15 HCSB)

Take5forHIM

JUNE 29
On a Mission

Ella Ruth is an inspirational college student with a passion for spreading the gospel in Kenya. After a two-week mission trip in Summer 2017, she wanted to go back a second time but for an extended 10-week commitment as a core leader. Fundraising was a challenge when the cost was nearly a third more than her first trip.

Months before her departure, she was thousands of dollars from meeting the expense. Six weeks passed with zero notifications of donations. However, she was determined to get there, so she got creative. Besides mailing letters to possible supporters, she purchased trendy t-shirts to sell, which were all the rage. Ella Ruth also posted an "Adopt-a-Box" calendar on social media asking people to pick a number representing the dollar amount donation. It didn't immediately catch on, but after multiple posts, she received more donations. It wasn't until then when a close family friend told her not to worry, that they would cover any extra cost she had if needed. That encouragement kept her going. For the final push, a hometown friend hosted a clothing percentage party, which furnished the last bit of needed funds and an opportunity to speak to locals about her heart for Kenya.

When Ella Ruth was accepted as a core leader, the fundraising wasn't the only stumbling block. Her parents pushed back discussions of a second mission trip plus the long summer stay. Her excitement was squashed, so she kept it quiet for a while. With each passing month, her parents slowly came around as she was persistent with raising money. Ella Ruth's blogs express what any parent hopes for their child: an inexpressible love for Jesus.

T5: What did you learn most from the mission trip?
ER: *"This summer was the first time in my life where I truly fell in love with the Word. I remember (and this still happens) being excited to go to sleep because I was exhausted, and sleep meant I was closer to morning, where I would be back in the Word. It didn't feel like I was checking off a box. It was actually a MUST. If I didn't spend time with Jesus, I truly wouldn't make it through the day. And not only that, but everyone around me would notice through my attitude."*

T5: Was there a specific passage that spoke to you during the trip?
ER: *"I did a lot of praying over God's revealed character in the Psalms: Provider, Protector, Giver, Restorer, Champion, loyal, worthy of praise, sovereign, full of grace."*

Youthful spirits rev me up! The determination, the drive, the ambition, the opportunities! YES!

Take5forHIM

Fundraising a mission trip is a huge undertaking of faith. It's my pleasure to set aside up to 10% of book sale profits to assist mission trip funding. Take5 wants to partner with girls (and boys) like ER in the Great Commission. Providing to this generation of missionaries is thrilling as bright-eyed and excited spirits dash on planes to third world countries to spread the gospel.

"And this gospel of the kingdom will be preached in the whole world as a testimony to all nations, and then the end will come."
(Matthew 24:14 NIV)

Take5forHIM

JUNE 30

I can't let yesterday's uplifting message on missions fundraising leave you hanging in wonderment. Today's devotional was written by Ella Ruth to summarize what ten weeks in a foreign land impressed on her the most.

I don't think that any sum of words can adequately define this summer. No amount of gratitude, lessons learned, flaws exposed, humility received, memories or friendships made can give you a clear picture of Kenya 2018.

My life was changed is a familiar response from western Christians coming home from a short-term mission trip. I've grown to despise that phrase, because I think it's a cop-out. It's so easy to speak about life-change without aligning it with scripture and living it out.

This summer didn't change my life in the sense that I am going to be a completely different person now that I'm home. 2 Corinthians 5 says that I am *already* a new creation because of Christ, so my life changed when I accepted the gospel, not when I spent a summer in Kenya.

However, the Lord was faithful to reveal a lot of things in my life that I *do* need to change. He revealed my selfish desire to do whatever I want, whenever I want. With that, He showed me again and again that time is a man-made idea. His life isn't ruled by the hours in a day and how to fill them. Nor is He concerned with whether or not I'm late or didn't get enough time to myself that day. Even in Kenya – with limited distractions – I was fighting to be present.

He revealed to me that love is a *choice* and fighting for unity is up to *me*. This was a constant conversation among me and the other three members of Core Team. I could choose to love them, or I could choose to be annoyed that they didn't meet my expectations. The four of us could not have been more different, so this was *hard* to do. Late night confrontations did not go undiscussed and exposed flaws were never swept under the rug. I didn't always call them my best friends, but DANG did the four of us become family.

God revealed a long list of things to me, but far at the top of that list is that I am unconditionally, irrevocably, recklessly, relentlessly, and fearlessly loved by the Father. I am fully seen, fully known, fully accepted, and fully loved. My quick temper doesn't make me unworthy of grace, and I am far better than I

Take5forHIM

give myself credit. This isn't me writing how great I am... these are BIG STEPS for me to understand the grace of the Cross.

Will I be back in Kenya? I have no idea. That place is close to my heart and the people there are even closer, but I am so sure that God loves Kenya far more than I do. If He wants me there, there's nothing I can do to alter that.

Thank you, sweet Jesus, for a summer where I was daily reminded how much you love me and how you see me – chosen, worthy, redeemed, and in the process of being sanctified and restored. Summer of a lifetime.

Be energized to be deep-seated in a personal relationship with Jesus. We live in a fast-paced world, but three months in a third-world country shouldn't be the requirement to slow down. That sweet friendship is obtainable right where God has rooted you today.

Take5forHIM

JULY

"Without God, there is no virtue because there's no prompting of the conscience. And without God, democracy will not and cannot long endure. If we ever forget that we're one nation under God, then we will be a nation gone under."

-Ronald Reagan

Take5forHIM

JULY 1

Proverbs is the book of wisdom, but check this out:

> *"But the wisdom from above is first pure,*
> *then peaceable, gentle, reasonable,*
> *full of mercy and good fruits,*
> *unwavering without hypocrisy."*
> *(James 3:17 NAS)*

Read James 3:12-18. Let's moniker verse 17 as the fruits of wisdom (instead of fruits of the spirit). Write it on the bathroom mirror and keep it in the car. If we could live by this verse, we'd be world changers. Christ would be plastered all over us. Our world needs more people who *simply* live their faith.

JULY 2

There are several Bible passages which highly encourage marriages to be equally yoked. The symbolism refers to a wooden beam that's normally fitted on the shoulders of two oxen. The yoked oxen can pull heavy carts or aid farmers to till soil. The strong oxen double the workload together, and the yoke and its fastened harness promote teamwork. Make sense already?

Biblical Background: In Deuteronomy 7, Moses briefed the Israelites on numerous responsibilities as God's people before they entered the Promised Land. One strong point he relayed was God's instruction not to marry outside the Israelite heritage. *"Do not intermarry with them. Do not give your daughters to their sons or take their daughters for your sons, because they will turn your sons away from Me to worship their gods." (Deuteronomy 7:3-4 HCSB).* Hundreds of years later, many Israelites rebelled (Judges 3:5-6 NIV).

Maybe the guys were excited about a new crop of young women, so it seemed harmless at first. However rationalized, the Israelites disobeyed God's command to protect them from straying away. There are many biblical examples of downfall when godly men succumbed to unbelieving women (see the stories of Samson and Solomon).

Paul issued the same command to the people of Corinth who were struggling in their new faith. 2 Corinthians 6:14 is the most cited verse calling believers to be equally yoked. *"Do not be bound together with unbelievers, for what partnership have righteousness and lawlessness, or what fellowship has light with darkness? Or what harmony has Christ with Belial or what has a believer in common with an unbeliever?" (2 Corinthians 6:14-15 NAS).* It's dangerous and unwise.

Genesis 2:24 describes a man and woman's marriage as one flesh- the closest relationship one can have with another. The union of a believer with an unbeliever is the blending of opposites; therefore, it's worth waiting for someone who shares spiritual beliefs. God has high standards for His children, and you should aim for nothing less. An equally yoked couple encourages each other in their faith, carry the load of heaviness, and strengthen as they team up for a lifelong commitment.

> *"You shall not plow with an ox and a donkey together."*
> *(Deuteronomy 22:10 NAS)*

Additional verses: Ezra 9:2 and 1 Corinthians 7:39.

Take5forHIM

JULY 3

David's son Solomon became king after his reign. You'll read a steamy devotional on Solomon and his future wife in August. Times were good for Israel under Solomon's reign. Word traveled quickly to far-away places about the thriving kingdom and wisdom of King Solomon. The Queen of Sheba traveled around 1,200 miles to meet Solomon for herself. Read 2 Chronicles 9:1-12.

The Queen was rich and powerful but impressed with Solomon's answers to her questions, which he comfortably answered. There's no evidence that she accepted the Lord as her own, but she traveled a great distance to see the blessings of the land reserved for God's people and to talk with its King. Many people go to great lengths to find answers, constantly searching for someone well-respected to explain the truth.

"She came to Solomon and spoke with him about everything that was on her mind. So Solomon answered all her questions; nothing was too difficult for Solomon to explain to her. When the queen of Sheba observed Solomon's wisdom, the palace he had built, the food at his table, his servants' residence, his attendants' service and their attire, his cupbearers and their attire, and the burnt offerings he offered at the Lord's temple, it took her breath away.

"And she said to the king, 'The report I heard in my own country about your words and about your wisdom is true. But I didn't believe their reports until I came and saw with my own eyes. Indeed, I was not even told half of your great wisdom! You far exceed the report I heard." (2 Chronicles 9:1b-6 CSB)

She brought gifts of algum wood and precious stones which the king used for the Lord's temple and the palace. In return, he sent the queen home with more than she gifted. That's hospitality!

Take5forHIM

JULY 4
Happy Birthday America!

A committee of five men drafted the Declaration of Independence beginning in mid-June. They debated and edited before finalizing it with 56 signatures on July 4th. The founding fathers had no idea what they had embarked nor the future that was in store for the new country. They simply wanted a better life apart from what had been lived in Britain.

"We hold these truths to be self-evident, that all men are created equal, that they are endowed by their Creator with certain unalienable rights, that among these are Life, Liberty and the pursuit of Happiness." (US 1776)

The most beautiful and well-known sentence in the history of our nation. The passage represents a moral standard for the United States to strive. Throughout the Declaration, God's name is referred. The last paragraph states:

"We, therefore, the Representatives of the United States of America, in General Congress, Assembled, appealing to the Supreme Judge of the world for the rectitude of our intentions, do, in the Name,......And for the support of this Declaration, with a firm reliance on the protection of Divine Providence, we mutually pledge to each other our Lives, our Fortunes, and our sacred Honor." (US 1776)

The Pledge of Allegiance was written over a hundred years later in 1892 also declares we are ONE NATION UNDER GOD.

Our money is stamped "In God We Trust" which can be interpreted that we will trust the Lord with our finances, the health of economy, and His hands on the nation.

What's not written in many history books is that life wasn't all waltzes and Betsy Ross sewing the flag after the big signing day. Like military men and women who have died in battle, signing the document required great sacrifice, suffering and even death for some of the founding fathers. History books have embellished the early years as sweet, starry eyed fiction, but it absolutely was not.

Through it all, God was in the center of the newly formed government. Over 200 years later, our country is divided politically and socially. We have challenges that seem impossible to resolve. It's complicated in a highly populated country with a conglomerate of ideas and cultures, but there were hardships in the early years with a much lesser population. On this day of celebration, let us remember the sacrifices our forefathers made in the name of God, country, and fellow man.

Take5forHIM

Dear Heavenly Father,

Thank you for the sacrifices that were made by our founding fathers and the military men and women over the centuries. We pray for honesty, integrity, level-headed decision making, selflessness, wisdom, and hard work ethic among our nation's leaders. We pray they will make decisions which will be in the best interest of the citizens. Speak in their ears with godly answers to resolve issues such as violence, crime, terrorism, moral ethics, foreign relations, and the healthcare crisis. We pray for ambassadors who will represent the country well on international relations. We pray for the military who are serving across the world on behalf of stamping out drug lords, terrorism, and matters which affect our country's soil. We pray for a revival to spread from border to border with people who call on Your Name. In Christ's Name, Amen.

"Let every person be subject to the governing authorities. For there is no authority except from God, and those that exist have been instituted by God."
(Romans 13:1 ESV)

"If my people who are called by my name humble themselves,
and pray and seek my face and turn from their wicked ways,
then I will hear from heaven and will forgive their sin and heal their land."
(2 Chronicles 7:14 ESV)

"He makes nations great, and he destroys them; he enlarges nations,
and leads them away. He takes away understanding from the chiefs
of the people of the earth and makes them wander in a pathless waste. They grope
in the dark without light, and he makes them stagger like a drunken man."
(Job 12:23-25 ESV)

"Blessed is the nation whose God is the Lord."
(Psalm 33:12 ESV)

Take5forHIM

JULY 5

There are times when life takes a toll. We don't see an out. Problems loom at every turn. The culmination of troubles weighs heavy on shoulders, and there's a daily reminder of the hefty load.

A puny, out of shape bush is given new life when it's hedged; so, have no fear, God's pruning when there are thorny branches. He's building muscles of faith for the upcoming rosebuds. The turning point may be the moment you scream out to God, lay face down, wailing that you cannot handle it [alone]. TBH, it's extremely difficult to give thanks for the trials, but when relief comes you will do just that.

"The righteous cry out, and the Lord hears,
and delivers them from all their troubles.
The Lord is near the brokenhearted; He saves those crushed in spirit."
(Psalm 34:17-18 ESV)

JULY 6

Pre-vaccine years, my mother had me play with neighborhood kids with chicken pox because, back then, everybody wanted their kid to get C.P. because it was a fact you'd have them at some point. The older, the worse the outbreak.

As a college student, the chicken pox vaccine became available for young children. When I was married and seventeen weeks pregnant with our first baby, I came down with flu-like symptoms. Within 24 hours, my body was covered with chicken pox with barely any space between bumps. It was a physically and mentally challenging two weeks as there were serious concerns for the baby's health. The OBGYN provided very little info except, "If you had been in the first term of pregnancy or the last few weeks of pregnancy, there could be deformities or stunted growth." I'm an advocate of journaling, so thankfully I can re-read through that horrible time.

> 11:20 a.m.- It's been lonely and depressing. When I changed into a fresh pair of pjs, I was disgusted at how the bumps have multiplied on my face and chest. I have ruddy complexion with a few on my face. I broke down a few minutes ago about the whole situation. The Lord is my strength, the Lord is my strength- I repeat over & over.

> 2:30 p.m.- I watched "Regis & Kathie Lee" today. Someone in the audience held a banner that said Nehemiah 8:10. I pulled out my Bible, "The joy of the Lord is your strength. Don't be grieved...Do not mourn or weep."

> Next morning: I'm miserable! I won't ever forget this, so I don't have to write the details. It is so humiliating to have my husband rub calamine lotion on each of the 100 or more red bumps on my back and fanny. I'm his "Bride of Frankenstein."

> My ears have them; therefore, I had a difficult time sleeping- no nap either. They're ringing and feel like they've been beaten with a baseball bat. I have no appetite because it's hard to swallow because of the ear pressure and I may have sores in my throat. My face looks like a pizza with big craters all over it. I can't wash my hair because I have four in my scalp.

> It has been a special time with the Lord. A time to trust and listen. I have taken my thoughts and mind consumption off myself and on our baby's health. I pray for His protection of the baby from any effects of this horrible disease. It's been a time for us to have faith that He is the Great Physician, and He knows what's best.

Take5forHIM

Our baby girl was born with a mysterious virus, but she recovered quickly. Months later, milk and peanut allergies, eczema, and slow growth were evidenced- possibly, but not confirmed, from the chicken pox. Grandmothers drove me to the looney tune farm over getting her to eat anytime her little mouth opened. I walked around the house with snacks trying to fatten her up. My mother-in-law even struck fear around her first birthday that she wasn't alert and active as she should be; maybe because her body wasn't getting the proper nutrients for brain development. I'm not exaggerating when I say my child's health was an extended family obsession. I felt inadequate in the eyes of the grandmothers who questioned, "Why is she so small? She's a year old and only weighs 14 pounds!"

Now in her 20's, she's beautifully petite with delicate features, evenly proportioned, intelligent, and a health and exercise nut.

I'm thankful for the journal of details, and smile while batting watery eyes. Priceless! I encourage writing thoughts, goals, dreams, life happenings, and prayers in booklet form whether hard-bound or a spiral composition. Minute details are hastily forgotten as we transition from one life occurrence to the next. It's a blessing to look back at the roads God walked you through and the answered prayers you'd forgotten were prayed.

"For the word of God is living and effective and sharper than any double-edged sword; penetrating as far as the separation of soul and spirit, joints and marrow. It is able to judge the ideas and thoughts of the heart. No creature is hidden from Him, but all things are naked and exposed to the eyes of Him to whom we must give an account." (Hebrews 4:12-13 HCSB)

Take5forHIM

JULY 7

It's repelling when people toot their own horns, bragging publicly on social media their greatness. Ya know what I mean? Gotta few in mind? Regularly, they commend themselves for their ministries, the impacted lives, how beautiful their family, and how super blessed. This proverb speaks to the puffed up. We're called to be humble and let compliments come out of the mouths of others. Even then, the response should be a modest "thank you."

"Let someone else praise you, and not your own mouth;
an outsider, and not your own lips."
(Proverbs 27:2 NIV)

JULY 8

Sabbatical- (from the Hebrew word shabbat) to cease from work to rest for an extended period.

BURNOUT. Running in a rat race at 90 mph to study, chores, go, do, grow, and disciple will suck the life right outta you after a while. The crash hits hard after a long stint. That's when a sabbatical is vital- not from the Lord, but from excessive activity. If this describes how you're feeling, cover ears to comments that you're out of line to also step back from areas of ministry as long as you're not taking a vacation from the Lord. The result of spinning too many plates causes brain overload, a bad case of the blahs, or a rotten attitude because you're simply zapped. Chillin' is good for the soul. A sabbatical is a time to regroup.

"Come to me, all you who are weary and burdened, and I will give you rest. Take my yoke upon you and learn from me, for I am gentle and humble in heart, and you will find rest for your souls. For my yoke is easy and my burden is light."
(Matthew 11:28-30 NIV)

"I said, 'Oh, that I had the wings of a dove! I would fly away and be at rest.'"
(Psalm 55:6 NIV)

JULY 9

"The Son is the image of the invisible God, the firstborn over all creation. For in him all things were created; things in heaven and on earth, visible and invisible, whether thrones or powers or rulers or authorities; all things have been created through him and for him. He is before all things, and in him all things hold together. And he is the head of the body, the church; he is the beginning and the firstborn from among the dead, so that in everything he might have the supremacy. For God was pleased to have all his fullness dwell in him, and through him to reconcile to himself all things, whether things on earth or things in heaven, by making peace through his blood, shed on the cross.

Once you were alienated from God and were enemies in your minds because of your evil behavior. But now he has reconciled you by Christ's physical body through death to present you holy in his sight, without blemish and free from accusation- if you continue in your faith, established and firm, and do not move from the hope held out in the gospel. This is the gospel that you heard and that has been proclaimed to every creature under heaven, and of which I, Paul, have become a servant." (Colossians 1:15-23 NIV)

The eloquent verbiage of the apostles is absolutely astounding. Paul was not educated at an Ivy League but an enthusiastic believer in the Lord Jesus Christ. He was fervent about Jesus as he spoke and wrote letters. He lived in and out of prison, persecuted, exiled, and died the death of a martyr. The above passage beautifully describes the incomparable Son of God.

Take5forHIM

JULY 10
Are you a Mary or a Martha?

"While they were traveling, He entered a village, and a woman named Martha welcomed Him into her home. She had a sister named Mary, who also sat at the Lord's feet and was listening to what He said. But Martha was distracted by her many tasks, and she came up and asked, 'Lord, don't You care that my sister has left me to serve alone? So tell her to give me a hand.' The Lord answered her, 'Martha, Martha, you are worried and upset about many things, but one thing is necessary. Mary has made the right choice, and it will not be taken away from her.'" (Luke 10:38-42 HCSB)

Some of the best lessons in the Bible are just a few verses long.

I AM MARTHA, BUT I WANT TO BE MARY. I'm guilty of resembling Martha when guests are coming over. I run from one end of the house to the other in a dash with the clock to make everything perfect. True at any age, women (and young ladies) stay busy cooking, doing laundry, running errands, straightening the house. It's important to take care of a home and family, but we often go overboard on the extras that DON'T MATTER. Females have a natural domestic tilt to pretty things up, but in many cases, we miss the BIG STUFF while doing the little tasks we THINK MAKE A DIFFERENCE. There could be once in a lifetime MISSED OPPORTUNITIES that never come back around. We're OCD trying to make an impression when many details DON'T MATTER in the big picture. Ask, "Is this going to make a difference in 100 years? 5 years? Tomorrow?"

Can you imagine having Jesus as a guest in your home and not sopping up every word out of His mouth? Martha knew who Jesus was and probably wanted to prepare a meal fit for a king, but she was missing a matchless opportunity. We do it every single day because His presence is with us, but we're TOO BUSY to spend time letting Him speak to us. Don't miss the occasion to enrich your day by investing precious time on piddly undertakings. Be a Mary!

Take5forHIM

JULY 11

A talking donkey?? Come on...is this an animated movie?

In Numbers 20, there's a guy named Balaam who lived at Pethor (a Moabite territory). Although he wasn't a Hebrew, He was used by God as a prophet. Balak, king of Moab, didn't serve God either but feared Him as news of the Hebrews release from Egypt was spreading. He was frightened that God's hand would be against the Moabites as the Hebrews, who were great in number, fought for their birthright land. Balak sent messengers to the prophet Balaam asking him to put a curse on the Hebrews. Balaam asked the Lord what he should do, and the Lord said NOT to curse His blessed people. Balak asked him three times to curse the Hebrews and offered him gold as a reward. The Lord told him not, but the money was tempting so he arose one morning with his donkey to do as the Moabites had employed him.

Balaam saddled up on his long-term faithful donkey. He wanted to take a certain route, but the donkey took the split in the road. Balaam was angry, so he beat the donkey. This continued for two more rounds, and Balaam beat his donkey each time. Then the Lord opened the donkey's mouth and said, "........." Actually, that's the gist of the backstory. Open up Numbers 22:22-41 because you've gotta read this for yourself.

The donkey was loyal to protect his master from death by the angel of the Lord. The donkey's voice got Balaam's attention when nothing else did. It caused Balaam to open his ears to the Lord and fall prostrate on the ground to the Lord's calling.

While a talking donkey is gargantuan, Numbers 23-24 concludes the narrative as Balaam sticks to the Lord's specifications despite Balak's pleas. Balak respected Balaam's dependence on the Lord's insistence by permitting Balaam to return to his homeland.

What can be learned from this passage when you're prodded repetitively? Great discussion topic.

Take5forHIM

JULY 12

"Should I or shouldn't I?"
"I'm going to be left out if I don't."
"If I don't drink, who'll be my friends?"
"It's not going to hurt anybody, and I'll be responsible."
"I'm young. These are the best days of my life. I want to have fun."

I didn't drink until a month before high school graduation after I started dating a naughty boy. WARNING: boyfriends influence. From that point, I was an occasional drinker and then in college it was almost every weekend. I never did or said anything to be ashamed, but it became a lifestyle.

I asked Jesus in my heart at VBS and then had a recommitment stretch in high school, but I didn't walk around like Suzy Christian. My husband and I dated in college. We'd drink on Saturday Nights after the Bulldogs LOST in Sanford Stadium, and sit in a church pew on Sunday mornings. We were the only set of our friends who attended church every single Sunday. Going to church was the way we were raised. It was a tradition more than anything, but that didn't make it right. At the time, my relationship with Jesus was not what it should have been.

After college, God started working in us separately. Partying days were in the past, but we never stated, "Thou shalt not drink because our Baptist Church says if you drink a beer you're heading straight to hell!" We stopped because we were more interested in our faith and building careers. With that out in the open....

Drinking alcohol is NOT a sin but getting drunk is a sin and can lead to other things. Under-age drinking is illegal and if you're under 21 years old, most of you aren't mature enough to handle the adverse reactions. My concerns are always:

-Alcohol loosens and opens you up to doing things you may not normally do, specifically sexual sin. One thing leads to another. Kissing leads to heavy kissing and then to sex whether traditional, oral or roaming hands.
-Drinking can become the only option for entertainment. It can also open you up to weed, and then what?
-Quickly, priorities change and before you know it you've become a totally different person.

I'm not judging because I've tasted that life. I recovered, but there's no guarantee you will later. What does the Bible say [because that's the only true source of wisdom and advice]?

Take5forHIM

"....And don't get drunk with wine, which leads to reckless actions but be filled by the Spirit...."
(Ephesians 5:18 HCSB)

Read Galatians 5:16-26. There's a long list. It's specific, convicting, and revitalizing- all in one passage.

Big shoes to fill? Does it feel overwhelming and impossible? It is overwhelming but not impossible. PLEASE don't be judgmental of peers who make bad choices. You're responsible for yourself- not them. Be a friend. Love them.

Take5forHIM

JULY 13
Esther: "For such a time as this"

Background: Jews were one of many minorities in ancient Persia (stretching from India to Egypt). They were exiled out of their homeland years prior, *but they were God's chosen people regardless of where they lived.*

After her parents died, Esther was adopted by family member Mordecai and the family moved to Persia to live. Mordecai was a citadel at the palace of King Xerxes. It tells a lot about the times and the king's reputation that he kicked out Queen Vashti after she refused to parade around for the pleasure of a bunch of drunk men at the end of a week-long feast. The King [and his advisors] felt Vashti was unworthy of royalty, so a search was made across the vast kingdom for a suitable replacement. Esther and many other young women were taken to the palace for the king's selection. She was a beautiful and articulate Jewish girl, but she hid that important tidbit upon the insistence of Uncle Mordecai. Of all the girls in the haram, Esther was highly favored, so she was crowned the chosen queen. King Xerxes was so pleased that he hosted a lavish banquet (called Esther's Banquet) and proclaimed a holiday in her honor.

Trouble came when a guy named Haman was promoted to the highest ranking noble. Royal officers bowed down to Haman when he entered their presence, but Mordecai refused (although the reason is uncertain). Enraged, he despised Mordecai's disrespect; therefore, plotted to kill Mordecai and wipe out all the Jews as a vengeance. Haman sweet talked the king into signing a decree saying,

"There is a certain people scattered abroad and dispersed among the peoples in all the provinces of your kingdom. Their laws are different from those of every other people, and they do not keep the king's laws, so that it is not to the king's profit to tolerate them. If it pleases the king, let it be decreed that they be destroyed, and I will pay 10,000 talents of silver into the hands of those who have charge of the king's business, that they may put it into the king's treasuries." (Esther 3:8-9 ESV)

When Mordecai heard of the conspiracy, he pleaded with Esther to tell the king about Haman's plot---basically to turn him in and save the Jews (numbering about 100,000 people) from death. Talking to the king without being summoned was unheard of, even if she was The Queen.

"'For if you remain completely silent at this time, relief and deliverance will arise for the Jews from another place, but you and your father's family will perish. Yet who knows whether you have come to the kingdom for such a time as this?' Then Esther

Take5forHIM

told them to reply to Mordecai: 'Go gather together all the Jews who are present in Shushan, and fast for me; neither eat nor drink for three days, night or day. My maids and I will fast likewise. And so I will go to the king, which is against the law; and if I perish, I perish!' So Mordecai went his way and did according to all that Esther commanded him." (Esther 4: 14-17 NKJV)

After three days, she went to the king. Once again, she found favor. He listened and was appalled that he'd been tricked by Haman. He reversed the decree, so the Jews were spared (and Haman was killed).

To this day, the Jewish people celebrate Esther as a hero. It took courage to confront the king about the conspiracy and confess her origin. She was the right person at the right time.

What can be learned from Esther?

She fasted (and most likely prayed) for three days. She didn't act hastily or irrationally. She took several days to compose herself. She put God in the center, waiting for His confirmation.

Her demeanor. Although King Xerxes had many beautiful choices, she was the one who stuck out in the crowd to be his queen; therefore, he evidently respected her on many levels.

Have you ever been the bearer of bad news OR the one appointed to act on behalf of a group? You may be called to step forward when something is erring. The way you live is a forerunner for the confrontation which may alter the end-result.

When you pray and feel the peace of God telling you to do something, what's to fear?

> "What then shall we say to these things?
> If God is for us, who can be against us?"
> (Romans 8:31 NKJV)

This is the condensed version. There's much more. Read the Book of Esther for a thrilling ten-chapter story.

Take5forHIM

JULY 14

Time is disconcerting. How many remember bits & pieces of toddler years? Maybe a day, moment, or special occasion that may be vague but still a distant memory. Does it seem that far away? Ever thought about how there was a time when you didn't exist before you were born into this world? Eerie? Does it seem like time is traveling at the speed of a bullet? Days run into weeks and seasons pass quickly? Did it seem like there was a wide gap of time between Christmases and now it rolls around more often? Why is that? Busier or is time snapping?

With age, the accumulation of habitual traditions will occur more frequently, and you'll be shocked when you reach 20 years old. You'll look back at how much you've changed in a decade, and how you barely remember turning 10 except for the birthday video and photos. At the big 3-0 milestone, you'll reflect on all that was accomplished in the 20s and hopes for the next decade. Ten years later, you'll look in the mirror and notice tiny lines forming around your eyes, crow's feet, and maybe even a grey hair or two. Decisions on cosmetic aging treatments become the predicament as we face the mirror daily and compare to more youthful years.

Although it should not pre-occupy thoughts, we even notice how much our parents have changed over the years in appearance and physical endurance.

Life is fleeting, and time on earth is a vapor. These devotions are meant to be inspirational and not a drag, so stick with it as it takes a positive direction. Every day that you wake up is a gift from God. Don't live by the calendar. Make happy memories. Maintain a good outlook, so you'll see God's hand working for good instead of stumbling on the cracks in the pavement.

"You don't even know what tomorrow will bring- what your life will be!
For you are like smoke that appears for a little while, then vanishes."
(James 4:14 HCSB)

"For physical training is of some value, but godliness has value for all things,
holding promise for both the present life and the life to come."
1 Timothy 4:8

Enrichment verses: Psalm 144:4; Psalm 39:4; 1 Corinthians 10:31.

Take5forHIM

JULY 15

A birthday party rolls around and classmates begin chattering about the upcoming event, but you didn't receive an invitation. Or, you see on social media that friends had a boating day without you. You investigate who was invited, hoping for an explanation.

RESULT: HURT FEELINGS erupt volcanic size sin. Bitterness, poor judgment of words, not accepting apologies; therefore, division occurs. The monstrous comes out because you feel slighted. Many times, it was miscommunication or unintentional. If you allow the beast to materialize, you'll be included less and less.

ADVICE: Smile, be gracious, and bite your tongue. Regarding the hurt, pray and move on.

"Death and life are in the power of the tongue...."
(Proverbs 18:21 ESV)

JULY 16

God is not a lucky charm so don't treat Him like a coin toss. Don't drag Him off the shelf when you need an answered prayer. And, He's not the old man upstairs!

God is holy and righteous. He deserves respect. Get to know His character so you will not fall into the above notions of taking His majesty lightly. He is the Alpha and Omega, Beginning and the End, Omnipresent, Omniscient, never changing, Shepherd, Healer, Almighty God, King of Heaven and Earth, the Maker of Heaven and Earth. He knew you before He created the world. He is fair and just. Get to know His attributes! An excellent place to learn is by starting in Genesis.

JULY 17

Words can build up, tear down, encourage, gossip, affirm, love. I "eat crow" every time I open my big fat mouth. Too bad there's not a rewind button. The only way to remedy it is by apologizing. Your character to ask forgiveness will be appreciated and esteem will be rebuilt.

"Every sea creature, reptile, bird, or animal is tamed and has been tamed by man, but no man can tame the tongue. It is a restless evil full of deadly poison. We praise our Lord and Father with it, and we curse men who are made in God's likeness with it. Praising and cursing come out of the same mouth. My brothers, these things should not be this way. Does a spring pour out sweet and bitter water from the same opening? Can a fig tree produce olives, my brothers, or a grapevine produce figs? Neither can a saltwater spring yield fresh water." (James 3:8-12 HCSB)

JULY 18

Thinking back on my own dating life, I wish someone had yanked me away from a couple of guys. My dad's disgust regarding my senior year/first year college BF is the only feedback I *ever* received. "That son of a gun is undressing you with his eyes. I don't trust him." To which Mama replied, "He's the type who will cheat on you in a heartbeat, and he'll definitely cheat on his wife." Yep, that's just what he did.

As an adult, I have a totally different view than I did at 17, and I'm sure your thoughts are of a typical 14 – 22-year old girl. I didn't have a mentor even though I was in a youth group. Nobody warned, nor do I ever remember a youth pastor teaching on it.

My story is a perfect example of a Christian girl falling for a rowdy boy. I was on the rebound after the breakup of a one-year relationship. Every day with him was new and exciting: super handsome guy with cat eyes, unbelievable romance, sweet surprises, love notes, and the introduction to alcohol. He idolized me yet cheated and lied. After multiple forgiveness, I dropped the breakup bomb. I severed it and never questioned myself. I had strayed from God and it took a long while to recoup.

"Remember your leaders, those who spoke to you the word of God.
Consider the outcome of their way of life and imitate their faith."
(Hebrews 13:7 ESV)

"Know well the condition of your flocks,
and give attention to your herds."
(Proverbs 27:23 ESV)

Take5forHIM

JULY 19

"So if you have been raised with the Messiah, seek what is above, where the Messiah is seated at the right hand of God. Set your minds on what is above, not what is on earth. For you have died, and your life is hidden with the Messiah in God. When the Messiah, who is your life, is revealed, then you also will be revealed with Him in glory. Therefore, put to death what belong to your worldly nature; sexual immorality, impurity, lust, evil desire, and greed, which is idolatry. Because of these, God's wrath comes on the disobedient, and you once walked in these things when you were living in them. But now you must also put away the following: anger, wrath, malice, slander, and filthy language from your mouth. Do not lie to one another, since you have put on the new self with its practices and have put on the new self. You are being renewed in knowledge according to the image of your Creator. In Christ, there is not Greek or Jew, circumcision or uncircumcision, barbarian, Scythian, slave and free, but Christ is all and in all." (Colossians 3:1-11 HCSB)

JULY 20

What's your label? Are you a cheerleader? Dancer? Majorette? ADPi? Chi O? Class President? Homecoming Queen? Track Star? Merit Scholar? John and Suzanne's daughter? Spanish Club social chair? It seems like no one can be introduced without adding a tagline. Even as an adult, one is described as, "She's a doctor." "She's a realtor." "She's Anna's mom." "She was a Tri Delt at Georgia."

Labels are wrapped and tied with a bow on extracurricular activities and careers when our focus should be on who we are in Christ. You are a child of God; a daughter of the name above all names. Yet on earth, the dazzle of being on the dance team or a beauty queen is much more impressive in our eyes (and others')?

Titles fade. One day, it's forgotten, or you're known as a "has been." That's a struggle in college after being a high school standout. New college acquaintances are unimpressed by past titles, and it's hard to reach super star level in college with so much competition for positions. Therefore, many crash and ask, "Who am I?"

If you're a Christian, all insecurities should vanish because your identity label is "Christ Follower." Whether vocal or if it's a quiet relationship between you and Jesus, you've found the eternal security of knowing HIM. When asked, be unashamed to share your faith, but there's no need to be loud or get a pat on the back because it's between you and HIM. There's inner satisfaction when the only label you need is the one Christ has given you- daughter.

"See what great love the Father has lavished on us,
that we should be called children of God! And that is what we are!
The reason the world does not know us is that it did not know Him.
Dear friends, now we are children of God, and what we will be
has not yet been made known. But we know that when Christ appears,
we shall be like Him, for we shall see Him as He is."
(1 John 3:1-2 NIV)

"Since, then, you have been raised with Christ, set your hearts on things above,
where Christ is, seated at the right hand of God. Set your minds on things above,
not on earthly things. For you died, and your life is not hidden with Christ in God."
(Colossians 3: 1-3 NIV)

"....the unfading beauty of a gentle and quiet spirit,
which is of great worth in God's sight."
(1 Peter 3:3-4 NIV)

Take5forHIM

JULY 21

"Wait for the Lord; be strong and let your heart take courage; wait for the Lord."
(Psalm 27:14 ESV)

Many verses in Psalms are when David was in exile- on the run for his life. The passages are full of verses on waiting, trusting, and walking with the Lord. Waiting takes resiliency. We're impatient and lack understanding because we wish for immediate results. Unanswered prayers can be halted for years leaving you to question if God is listening. Or worse, if He's forgotten. He never forgets, but it's always in His perfect timing. We're not on God's clock. Wait. He knows what's best and when.

JULY 22

Driving home one afternoon, a teenage boy walking on the sidewalk caught my attention with his body language. He waved his hands high in then lowered them to his waistline. He punched the air with his right fist and then his left. He was singing his heart out and glowing with excitement. Who knows if he was praising Jesus or rappin', but he was animated, for sure. Some drivers probably snickered and thought he had some screws loose. I, on the other hand, could not shake the young face full of pure delight.

Whatever was the source of the expressions, shouldn't we be the same about the gospel? We should be ecstatic with the good news of the risen Lord. We have the privilege of a relationship with the King of Kings. His spirit goes wherever we go.

"Shout triumphantly to the Lord, all the earth. Serve the Lord with gladness; come before Him with joyful songs. Acknowledge Yahweh is God. He made us, and we are His people, the sheep of His pasture....."
(Psalm 100 ESV)

JULY 23

Being on a spiritual high after a retreat is like nothing else. The songs, the new friend connections, the memories, the time sitting by a pine tree praying. The temptation from Satan when you return is real. It's easy to slide into old habits and gradually lose the thrill. That's Satan's challenge.

We're in a battle. It's an everyday commitment to take up a cross and follow Jesus. Band with devoted Christian followers, read The Word, and pray about everything! It's a cold, cruel world out there.

"Let us hold on to the confession of our hope without wavering,
for He who promised is faithful."
(Hebrews 10:23 HCSB)

"So faith comes from hearing, and hearing through the word of Christ."
(Romans 10:17 ESV)

Take5forHIM

JULY 24

Who do you admire and why? A good role model has a dynamic way of perking ears with interest because when she speaks, you want to listen. Interestingly, do a web search to compare who you identify as a role model vs. who the world considers.

*"Strength and dignity are her clothing, and she laughs at the time to come.
She opens her mouth with wisdom, and the teaching of kindness is on her tongue."
(Proverbs 31:25-26 ESV)*

Many teenagers are deprived a positive role model- a woman to look up to as someone who has it all together. Don't confuse the title with a beautiful woman because anyone can put on a facade with stylish clothes and an attractive face.

*"Charm is deceitful and beauty is vain,
but a woman who fears the Lord is to be praised."
(Proverbs 31:30 ESV)*

Admire and seek to be a woman who is strong and well respected; optimistic about the future knowing God is in control; kind and encouraging; and points to Christ.

Does a certain face come to mind? Mom? Teacher? Coach? Someone in your interested career field? Cancer survivor? She may be an ordinary person who is extraordinary in a rare way. Whoever she may be, stand back and watch. Don't resist asking for advice, direction, or if she's willing to meet regularly. Learn life lessons from her and the Proverbs verses. In turn, you'll grow into a role model for a younger generation girl which is extremely rewarding.

Find a role model -------> Become one.

JULY 25

Days melt into days and years. Life gets mundane and routines resemble robotic behaviors. Metaphorically, the sunsets and sunrises are the high points, and the daily grind becomes like sandpaper wearing us down little by little. That's why we NEED sunsets and sunrises to brighten our days and make an indelible mark of Who paints the sky.

The cotton candy and blood orange sight of a sunset revives the end of a day. When driving, eyes are drawn to the loveliness and it's impossible to turn away from its allurement. Cars pull off to the side of the road to capture the beauty, but even the fanciest cameras cannot snatch the indescribable artistry. It's a day changer and pushes the weight of the day behind for a few moments.

The same is true with the sunrise. There's something special about waking up in the dark, driving to a beautiful spot such as the waterfront, and watching the sun slowly creep from darkness to a bright light. The stillness of the early morning is peaceful. When it pops up over the horizon, it's vivid and eye squinting as if it's been up for hours. "Hello, World!"

Neither last long, but it affects a day and slows us down- in a good way. Both the rising and the setting confirm that surely all that's seen cannot be by accident. Like a quick whiff of sweet gardenias, it doesn't last long but refreshes a routine, monotonous, chaotic, stressful, and noisy day. By His grace, He gives us a new day to breathe. Life is erratic, but we can count on the sun to rise and set. Sometimes it's extremely colorful and breathtaking, and sometimes hiding behind cumulous dark clouds.

It's Summer! Alone or with a friend, grab a big blanket and catch the rays of exquisite beauty. Praise His Holy Name.

"The steadfast love of the Lord never ceases; his mercies never come to an end;
they are new every morning; great is your faithfulness."
(Lamentations 3:22-23 ESV)

"From the rising of the sun to its setting, the name of the Lord is to be praised!
The Lord is high above all nations, his glory above the heavens!
Who is like the Lord our God, who is seated on high,
who looks far down on the heavens and the earth?"
Psalm 113:3-6

Additional verses: Psalm 19:1; Jeremiah 31:35; Romans 1:20; Psalm 65:8; Genesis 1:16-18; Psalm 50:1; 2 Corinthians 4:6.

Take5forHIM

JULY 26

QUESTION: If you could have dinner with one person from the Bible besides Jesus, who would it be? Take5forHIM is brimming of devotionals on men and women who've made an imprint on biblical history. My choice would be David. I envision the personality and charisma of David. The conversation could last for hours as he would undoubtedly be a vivid story-teller.

Here's a condensed synopsis on the life of David.

God rejected Israel's first king, Saul, for poor leadership choices. God gave the prophet Samuel the task to go to Jesse's house [in Bethlehem] to anoint a new king. After Samuel saw six of Jesse's sons, God said no to all. Jesse sent for his youngest son who was tending sheep. When the boy came, God said, "Rise and anoint him; this is the one." David was a boy not a man.

For a while, David was an armor bearer for King Saul. During this time, there was a battle with the Philistines. A giant warrior named Goliath, estimated to be close to 7 feet tall, intimidated the Israel soldiers by daring a one-on-one fight. The men were terrified, but boy David rose up without trembling to accept the challenge. Saul discouraged him, but David was confidently determined. David appeared to Goliath with five smooth stones and a slingshot. Goliath laughed at the boy and exuded trash talk. David said, "You come to me with sword and spear and javelin, but I come against you in the name of the Lord Almighty." (NIV) After a robust speech, David killed the giant after slinging the first smooth stone. Take a few minutes to re-read this familiar story in 1 Samuel 17.

After the Goliath killing, King Saul and others took notice of David. Even though David defeated an enemy force, Saul was jealous and concerned for his royal position because of the rising young warrior. And then, David and Saul's son Jonathan became the best of friends which didn't help matters. David spent lots of time on the run as Saul wanted David dead. As David feared his life, he wrote much of Psalms which are abundant praises, poems, and prayers- so beautifully written. David's poetry are the most read poems in all of history.

David was noted as a man after God's own heart (1 Samuel 13:14). He loved the Lord yet had an affair with Bathsheba and killed her husband so that he could have her as his own. His human desires wandered him from the Lord. There are consequences for sin which are not always immediate, but David and Bathsheba mourned greatly when their young child became ill and died days later. God got David's attention. He fasted and wept while the child's health quickly declined. When the child died, he went to the house of the Lord and worshiped.

Take5forHIM

Years later, he grieved the loss of two adult sons: Amnon and Absalom. Amnon was killed by his half-brother Absalom. And then Absalom was later was killed in battle after abandoning conflict with David.

David wrote a beautiful song of praise (1 Samuel 22 and Psalm 18) after the Lord delivered him from military enemies, but also as a testament to God when reminiscing on the battles and trials of his life. *"The Lord is my rock, my fortress and my deliverer: my God is my rock, in whom I take refuge, my shield and the horn of my salvation. He is my stronghold, my refuge and my savior- from violent people you save me. I called to the Lord, who is worthy of praise.....verse 46- The Lord lives! Praise be to my Rock! Exalted be my God, the Rock, my Savior! ...."* (Psalm 18:2-3, 4646 NIV) The fifty verses are repetitive praise and thankfulness to His Great God. He was a man of continuous love for the Lord and exalted God for His goodness and Israel's success during his reign. David was a popular leader, a master warrior, and an eloquent speaker. God favored him as he led a successful nation, but life wasn't all roses. The thorns grew dependence on the Lord closer.

I could sit on the edge of my seat for hours without tasting a bite of food while listening to David's recollections. Never a dull moment. What a life!

Take5forHIM

JULY 27

Day 2: Studying David

There are many rich stories exhibiting David in 1st & 2nd Samuel, 1 Kings, 1 Chronicles, and Psalms. Good character shines in today's devotional.

After David killed Goliath, the people praised David's big win. Although Saul was impressed by the young warrior, he quickly became jealous because David's heroism was the buzz around town. It didn't take long before Saul felt intimidated that David would take over the royal throne, so he wanted to get rid of him. David fled to save his life. He was on the run for years. While a fearful time, David was dependent on the Lord's protection. His faith grew as evidenced in the poetry of Psalms.

Psalms 57 was written during his time hiding in a cave. *"Have mercy on me, my God, have mercy on me, for in you I take refuge. I will take refuge in the shadow of your wings until the disaster has passed. I cry out to God Most High, to God, who vindicates me. He sends from heaven and saves me, rebuking those who hotly pursue me....I am in the midst of lions; I am forced to dwell among ravenous beasts—men whose teeth are spears and arrows, whose tongues are sharp swords. Be exalted, O God, above the heavens; let your glory be over all the earth....I will praise you, Lord, among the nations; I will sing of you among the peoples. For great is your love, reaching to the heavens; your faithfulness reaches to the skies...."* (Psalm 57:1-5,9-10 NIV)

In 1 Samuel 24, Saul and his men discovered David was hiding out in the cave. Assuming it was very dark, David had an opportunity to attack and kill Saul. David could've/should've killed Saul when he had the chance but instead showed mercy.

"Then David went out of the cave and called out to Saul, 'My lord the king!' When Saul looked behind him, David bowed down and prostrated himself with his face to the ground....'This day you have seen with your own eyes how the Lord delivered you into my hands in the cave. Some urged me to kill you, but I spared you; I said, 'I will not lay my hand on my lord, because he is the Lord's anointed. See, my father, look at this piece of your robe in my hand! I cut off the corner of your robe but did not kill you. See that there is nothing in my hand to indicate that I am guilty of wrongdoing or rebellion. I have not wronged you, but you are hunting me down to take my life. May the Lord judge between you and me. And may the Lord avenge the wrongs you have done to me, but my hand will not touch you......Against whom has the king of Israel come out? Who are you pursuing? A dead dog? A flea? May the Lord be our judge and decide between us. May he consider my cause and uphold it; may he vindicate me by delivering me from your hand.'" Saul's heart melted and said, "'You are more righteous than I,' he said, 'You have treated me well, but I have treated you badly. You have just

Take5forHIM

told me about the good you did to me, the Lord delivered me into your hands, but you did not kill me. When a man finds his enemy, does he let him get away unharmed? May the Lord reward you well for the way you treated me today. I know that you will surely be king and that the kingdom of Israel will be established in your hands. Now swear to me by the Lord that you will not kill off my descendants or wipe out my name from my father's family.' So David gave his oath to Saul." (1 Samuel 24:8-22 NIV)

That, my friend, is a reconciler! David experienced dark times while on the run, but his faith flourished. It developed him for the future that was laid out before him. If he'd lived a sing-song life, maybe he would've been a shaky king like Saul. His reliance evolved a heart for the man who was out to take his life- calling him lord and father. Saul could've also seized the opportunity to kill David, too, but how could he when David paid homage to the King of Israel?

What does this story teach about how to treat enemies?

Day 3: Studying David

As we're learning, David had strengths and weaknesses. David had many wives (eight to be exact) which was never God's plan (Genesis 2:22-25). Although there isn't a passage where God addresses David's love for wives, it must've been disappointing. As a result of polygamy, there was indirect conflict that's underlying but never written in black and white. The story of David's daughter Tamar is one of them.

Read the onset passage in 2 Samuel 13:1-5.

David was blind to what was going on, so he sent word to Tamar to tend to Amnon's health. When Tamar showed up, Amnon sent everyone out of his house. He told her to make a meal and feed it to him. When she brought homemade bread, he grabbed her and said, "Come to bed with me, my sister." She resisted and tried to talk him out of it.

"'Don't force me! Such a thing should not be done in Israel! Don't do this wicked thing. What about me? Where could I get rid of my disgrace? And what about you? You would be like one of the wicked fools in Israel. Please speak to the king, he will not keep me from being married to you.' But he refused to listen to her, and since he was stronger than she, he raped her. Then Amnon hated her with intense hatred. In fact, he hated her more than he had loved her. Amnon said to her, 'Get up and get out!'" (2 Samuel 13:12-15 NIV)

Amnon called his servants to kick her out and bolted the door behind. She was wearing an ornate robe which signified virginity. She was degraded, put ashes on her head, and tore the robe. She was hurt, ashamed, and abused. When Absalom saw her, he suspected what had happened and told her to keep quiet. The Bible says, *"And Tamar, lived in her brother Absalom's house, a desolate woman."* (2 Samuel 13:20 NIV)

"When King David heard all of this, he was furious. And Absalom never said a word to Amnon, either good or bad; he hated Amnon because he had disgraced his sister Tamar." (2 Samuel 13:21 NIV)

The Bible doesn't share info as to whether David addressed the incident with Amnon. It's presumed that he fumed but let it go. The next paragraph expresses Absalom's festering bitterness towards David and Amnon as years passed. The condensed story is that Absalom took justice on his own by having his men kill Amnon. Sketchy Jonadab had the pleasure of reporting the bad news to King David. Absalom fled for three years after the killing, and the father/son relationship suffered in the years to come.

Rape is a horrible act. Absalom consoled his sister by taking her into his home. He burned with hatred knowing her virginity was robbed by their half-brother who chewed her up and then spit her out. She no longer wore the ornate robe signifying purity for prospective husbands. Tamar's dignity and future were stolen by a lustful, selfish, deceitful, hungry man.

Sin has a ripple effect, so be cautioned not to develop an attitude of "I'm not hurting anybody. It's my life to do what I want to do with it." This story exemplifies how many lives were affected by one man's sin.

Read the full play-by-play story in 2 Samuel 13.

Day 4: Studying David

Despite the clash with King Saul, David was best friends with Saul's son Jonathan. It's one of the most outstanding stories of a best friend bond in the Bible. They were tight bros in spirit. Sadly, Jonathan was killed in battle against the Philistines. Note, there was always a war going on with the Philistines. Jonathan's son Mephibosheth was five years old when his grandfather died. Upon hearing of his death, a nurse picked up Meph (for short) and ran in fear of the Philistines harming him. The nurse accidentally dropped the boy on his feet and he was crippled for the rest of his life (2 Samuel 4:4). There's a short and sweet passage which displays David's loyalty to his deceased best friend (and Saul, for that matter).

Stop to read 2 Samuel 9.

Meph referred to himself as a dog because of lameness or unknown reasons, but David considered him as the Lord did- a valuable human being. He was the former king's grandson, but it's implied he'd been tossed on the side of the road, so to speak. Disability and home health services weren't provided, so invalids were cared for by family as best possible. David's allegiance to his predecessor and best friend is commendable because he could've gone about his business without ever giving a thought to remaining family members. He said, *"Is there anyone still left of the house of Saul to whom I can show kindness for Jonathan's sake?" (2 Samuel 9:1 NIV)* The fact that Meph was crippled had nothing to do with the story. David's intention wasn't pity. It just so happened that the family member who needed support was a lame man. David wanted to share God's kindness to whoever was left. And, he was not forgotten for he ate at the king's table as if he'd been adopted. To be treated like family of the king brought dignity to a man whose self-esteem was exposed as a dog.

Take-away: Today's devotional affirmed that I need to show kindness to _____. Is there someone who has been left by the wayside by family who needs a helping hand?

Take5forHIM

JULY 30

Day 5: Studying David

After war, the ark of the covenant was taken from Israel by the Philistines for seven months. The Philistines had one calamity after another when it was in their possession, so they gladly delivered it back to Israel (1 Samuel 6). Then the ark was kept at the house of Abinadab for 20 years and eventually resided in a tent in Jerusalem. When David became king, he disclosed to the prophet Nathan his dream to build a temple for the ark. That evening the Lord spoke to Nathan to pass along to David that a temple would not be built under his leadership.

Nathan's conversation with David: *"I declare to you that the Lord will build a house for you: When your days are over and you go to be with your ancestors, I will raise up your offspring to succeed you, one of your own sons, and I will establish his kingdom. He is the one who will build a house for me, and I will establish his throne forever. I will be his father, and he will be my son. I will never take my love away from him, as I took it away from your predecessor (Saul). I will set him over my house and my kingdom forever; his throne will be established forever."* (1 Chronicles 17:11-14 NIV)

David's dream was to build the temple for the Lord, but God's plan was for his son Solomon to build a temple. God had a different purpose for David's reign. Side note: most likely neither David nor Nathan understood God's foretelling of Jesus' coming. David accepted the Lord's will in verses 16-27 with a prayer of adoration.

"You, my God, have revealed to your servant that you will build a house for him. So your servant has found courage to pray to you. You, Lord, are God! You have promised these good things to your servant. Now you have been pleased to bless the house of your servant, that it may continue forever in your sight; for you, Lord, have blessed it, and it will be blessed forever." (1 Chronicles 17:25-27 NIV)

Sometimes God's plans are for us to lay the foundation for someone else to do the exciting stuff. Read David's poignant speech to Jewish leaders regarding the temple in Chapter 28. From then, David and the leaders prepared the way for the future generation because the current moment was not God's timing. Even a heart with the best intentions cannot rush God's work.

What does today's message teach about crumbled, beaten down dreams?

Take5forHIM

Day 6: Studying David

David was known as a man after God's own heart. Jesus is even titled "Son of David" in addition to the Son of God. David certainly prayed beautiful prayers, wrote deep poetry, and demonstrated godly character. He unified the governance of the Twelve Tribes of Israel. The accolades are many, but what about Bathsheba? Not only did he have an affair with another man's wife, he had her husband Uriah killed so that he could marry her. He also bombed when he didn't discipline Amnon for raping Tamar, resulting additional domestic issues. He wasn't perfect, but he was called a man after God's heart. He had flaws because he was human. He loved the Lord and sought guidance and wisdom, but he was broken in many ways, too. He was anointed King of Israel, but he wasn't the Messiah, so the junk in between shouldn't be surprising. He wasn't perfect, but he repented.

"So Samuel took the horn of oil and anointed him in the presence of his brothers,
and from that day on the Spirit of the Lord came powerfully upon David."
(1 Samuel 16:13 NIV)

"And when He had removed him (Saul), He raised up for them David as king,
to whom also He gave testimony and said,
'I have found David the son of Jesse, a man after My own heart;
who will do all My will.'"
(Acts 13:22 NKV)

Are you seeking to be known as a woman after God's heart? In blunders, repent; pick yourself up; don't blink an eye; and keep both eyes focused on the Lord Jesus.

AUGUST

*"It is the sweet, simple
things of life which are
the real ones after all."*

-Laura Ingalls Wilder

Take5forHIM

AUGUST 1

Today's consolation is that we can't be all things to all people.

At 18 years old, "What do you think your life will look like in 10 years?" My answer? "Get married; live a financially comfortable life; have two kids; a house with a big front porch and dormer windows; a pool; enjoy the simple things; and have a great relationship with family." How many dreams can I put a big check mark? By reading, perhaps you envision open ended, long convos on the couch with my kids laying it all down about life, faith, God sightings, as well as the day's activities. It's lamenting, but it's not the case. I have more enriching discussions with girls over lunch than with my own precious ones. My kids know I love them more than life, but colloquies are strained. There was a breakdown somewhere- maybe because I wasn't the best mom for a few years when I suffered depression. During that time, I got bent out of a shape and flew off the handle over the least little things. I spanked, screamed, and came down hard when they didn't clean up their messes. Best defined as crabby and ornery, but I answered friends' phone calls with a chipper "hello." I've apologized umpteen times, but mending scars takes years. I over-exert to be involved in their (current) college lives, empathetic, listen, and cheer. As I receive impromptu hugs at a high school football game, my heart leaps but in the back of my mind I ache for my own kids to do the same. Oh, how I wish I was the mother of today in the growing years! It brings me to my knees.

David had the make-up of a great king, but it's presumed his family life was not reflective of the same person [based on what's written]. Very few can excel in all areas of life. No one can be all things to all people. Without spreading yourself too thin, be the best you can be with the people you love the most. Friends and careers are chosen, but family is for life. Endow in kinship wholeheartedly.

"Now therefore fear the Lord and serve him in sincerity and in faithfulness. Put away the gods that your fathers served beyond the River and in Egypt, and serve the Lord. And if it is evil in your eyes to serve the Lord, choose this day whom you will serve, whether the gods your fathers served in the region beyond the River, or the gods of the Amorites in whose land you dwell. But as for me and my house, we will serve the Lord." (Joshua 24:14-15 ESV)

Take5forHIM

AUGUST 2

Time is ticking 'til school starts. It's a clean slate whether beginning high school, college, or returning to the same school. What's going to be different? Today's message is an uplifting prayer as you embark on a fresh beginning. May this be the school year that strengthens your path with Christ.

Dear Lord Jesus,

I pray for the girls reading this prayer. Go before them and hand pick teachers, professors, and students in their classrooms and dorm hallways. Surround them with Christians who will encourage them daily in their studies. Prove that the Body of Christ is everywhere they go. I pray each one as she steps into the life of a freshman (high school or college) thru senior (high school or college). Every year is a mile marker, and I pray they will live it to the fullest and to Your Glory. Give them confidence in who they are in You, and may they live boldly to fulfill dreams You have instilled in them. With You on their side, let them be encouraged as You light their paths and accommodate their needs. Opportunities are expensive, so afford ways to experience extracurricular activities and travel opportunities. Wherever they go, align their voyage. Guide them and may they always acknowledge You as THE PROVIDER.

John 13:35 says others will know we are Christians by our love. Lord, I pray all walks of life will be drawn to these girls because of their actions, speech, demeanor, and attitude. I pray they will be great examples of showering unconditional love to all they come in contact. We pray a Titus 2:7 prayer, "In everything set them an example by doing what is good. In your teaching let them show integrity, seriousness and soundness of speech that cannot be condemned, so that those who oppose You may be ashamed because they have nothing bad to say about us." (Titus 2:7-8 NKJV) Let them be genuine as they show kindness and the right words to comfort those who are hurting.

Do not allow these girls to be persuaded by atheists, agnostics, and wishy-washy-name-only Christians that You're a myth. Come alive so they will not be shaky but stand on the solid ground of the Almighty God.

You give us free will, and I pray these girls will make choices that honor Your Name and Your People. I pray they will take ownership of their Christianity and be committed to say "no" when peers tell them it's okay to participate in immoral behavior. I pray they will not buy into the lie that it's perfectly fine to stray and come back later. It's not permissible because choices affect futures. Draw them to Yourself so they will not wander away- even for a night- because true joy & happiness is living in Your will. Let them not be morally good, but let their guts yearn for what is pleasing

Take5forHIM

in Your sight. Lord, let them cry out for clear insight and ask for understanding, so they will know what it means to fear You and gain knowledge from You. (Proverbs 2: 3,5)

Lastly, we pray for academic success. While they're in school for an education, it's not the highest ambition. Some may argue that straight A's and a GPA is the ticket, but it means nothing without You. A high dollar paycheck after college graduation is not the big prize either. So, I pray these girls will seek first the kingdom of God and believe everything else will be added unto them (Matthew 6:33).

We give YOU this school year, trusting You will do mighty things. Jesus, permeate their souls to mold them into the godly women YOU created them to be! Work, Lord Jesus, work! In Christ's Name, Amen.

AUGUST 3

Like a calendar year, a new school year (or college) is the perfect term to evaluate who you're hangin' around.

Do you have friends who are preventing you from being the Jesus follower you want to be? If you have a friend who's dragging you in the mud, now is the best time to shake her/him off. What about negativity? Are you surrounded with positive influences? Unfortunately, we tend to adopt the traits of those around us no matter how strong our personality. A resolution to overcome bad company is hard to carry through, but hopefully this message will be inciteful how to make a clean break from toxic relationships. The goal is to breach with minimal strife. How?

-Don't bad mouth. That's the worst thing, so keep your lips zipped!
-Pray before you say/do anything.
-Gradually pull away without arguing.
-When asked why you never get together, be honest. Say something like, "I've changed and feel like this is unhealthy. We have different views, so I'm not having fun together anymore." "I don't approve of the things you are doing nor the people you are following. I don't want to go in that direction."

Sound stupid? Brutal? Unrealistic? Canned? Maybe. However, say it- DON'T TEXT IT. Say it and be honest. There will be achy feelings but handling it with maturity will help the wounds heal, so both of you can move on different paths.

Friends come and go through the years and only a handful will be friends in 2-5 years. Don't be afraid to graciously walk away. There's a right and wrong way to do it. Read James 1 on wisdom.

The Word is full of advice on friendships. Search the internet or the back of the Bible.

Take5forHIM

AUGUST 4

Daily fatal shootings in schools and public places is a reminder of the fallen world we live. It also calls attention to the fragility of life. It's oblivious what the day has in store. We take lightly simple pleasures throughout the day.

When we know Christ, we should be ready unknowing if it's our last day or a family member's. Be prepared to meet our Savior at any moment.

"Yea, though I walk through the valley of the shadow of death, I will fear no evil;
For You are with me; Your rod and Your staff, they comfort me."
(Psalm 23:4 NKJV)

Take5forHIM

AUGUST 5

Do you ever wonder what's your purpose? Your purpose is to glorify God. Simple. Period. He does not need you; you need Him. He knew you before He created the world. You are unique and special, but He does not depend on you for existence, you depend on Him. You are a one of a kind creation, but you need Him to give your life meaning.

Many spend too much time scratching their heads wondering why they're on earth, when the answer is uncomplicated. When you accept this straightforward statement, your heart will be more aware of glorifying Him through your actions.

"That the proof of your faith, being more precious than gold which is perishable, even though tested by fire, may be found to result in praise and glory and honor at the revelation of Jesus and though you have not seen Him, you love him, and though you do not see Him now, but believe in Him, you greatly rejoice with joy inexpressible and full of glory, obtaining as the outcome of your faith the salvation of your souls." (1 Peter 1: 7-9 NAS)

A prayer:
"I have not stopped giving thanks for you, remembering you in my prayers. I keep asking that the God of our Lord Jesus Christ, the glorious Father, may give you the Spirit of wisdom and revelation, so that you may know Him better. I pray that the eyes of your heart may be enlightened in order that you may know the hope to which He has called you, the riches of His glorious inheritance in His holy people, and His incomparably great power for us who believe." (Ephesians 1:16-20 NIV)

AUGUST 6

So if you're wondering how Take5forHIM *started.......*

On a Wednesday Night in July 2015, the youth pastor preached about knowing God's Word. I was involved in youth group as a breakout leader. That night when our breakout group met at a picnic table on the playground, I asked how many read the Bible regularly. The answer was obvious when eyes darted everywhere but to mine. Further discussion disclosed that the Bible is boring and oftentimes irrelevant.

A few days later, I sat on my back-porch swing and prayed asking God to give the girls a desire to read His written words. He spoke to me in a big way- "WRITE CARDS." Not knowing what to write, I grabbed a stack of bright colored index cards. For over two hours, I wrote twenty-six cards without stopping. I thumbed through the Bible and never wondered what to write next. Each card had a Bible passage and a relatable message to spark interests. I wish I had scanned the original set because it was an unforgettable morning. It was the beginning of passing out weekly notecards to girls at church and wherever I bumped into them during the week.

There was a time when the church youth group was bursting at the seams. Wednesday Nights were the place to be, and nobody missed without a good reason. My own breakout group was in a cozy, homey, inviting room huddled tight around a table. When the church outgrew the large group meeting space, youth group moved to Sunday Nights in a re-designed Fellowship Hall. The venue and night change threw a wrench in routines, and attendance plummeted.

During the summer when I finally had a chunk of time to look at my son's school yearbook, I grabbed it. As I flipped through the pages, my eyes swelled. Girls I had not seen in months were on every page. I cried out, "God, this is awful! They're going to totally lose interest [in You] if somebody doesn't do something! Somebody's gotta do something fast!" A few days later as I was exercise walking, God said, "EMAIL." I shuttered and kept moving, but God kept ringing "EMAIL" in my ears all during the day. "Email what?" I didn't expect Him to direct me to do anything more than pray about the situation. That's the church's responsibility, right?

Then, He started pouring a vision in front of me that was so vivid & clear. My mind raced. I thought about a trendy blog. He said, "EMAIL." Within days God, pulled it all together. The name popped in my head for quick five-minute powerful messages with some meat to chew, so to speak. Take5forHim was the email address; thus, the catchy name stuck. Girls signed up and I got it started three weeks later.

As time passed, college roommates signed up for the weekly emails. Sorority sisters

Take5forHIM

popped a sign-up email. Old neighbors' daughters and friends. Former classmates of my kids who had moved away. It was thrilling as even moms asked to join as an opportunity to have spiritual discussions with their daughters.

Then God called me to disciple you through a printed book. God works in ordinary people to do His unexpected work.

> *"Trust in the Lord with all your heart, and do not lean not on*
> *your own understanding. In all your ways acknowledge Him,*
> *and He will make your paths straight."*
> *(Proverbs 3:5-6 NAS)*

AUGUST 7
Do not stir up or awaken love until the appropriate time."
(Song of Solomon 2:7 and 3:5 HCSB)

Song of Solomon (a.k.a. Song of Songs) is a juicy book tucked in the middle of the Old Testament describing two young hearts. The young woman is head over heels for young King Solomon and begins the Book with her finding a way to spend time with him as he tends a flock of sheep. As the book progresses, the two write love letters comparing their fondness to each other to the beauty of the nature around them. Describing her beauty and his handsomeness in a way that makes us giggle; they were madly in love. The entire book describes how God intends a man and woman to fall in love. They were absolutely smitten and could not wait to be husband and wife, abstaining from physical intimacy until they were united in marriage.

Purity is God's best plan. In plain honest girl talk, the sexual experience in an unmarried relationship does not compare to the beauty of sex inside of marriage! *"Do not stir up or awaken love until the appropriate time." (Song of Solomon 2:7 and 3:5 HCSB)* The appropriate time is when you say, "I do."

Your future husband may not describe your teeth as a flock of sheep shorn, coming up from the washing (NAS), but he will hopefully love, adore, and compliment your beauty in his own way. The endearing love is the form of romantic love a girl longs for, and later the kind of physical intimacy that seals a marriage.

Did you know this was in the Bible? Read Song of Solomon and the commentaries (notes) about the passages. Reading the eight chapters comparing legs to pillars of marble and a waist like a mound of wheat encircled by lilies- so worth reading.

"My beloved is mine and I am His."
(Song of Solomon 2: 16 and 6:3 NKJV)

Take5forHIM

AUGUST 8

Humanity's greatest problem is sin, but we serve a forgiving God. Who serves a God who is so easy to forgive, erases the file, and moves onward? We backtrack because it seems preposterous since our nature is slow to forgive, and unlikely to forget.

Today's verses are a prayer of adoration in Micah 7. Micah was inundated by the magnificence of God's consistent character of love and forgiveness. We'll have daily clashes with sin, but God is merciful to those who call upon His Name in the combat.

> *"Who is a God like You, removing iniquity and passing*
> *over rebellion for the remnant of His inheritance?*
> *He does not hold on to His anger forever because He delights in*
> *faithful love. He will again have compassion on us; He will vanquish*
> *our iniquities. You will cast all our sins into the depths of the sea."*
> *(Micah 7:18-19 HCSB)*

AUGUST 9

Did you grow up going to church with your family? Is this church stuff new to you? Have you explored other religions? Do you understand why Jesus died for our sins? Do you know why we say there is only one true God? What about when people say, "The Holy Spirit is living in you?" Lastly, spiritual warfare. Do you know what that means?

Today's devotional is based on a heavy passage. There's no sugar coating these verses. It stings, but we cannot skip over tough passages just to read the comforting ones about God's love. We must consume all of it. The crux is that we'll always be in a war between what the world tells us and what God's Word says. We can penetrate our souls with the darkness of the world or the Light of Christ. The best way to develop your faith is to read THE WORD. Know what you believe so you won't be tempted to slide from His truth.

WARNING: THIS IS HEAVY.
"For God's wrath is revealed from Heaven against all godlessness and unrighteousness of people who by their unrighteousness suppress the truth, since what can be known about God is evident among them, because God has shown it to them. For His invisible attributes, that is, eternal power and divine nature, have been clearly seen since the creation of the world, being understood through what He has made. As a result, people are without excuse. For though they knew God, they did not glorify Him or show gratitude. Instead, their thinking became nonsense, and their senseless minds were darkened. Claiming to be wise, they became fools and exchanged the glory of the immortal God for images resembling mortal man....
Therefore God delivered them over in the cravings of their hearts to sexual impurity, so that their bodies were degraded among themselves. They exchanged the truth of God for a lie, and worshiped and served something created instead of the Creator, who is praised forever.

This is why God delivered them over to degrading passions. For even their females exchanged natural relations for unnatural ones. The males in the same way also left natural relations with females and were inflamed in their lust for one another....they did not think it worthwhile to acknowledge God, God delivered them over to a worthless mind to do what is morally wrong. They are filled with all unrighteousness, evil, greed, and wickedness. They are full of envy, murder, quarrels, deceits, and malice. They are gossips, slanderers, God haters, arrogant, proud, boastful, inventors of evil, disobedient to parents...." (Romans 1:18-32 HCSB)

Verse 22- Special emphasis on "claiming to be wise." Any one of us is a blink from turning our eyes from truth.

Take5forHIM

August 10

A South Georgia family's lives took a traumatic turn when their daughters, three years apart in age, were both diagnosed with cancerous brain tumors. August 10th is the indelible date when the high school junior had a seizure the first day of school which lead to a diagnosis. Weeks later, the college-age daughter had a terrible lingering headache which lead to an ER visit. She was also diagnosed with a different type brain tumor. Surgery successfully removed the tumor, but she had a similar treatment plan in order to completely zap the cancer.

How could this be? What's the likelihood of two sisters, in two geographic locations, could be diagnosed with a non-contagious illness? Both girls had been healthy with no symptoms whatsoever in the months prior. Then BAM, both girls' lives were rocked, but not shattered. Their sisterhood love bonded even tighter as they leaned on each other every step of the way. Both girls endured thirty radiation treatments after surgeries prior to chemo which is physically, mentally, and emotionally fatiguing.

The dad posted an amazing statement on social media that was a positive outlook on what would be a parent's nightmare. He said, "We have been blessed by friends and an unwavering faith that God is by our side and will get us through this dark time. We have to believe that God has a bigger plan for these incredible girls that has not been revealed yet. Please pray for Lilia to achieve complete healing. Pray for Saville as she embarks on the same journey as her sister which starts tomorrow morning with a difficult and lengthy surgery. Already, we have a deeper love and appreciation for God, the beauty of life itself, and the love of family."

Wow is an understatement.

BOTTOM LINE: Regardless of how perfect, how good, how beautiful, how much money is in our bank accounts- we will experience hardships. Hanging on to Biblical truths will keep us from drowning when the tide rises.

"I have told you these things, so that in Me you may have peace.
In this world you will have trouble. But take heart! I have overcome the world."
(John 16:33 NIV)

"Peace I leave with you; My peace I give to you; not as the world gives,
do I give to you. Let not your heart be troubled, nor let it be fearful."
(John 14:27 NAS)

Cling to these additional verses: 2 Corinthians 2:14; 2 Corinthians 6:4.

Take5forHIM

AUGUST 11

A Guatemalan girl was on a chicken bus one afternoon on her way home from work. The bus was hi-jacked by four robbers armed with guns. The girl began to pray as the robbers were demanding the passenger to empty their bags of everything or they would shoot. Then men violently screamed and pounded their guns on the bus ceiling. One gunman stood right next to her. She kept her head down and started silently praying, "Please God, make me invisible. Please God, make me invisible." The gunman next to her reached across her body with the gun and scratched her wrist to take the belongings from the persons on both sides of her, and it was like he never saw her! She was the only passenger they never acknowledged or approached!

Our God hears our minds as we pray silently. What other religion can testify to such a story! Only the one true God could answer a silent prayer. Trust Him to care for you even when you cannot speak!

> *"O Lord, you have searched me and you know me! You know when I sit*
> *and when I rise up; you discern my thoughts from afar. You search out*
> *my path and my lying down and are acquainted with all my ways.*
> *Even before a word is on my tongue, behold O Lord,*
> *you know it altogether."*
> *(Psalm 139: 1-4 ESV)*

> *"My sheep hear my voice, and I know them,*
> *and they follow me."*
> *(John 10:27 ESV)*

What the heck is a chicken bus? *A chicken bus is a brightly painted school bus re-vamped for cheap public transportation in Guatemala. It doesn't carry chickens at all—just people & goods.* Stories like this one reminds us that God's people are all over the world and He's working. His omnipotence (unlimited power) and omnipresence (presence everywhere at the same time) are staggering. His people may speak hundreds of languages & live different cultures, but we serve the same Almighty God.

Take5forHIM

AUGUST 12

Being happy and having joy are two different feelings. Happiness is a temporary emotion while joy is a long-lasting emotion that explodes from the spirit living inside. True joy is knowing where you've been, putting the past being, living in contentment with the present, and looking positively towards the future. True joy is humble and thankful there is no condemnation for the past and that Christ has freed you from bondage. True joy illuminates in your attitude, actions, and face.

"These things I have spoken to you, that my joy may be in you,
and that your joy may be full."
(John 15:11 ESV)

AUGUST 13

"The kingdom of heaven is like a mustard seed which a man took and
sowed in his field, and this is smaller than all other seeds,
but when it is full grown, it is larger than the garden plants,
and becomes a tree, so that the birds of the air come and nest in its branches."
(Matthew 13:31-32 NAS)

The meaning of this parable? Having the faith of a mustard seed means your faith starts small and grows until it flourishes. It's like a fine wine; it takes time to age. The tiny speck sized seed grows into a huge, beautiful, luscious plant. Google it!

Take5forHIM

AUGUST 14

What's being a good friend? Do you call yourself a good friend to all (emphasis on ALL)? Are there times when you don't want to be bothered with problems? Are some girls' issues bigger than you care to be involved? If you're a senior, are there people you cannot wait to never see again? Were these once great friends? How do you treat ex-friends?

Christ calls us to love our neighbor as ourselves----MORE than ourselves. We should be flexible for an urgent text. No appointment necessary. When issues reach their height, some things cannot wait. When you know it's an ordeal to arrange talk time, then it's too late. True friends push busyness aside and make room to be a friend.

With that in mind, would you run to a friend's aid to pick her up at 2 a.m. if she's drunk with vomit all over her clothes? Would you clean up the puke, wash her up, get her in the car, and deliver her to safety? The next day, would you call to ask if she's alright? Would you listen to the drama story attached to the previous night? Advise her? And then at school on Monday, would you sit with her at lunch? Then when Friday rolls around, would you invite her to a movie and dinner instead of the next banger? If she's a believer, would you hold her accountable for poor choices?

What about the classmate who has no friends? Maybe she's a wallflower. Maybe she's not college bound. Maybe she's a little chubby and out of shape. Maybe her family life is unstable. Maybe she's handicapped. Maybe she has a bad reputation. Maybe she's hurting for money. Maybe a parent just passed away. Maybe other people call her annoying, but you feel like God is calling you to be kind. Would you be a friend even if it's unpopular in the eyes of others? Would you give a smile or invite her to grab a smoothie after school? Without going overboard with WWJD (which was a 1990's movement before you were born- WHAT WOULD JESUS DO), but Jesus did hang with the unpopular. He hung out with all kinds of people. Nobody's perfect so why should we hang with a closed group of people.

"One gives freely, yet grows all the richer; another withholds what he should give,
and only suffers want. Whoever brings blessing will be enriched,
and one who waters will himself be watered."
(Proverbs 11: 24-25 ESV)

"And he answered and said, "You shall love the Lord your God with all your heart
and with all your soul and with all your strength, and with all your mind,
and your neighbor as yourself."
(Luke 10:27 NAS)

Take5forHIM

AUGUST 15

When mom and dad suffer financial downfall, it filters straight down to the kids. It adds a lot of stress on a family when the money flow is weak. Parents may say, "You've gotta get a job because we cannot afford to buy all you want and need."

A job teaches a lot about real life, the value of a dollar, building confidence, submitting to the authority of a boss, and responsibility.

Get a job and tithe. It's only 10 cents of every dollar. Make it a priority. God honors it. It's biblical, and He'll stretch your finances, so you don't notice it's gone.

Money problems are the worst when you're in it, but it will relieve your parents and be an excellent lesson in maturity. It's a win-win.

"Bring the full tithe into the storehouse, that there may be food in my house. And thereby put me to the test, says the Lord of hosts, if I will not open the windows of heaven for you and pour down for you a blessing until there is no more need. I will rebuke the devourer for you, so that it will not destroy the fruits of your soil, and your vine in the field shall not fail to bear, says the Lord of hosts. Then all nations will call you blessed, for you will be a land of delight, says the Lord of hosts."(Malachai 3:10-12 ESV)

"In all toil there is profit, but mere talk tends only to poverty."
(Proverbs 14:23 ESV)

Take5forHIM

AUGUST 16

Like most moms, I have a love-hate relationship with our *"fourth child"*, Bella- a solid black, miniature dachshund with a patch of aging white hairs around her chin. One minute she brings laughter, and the next sentence I'm ready to drop her off on the side of a country road. She adds spice to our kitchen when she moves her head side to side as she intently listens to our dinner conversations. Yet I get so aggravated with her as she begs for food, digs for skinks, barks at lizards & squirrels, and runs in the opposite direction when her name is called. She has many expressions, and I can look into her deep brown eyes and know there's a soul. There is a running joke around our home that I'm jealous because my husband loves THE DOG more than ME. A dog truly is man's unconditional best friend. I could ramble. Emotions swing with our four-legged, high pitched yapping child. However, today's light-hearted message brings a huge smile on my face- a sweet, unforgettable memory.

One afternoon, I sat at the computer watching a video of one of my favorite praise songs. The words are powerful describing the death and resurrection of our King..."*The ground began to shake, the stone was rolled away.....*" Bella was living the good life napping with her chin resting on the rug next to me. As the vocalist belted out the song, so did I! As the song picked up the pace and got louder and stronger, Bella perched on her hind legs and started howling at the top of her lungs. Occasionally she would cut her brown eyes over to mine, and then raise them up to the ceiling as we sang a duet. She lifted her nose up and yelped through the rest of the song. It was ear piercing, but so was my singing.

When the song was over, she stopped and put her chin back on the rug. The next song came on, but she was worn out after praising her Lord. Do dogs and cats go to Heaven? I certainly hope so.

"Let everything that has breath praise the Lord."
(Psalm 150:6 NAS)

Take5forHIM

AUGUST 17

Girl: Is it ok to go to parties but not drink alcohol? Can I be the designated driver?

T5: Hmmmmmm......This is a tough one to answer and debatable. There are no specific scriptures to answer the dilemma except:

> "Do not be misled: 'Bad company corrupts good character.'
> Come back to your senses as you ought, and stop sinning; for there are
> some who are ignorant of God- I say this to your shame."
> (1 Corinthians 15:33-34 NIV)

> "Walk with the wise and become wise,
> for a companion of fools suffers harm."
> (Proverbs 13:20 NIV)

The old adage, "You're known by the company you keep," was likely stemmed from the above verses. There are two arguments for/against attending drinking parties. IF YOU CAN BE STRONG AND ABSTAIN FROM ALCOHOL (NOT EVEN HOLDING A CUP), go for it. More power to ya, girlfriend! Stand firm, socialize, be a part of the friend circle, and give safe rides home. However, being the only sober one at a party is lonely. While observing the absurd effects of alcohol consumption, there's a feeling of exclusion and the source of snide comments. It's arduous to attend and not participate. "After a while, I just gave in because they're my friends."

Final point: While no desire to drink or smoke with the crowd, there will be "guilty by association" rumors which pass through circles. Social media pics and gossip produce lots of chatter. *It doesn't matter what others think, but what's right in God's eyes.*

Take5forHIM

AUGUST 18

"Let no one look down on your youthfulness, but rather in speech, conduct, love, faith and purity, show yourself as an example of those who believe."
(1 Timothy 4:12 NAS)

Disregard the number age; don't let anyone make you feel less knowledgeable or like an immature Christian. Everyone's living out different levels of faith with unique journeys. Many of you are more excited for Jesus than any adults I know! You have a genuine faith, walk your talk, invite friends to church and small groups, and sincerely live for Jesus. I'm impressed by blogs and testimonies. This generation of believers is far from shallow.

AUGUST 19

"There is therefore now no condemnation to those who are in Christ Jesus,
who do not walk according to the flesh, but according to the Spirit.
For the law of the Spirit of life in Christ Jesus has made me
free from the law of sin and death."
(Romans 8:1 NKJV)

Do a happy dance. This is one to sing and shout. God forgives past sins and wipes them out with hurricane force winds. Hallelujah! Freedom!

Take5forHIM

AUGUST 20

Prayer for college girls....

Father, here's a rock-solid prayer for the college girls as they begin this school year. Be with each one who is transitioning from the comforts of home to a dorm or apartment. Extinguish any homesickness with the companionship of roommates, wholesome new friends, and excitement for what's to come. I pray they will not long for home but smile upon the fulfillment of goals You have paved ahead.

Whether the girls are away at college or local, draw them to compatible Christian friends who will bond tight as they are faced with the challenges of new-found freedom. Plug them into a college ministry, Bible Study or church. Set hearts on fire for Your truth and start revivals across college campuses. Guide them as they figure out who they are as an adult. May their identification be found in YOU, not in Greek status or a major. Thank you for their first eighteen years they spent growing up. They've been taught, mentored, and coached. Now it's time for them to spread their wings, rise up as Your Daughters, and ultimately the godly women You created them to be. Although I have not met them, I have a heart for each one and pray for successful college years. Let them be world changers.
In Christ's Name, Amen.

AUGUST 21

Do you know anyone carrying a chip (or boulder) that has settled deep in the heart, tearing her apart? Nobody likes being around her, and she can't live with herself either. She's been hurt deeply and has no clue how to recover. The fissure cracks deeper as time goes by. The person hasn't dealt with it. It's bottled up inside except instances when disparaging comments explode towards the culprit. Thus, the bitterness continues to grind until.......

A beautiful soul has a HEART OF STONE. Something is eating away down to the bones. It's rotting, and she doesn't how to eradicate it.

The frozen heart can be vocalized by anger, cussing, cynical jokes, and sarcasm. When a horrendous attitude gets to this point, there's no reasoning. The calendar takes a toll, and it becomes a HUGE PROBLEM.

Is there something gouging that YOU just cannot forgive and forget?
-Not making the team.
-Not winning the scholarship.
-X-ed from the #1 sorority.
-Excluded from a party.
-REJECTION
-A friend pushing you aside to spend more time with another friend.
-It's senior year and you've never had a date to Homecoming.
-You have a part-time job to pay for clothes, gas, car insurance, and your sport. Other parents have the money to give to their kids; yours does not.
-Hereditary genes explain your big rump and large thighs. No amount of exercise gets rid of it. "Other girls have perfect bodies."
-A situation was mishandled; therefore, there's resentment towards the church.
-"Someone said that she said...."
-"Nobody ever invites me to do anything. I have no friends."

Whatever's taxing, chisel the boulder. Ask God to soften the slab that's formed in your calloused chest. If your hardness is due to someone, begin praying for that person. When we pray for enemies, sore feelings naturally loosen up. There's no way to pray for someone and have acidity. It just doesn't work that way.

> "I will give you a new heart and put a new spirit within you; I
> will remove your heart of stone and give you a heart of flesh."
> (Ezekiel 36:26 CSB)

Read Proverbs 14:30; Proverbs 17:22.

Take5forHIM

AUGUST 22
Big Churchy Words

PROPITIATION- To cover or become the substitute for our sins. In so doing, a propitiation assumes the responsibility of our sin and reconciles it.

Bible Verses: *"My little children, I am writing you these things so that you may not sin. But if anyone does sin, we have an "advocate" with the Father- Jesus Christ the Righteous One. He Himself is the "propitiation" for our sins, and not only for ours, but also for those of the whole world." (1 John 2:1-2 HCSB)*

"Love consists in this: not that we loved God, but that He loved us and sent His Son to be the propitiation for our sins." (1 John 4:10 HCSB)

SANCTIFICATION- The processing of becoming holy.

Bible Verses: *"But we are bound to give thanks to God always for you, brethren beloved by the Lord, because God from the beginning chose you for salvation through sanctification by the Spirit and belief in the truth." (2 Thessalonians 2:13 NKJV)*

"And that is what some of you were. But you were washed, you were sanctified, you were justified in the name of the Lord Jesus Christ and by the Spirit of our God." (1 Corinthians 6:11 NIV)

Also 1 Corinthians 6:9-11; 1 Corinthians 1:2.

ATONEMENT- "That the Bible's central message is atonement, that is, that God has provided a way for humankind to come back into harmonious relation with him, is everywhere apparent in Scripture."[16]
In short, this word describes Jesus sacrificing in our place to bring us into the right relationship with God the Father.

Bible Verses:
"I am the good shepherd. The good shepherd lays down His life for the sheep." (John 10:11 NIV)

"Who does not need daily, as those high priests, to offer up sacrifices, first for His own sins and then for the people's, for this He did once for all when He offered up Himself." (Hebrews 7:27 NKJV)

Also read Romans 5:10.

Take5forHIM

REDEMPTION- the action of saving or being saved from sin, error, or evil.[17]

"The word redeem means "to buy out." The term was used specifically in reference to the purchase of a slave's freedom. The application of this term to Christ's death on the cross is quite telling. If we are "redeemed," then our prior condition was one of slavery. God has purchased our freedom, and we are no longer in bondage to sin or to the Old Testament law."[18]

SCRUPULOSITY- "A form of Obsessive-Compulsive Disorder (OCD) involving religious or moral obsessions. Scrupulous individuals are overly concerned that something they thought or did might be a sin or other violation of religious or moral doctrine."[19] From all I've read, it's best described as someone who thinks they're never good enough to receive God's grace.

SALVATION- *"If you confess with your mouth that Jesus is Lord and believe in your heart that God raised him from the dead, you will be saved. For it is with your heart that one believes and is justified, and with the mouth one confesses and is saved."* (Romans 10:9-10 ESV)

[16]Atonement. Elwell, Walter A. *"Entry for Atonement". "Evangelical Dictionary of Theology"*. 1997. *Bible Study Tools.* www.biblestudytools.com/dictionary/atonement.
[17]Redemption. *Google.* www.google.com/search.
[18]Redemption. *GotQuestions.org.* 2018. www.gotquestions.org/redemption,html.
[19] Scrupulosity. *Wikipedia.* 2018. https://en.wikipedia.org/wiki/Scrupulosity.

AUGUST 23

Today, we're reading Deuteronomy 28. It's long, but powerful. Stick with it as Moses is very descriptive about the blessings of following God's commands versus NOT. The first fourteen verses are the divine sanctions of following Him. Verses 15-68 are difficult to read because it's the opposite of the blessings- referred as curses. It's a very detailed list of an oppressive life following disobedience. God is a good God, but He's also a God of judgment.

The Blessings of Obedience: Read Deuteronomy 28:1-14.

Curses for Disobedience: Read Deuteronomy 28: 15-68.

Moses spoke sternly to the Israelites to live by God's commands. They knew they weren't spotless nor is anybody. That's why they sacrificed animals as a way of atoning sins.

You ask, "Does this apply to me today? Wasn't Moses speaking to the Israelites thousands of years ago?" Our God is the same God today as He was thousands of years ago. We are adopted into His covenant family, so we should not turn a deaf ear to these words.

AUGUST 24

Ever known someone who opposed an issue but suddenly took a drastic turnaround in favor of the agenda? A staunch Democrat who switches to the Republican Party and then runs for office. Or, how about Ebenezer Scrooge, the infamous fictitious character who turned a leaf from stingy and stone-hearted to a kind and giving man who loved Christmas. Saul was one of those people. As a fresh start, God even changed his name to Paul.

BEHIND THE STORY: Saul was a Pharisee who was on the extreme swing of the pendulum as Jews and Gentiles were converting to Christianity. The early church conversions multiplied rapidly, and Saul was one of the ardent Pharisees who persecuted Christians. In Acts 7, an amazing Christian named Stephen was stoned to death for his faith. Severe persecution broke out after his death. Saul burned with the desire to destroy the church, so he drug men and women out of their homes to imprison them. He was known for rebelling against Jesus' teaching and followers. He must've been a beast. Read Acts 9:1-18.

Have you ever known anyone who converted to Christianity so profoundly? I've known a few and it's spine-tingling. Paul was a rogue who believed he was fighting for a good cause- to preserve the Jewish faith. He passionately believed Christians were serving a false religion until God got a hold of him and shut him up for three solitary days. Not only was his heart softened, it was ignited. THE SCALES FELL OFF HIS EYES! It's unclear if that's figuratively or if a crust had formed over Saul's eyes, causing blindness. Scales are like a thick coat of armor on a fish. Now, read the below passage Paul wrote to the Philippians.

"Further, my brothers and sisters, rejoice in the Lord! It is no trouble for me to write the same things to you again, and it is a safeguard for you. Watch out for those dogs, those evildoers, those mutilators of the flesh. For it is we who are the circumcision, we who serve God by his Spirit, who boast in Christ Jesus, and who put no confidence in the flesh— though I myself have reasons for such confidence.

If someone else thinks they have reasons to put confidence in the flesh, I have more: circumcised on the eighth day, of the people of Israel, of the tribe of Benjamin, a Hebrew of Hebrews; in regard to the law, a Pharisee; as for zeal, persecuting the church; as for righteousness based on the law, faultless.

But whatever were gains to me I now consider loss for the sake of Christ. What is more, I consider everything a loss because of the surpassing worth of knowing Christ Jesus my Lord, for whose sake I have lost all things. I consider them garbage, that I may gain Christ and be found in him, not having a righteousness of my own that comes from the law, but that which is through faith in Christ—the righteousness that comes from God on the basis of faith. I want to know Christ—yes, to know the power of his resurrection and participation in his sufferings, becoming like him in his death, and so, somehow, attaining to the resurrection from the dead.

Not that I have already obtained all this, or have already arrived at my goal, but I press on to take hold of that for which Christ Jesus took hold of me. Brothers and sisters, I do not consider myself yet to have taken hold of it. But one thing I do: Forgetting what is behind and straining toward what is ahead, I press on toward the goal to win the prize for which God has called me heavenward in Christ Jesus." (Philippians 3:1-14 NIV)

Paul was an evangelist, missionary, prisoner, and died a martyr. The same man who assaulted Christianity made a complete role reversal.

Take5forHIM

AUGUST 25

Yesterday's devo mentioned Stephen being stoned. Acts 6 & 7 tell his gallant story. He was described as full of faith and of the Holy Spirit. The death produced an outcry of persecution which must've been a terrible time for the Christian community. Although it was gloom and doom, it caused new believers to scatter to other areas to safely worship their Lord Jesus. In midst of the bad, the gospel spread to new territories. It's a case similar to "man meant it for evil, but God meant it for good." God brings good works during bleak conditions. It's easy to casually skip over such points when reading, so it was important today to identify how Christianity advanced.

"On that day a great persecution broke out against the church in Jerusalem, and all except the apostles were scattered throughout Judea and Samaria. Godly men buried Stephen and mourned deeply for him. But Saul began to destroy the church. Going from house to house, he dragged off both men and women and put them in prison.

Those who had been scattered preached the word wherever they went. Philip went down to a city in Samaria and proclaimed the Messiah there. When the crowds heard Philip and saw the signs he performed, they all paid close attention to what he said. For with shrieks, impure spirits came out of many, and many who were paralyzed or lame were healed. So there was great joy in the city." (Acts 8:1-8 NIV)

AUGUST 26

"But the fruit of the Spirit is love, joy, peace, patience, kindness, goodness, faithfulness, gentleness and self-control. Against such things there is no law. Now those who belong to Christ Jesus have crucified the flesh with its passions and desires. Since we live by the Spirit, we must also follow the Spirit. We must not become conceited, provoking one another, envying one another." (Galatians 5:22-23 NIV)

Let's back up for more info on Paul's teaching on the fruits of the spirit because the full meaning cannot be appreciated without digging a little further for interpretation. Chapter 5 begins with *"Christ has liberated us to be free. Stand firm then and don't submit again to a yoke of slavery."* Paul goes on to tell the Galatians that it doesn't matter whether they are circumcised or not circumcised because their faith in Jesus is the greatest concern. Those in the church of Galatia were confused about their new faith and were trying to add works and legalistic Jewish laws as a means of working out their salvation, but Paul assured them that Jesus freed them from the bondage of the old laws when He died on the cross and resurrected from the dead. Paul said, *"For you were called to be free, brothers, only don't use this freedom as an opportunity for the flesh but serve one another through love. For the entire law is fulfilled in one statement: Love your neighbor as yourself."* (Galatians 5:13-14 HCSB) Paul taught that they would exhibit the fruits of the Spirit if they walk by the spirit rather than the rituals of religious laws.

A Christ follower is like a tree that blossoms and bears fruit. The fruit is the beautiful souls who naturally love their neighbors. The next time you're around an irritating person, think, "Love all people, love all people." And instead of whispering, "Get a job" about the homeless person begging for a few dollars on a street corner, say, "Love all people." Bearing fruit doesn't mean giving money to every charitable cause, but gleaming God's love to mankind by living a life of LOVE, JOY, PEACE, PATIENCE, KINDNESS, GOODNESS, FAITHFULNESS, AND SELF CONTROL. We've been crucified with Christ therefore we no longer live; Jesus Christ now lives in us. Jesus also used the fruit analogy, *"I am the vine, you are the branches. If you remain in me and I in you, you will bear much fruit; apart from me you can do nothing." (John 15:5 NIV)*

Smother the desires of the flesh and let fresh fruit ripen.

Take5forHIM

AUGUST 27

Repentance is being humbled and broken of sin, and then exiting with no intentions of returning. True repentance lays it down at Jesus' feet, accepting the forgiveness, and moving forward. It's welcomed, but a daily challenge to reprieve for degrading sins, yet we're taught God easily forgives. Feelings of unworthiness for the gift is normal. God holds us in His righteous right hand for assurance. Cease from the fatigue of repetitious requests. Repent and LET IT GO!

"Repent, then, and turn to God, so that He will forgive your sins."
(Acts 3:19 NIV)

"Jesus answered them, 'It is not the healthy who need a doctor, but the sick.
I have not come to call the righteous, but sinners to repentance.'"
(Luke 5:31-32 NIV)

"The Lord is not slow about His promise, as some count slowness,
but is patient toward you, not wishing for any to perish
but for all to come to repentance."
(2 Peter 3:9 NAS)

Don't get slack. I'm laying a foundation for eager learners. Also look up the following: 2 Peter 3:9; Matthew 3:2; Psalm 38:18; 2 Chronicles 7:14.

Take5forHIM

AUGUST 28

How do you do it? How do Christian youth separate themselves from pop culture trash? It's impossible to avoid when there's media on phones, computers, and TVs. Sexual innuendos fill up 99.99% of visual outlets. The older generation argues that times have changed, and it wasn't this bad 30+ years ago. Not true, older movies are laced with depravity. Watching videos and music artist interviews from the 70's to present day portray drugs, rampant lifestyles, and lost souls. How do you stay focused on God while enjoying secular music and current TV series without losing moral values of right and wrong? After all, we're not hermit crabs who come out only when it's safe. We're still living in a clear box even if we choose to stay inside a shell. It's onerous not to see and hear.

What goes in the mind corrupts the mind, but there's got to be a balance without being prudish. The nitty-gritty is to keep tabs on what's on your mind and language. No matter how much I adore God, Christian radio gets monotonous. Variety is good, but keeping Jesus #1 cannot be overemphasized enough. Be careful what you see, sing, and say to prevent conforming to a non-religious civilization.

"And do not conformed to this world, but be transformed by the renewing of your mind, that you may prove what is that good and acceptable and perfect will of God."
(Romans 12:2 NKJV)

"Do not love the world or the things in the world. If anyone loves the world, the love of the Father is not in him. For everything in the world- the lust of the flesh, the lust of the eyes, and the pride in one's possessions- is not from the Father, but is from the world. And the world with its lust is passing away, but the one who does the will of God remains forever." (1 John 2:15-17 CSB)

Take5forHIM

AUGUST 29

What are your expectations for this school year? At the end of the year, what will be the one word that defines it? Take today to be still. Set personal goals. Pray. Listen.

"Your ears shall hear a word behind you, saying, 'This is the way, walk in it,"
Whenever you turn to the right hand or whenever you turn to the left."
(Isaiah 30:21 NKJV)

"Whatever you do, do it heartily, as to the Lord and not to men."
(Colossians 3:23 NKJV)

Watch God work this school year.

AUGUST 30

Today's topic may strike a chord. I've mildly struggled since college with the number on the scale. In my 20's, I took laxatives on a regular basis to drop a few pounds- even though I was a pretty and petite 105 pounder. I could've easily fallen in the trap of an eating disorder as I've aged and longed for 1-0-5 again. Below is a testimony from an anonymous teenage girl in her battle to overcome bulimia.

"So right now, I'm ready to share a story that I rarely talk about yet has majorly impacted my life. Today I came to a major realization. The world is screwed up, and right now I can't change that, but I can change my world. This picture (on social media) shows the true me, a happy girl who just likes to dress nice and hang out with friends, but about 2 months ago I came home crying and admitted to my mom everything I was going through, and although I'm not ready to share everything on here that happened, I am ready to say this. I suffer from two eating disorders. Now I know that I'm only 16 and everyone 'goes through an I want to be skinny phase,' but I'm here to explain my story so more people who suffer from an eating disorder will save themselves like I am trying to do. I suffer from a commonly known, but un-talked about disorder called Bulimia. I've suffered from this since 7th grade and let's face it, that's quite a while. Bulimia is a life threatening and altering disease that takes over you until you feel worthless and unwanted because of how you look and what you put inside of you. It has led me to also skipping many meals until friends started to notice, and now many doctor appointments. Many people have asked me why I only go to three classes and why I have so many appointments, and my bulimia (and other things) is why. BUT BULIMIA IS NOT ME, I AM NOT BULIMIA. I had to scream that because it's hard for me to process that I am not my disorder. I also suffer from a disorder called ARFID which is avoidant, restrictive food intake disorder. I have a fear of new foods. I have panic attacks, gag-problems and other things that are caused by the fact that I fear food with different textures, smells, and colors. This may sound weird, but it's a psychological block in my brain that is trying to 'protect me' from these 'invaders' which is just food. It's strange to hear about this, I know, but people actually have this just like they have anxiety and other things. Eating disorders are one of the many things in today's world that need to be talked about, and I'm changing my life to make sure that they are brought up in a healthy way so the boys and girls who suffer from them feel okay with telling someone that they have one. Please, if you or somebody you know is suffering from an eating disorder or anything else, talk to a friend, parent, teacher, or anyone to make sure that that person stays safe and secure in their own bodies. This has been hard for me. I know this will put a major label on me, but I know the Lord is telling me that admitting this is the right thing to do for me and my progression with beating this disorder." - Anonymous

Take5forHIM

I spoke with this girl about the everyday war in her head that has been a long-haul recuperation. The disorders spurred additional health problems because she wasn't getting the proper nutrients her body needed as she purged daily meals. With God's help and supportive parents, she's winning the fight.

Eating disorders weren't a problem in biblical times, so there are no weighty verses to quote except God's Word says our bodies are the temple of the Lord. Eat sensibly. Exercise sensibly. Keep it healthy.

August 31

An anvil is a hard piece of steel or iron used as an anchor for a blacksmith to take a shapeless strip of fired up iron to form a horseshoe. Each part of the anvil has a purpose in shaping the horseshoe without the blacksmith touching the scorching piece. The anvil is the anchor which allows the artist (the blacksmith) to create a luxury for the horse- protection for his hoofs from rocks and all types of ground surfaces.

Sometimes we need to be on God's anvil so that He can mold and shape us to be the Christ followers He created us to be. In the trials we are weak, stretched, and formless, but as the weight of the trial is lifted (or relieved) we are strong as a cooled piece of iron.

"But we have this treasure in jars of clay, to show that the surpassing power belongs to God and not to us. We are afflicted in every way, but not crushed; perplexed, but not driven to despair; persecuted, but not forsaken; stuck down, but not destroyed; always carrying in the body the death of Jesus, so that the life of Jesus may also be manifested in our bodies." (2 Corinthians 4: 8-10 ESV)

SEPTEMBER

"Spread love everywhere you go. Let no one ever come to you without leaving happier."

-Mother Teresa

Take5forHIM

SEPTEMBER 1

Teenagers complain about what jerks their coaches can be- regardless of the organized sport. I've personally observed coaches from Little League teams to high school. Like teachers and work supervisors, coaches are in authority for a season. Their purpose is to teach, coach, and win. All this to say, there's a fine line. You'll learn life lessons looking back, but ultimately God is in authority over successes/failures, and your life purpose is to glorify God alone- not a team coach. Be respectful but remember who's in control so that irritating remarks and bench time don't get under your skin.

If the thrill of the sport is dampened by an intense coach, there's nothing shameful about walking away. Parents encourage their kids not to be quitters, but when a coach has unrealistic training and expectations, it's a no-brainer.

"Finally, be strong in the Lord and in his mighty power. Put on the full armor of God, so that you can take your stand against the devil's schemes. For our struggle is not against flesh and blood, but against the rulers, against the authorities, against the power of this dark world and against the spiritual forces of evil in the heavenly realms. Therefore put on the full armor of God, so that when the day of evil comes, you may be able to stand your ground, and after you have done everything, to stand. Stand firm then, with the belt of truth buckled around your waist, with the breastplate of righteousness in place, and with your feet fitted with the readiness that comes from the gospel of peace. In addition to all this, take up the shield of faith with which you can extinguish all the flaming arrows of the evil one. Take the helmet of salvation and the sword of the Spirit which the word of God. And pray in the Spirit on all occasions with all kinds of prayers and requests. With this in mind, be alert and always keep on praying for all the Lord's people. Pray also for me, that whenever I speak, words may be give me so that I will fearlessly make known the mystery of the gospel for which I am an ambassador in chains. Pray that I may declare it fearlessly, as I should." (Paul-Ephesians 6:10-20 NIV)

Take5forHIM

SEPTEMBER 2

Hitler's Nazis killing Jews. **Blacks killing whites; whites** killing blacks. Cop killings. Extremists killing gays. Terrorisms. Haven't we learned anything over the decades? Is there any value in another human life? Why should anyone think they are better than someone else? God created us in His image, but the sin of thinking higher of ourselves and less of others wreaks havoc.

Today's message was inspired by a testimony from a girl who attended a local mission trip. She gets it. "In the eyes of God, we are all equal."

[The mission trip] "was one of the most impactful experiences I've ever had. I was blessed with the opportunity to work with the amazing girls from the children's home. My site was a lot different compared to others. I didn't paint signs or build ramps; I made relationships. Mission work can take a variety of different forms and I found this particular form a bit challenging at first. Instead of having a set task that could be completed through the week, we were there to serve the girls by way of fellowship and love. Through arts and crafts and hair braiding, we made real genuine friendships. The girls were amazing to say the least. Our prayer for the week was to be Jesus to these girls- not be preaching but by the ministry of presence. One of my favorite days of the week was when one of the girls opened up about her past. Now from a worldly perspective, you could say our lives were very different. In no way but by the grace of God would our paths cross. Yet there we were, hanging out, being teenage girls together. It was in this moment that I realized no matter what background she came from, regardless of what her past held, in the eyes of God we are all equal. We are all His sons and daughters. His love does not discriminate against different circumstances; it knows no end. We are all children of God. The bottom line is to love all. Love period."

Around mid-week, this girl was humbled and compassionate as she described her team's struggle finding a common thread connection to the girls in foster care at the children's home. Normally teenage girls would be chatting about college visits, summer trips, social media, and jobs. But these girls spent their lives physically and emotionally battered, tossed from one home to the next and longing for a "forever family." She and the team were determined to make a difference.

By the end of the week, the girls bonded by quality time. The home director said she witnessed a 180-degree change from Monday to Friday. The team found common ground. When you strip away backgrounds, we're all the same on the inside. If we could walk/talk/live/treat others as Jesus commanded, there would be a true revival of change. Read 1 Samuel 16:7 and James 2:2-10.

Take5forHIM

SEPTEMBER 3

Grace and mercy are used hand and hand, but what's the context?

Grace is the undeserving gift God bestows to us when we ask forgiveness. Asking is all that's required.

Mercy is requesting God to relinquish (or relieve) some of the pain associated with a trial. God is a merciful Father, and while we deserve the pain for our sins, often times He delivers us- whether by asking or not.

> *"Who is a God like you, who pardons sin and forgives the*
> *transgression of the remnant of His inheritance? You do not stay*
> *angry forever but delight to show mercy."*
> *(Micah 7:18 NIV)*

> *"Mankind, he has told each of you what is good and*
> *what it is the Lord requires of you; to act justly, to love faithfulness,*
> *and to walk humbly with your God."*
> *(Micah 6:8)*

SEPTEMBER 4

When you're young and beautiful, you want to show off as much as allowed for semi and formal events. If Moms will buy the dresses, why not? This is the wrong outlook and very unwise for a mom or daughter. Do you think Jesus approves of girls who claim to follow Him but wear low cut, tight fitting, dresses so short that panties [or bare butt cheeks] are uncovered? Do you think it's OK to say, "I'm going to be pure until I get married" yet wear clothing that exploits the body? What about all the guys who drool over the skimpy dresses? Is it right to tempt their minds? Guys struggle with porn temptations anyway, so seeing their "girl" friends dressed provocatively adds to the problem. Do you want guy friends to view you with those type of thoughts? It's something to consider on the next shopping venture for the perfect special occasion dress.

Jesus said, *"But I tell you that anyone who looks at a woman (or man) lustfully has already adultery of the heart with her in his heart."* (Matthew 5:28 NIV)

Take5forHIM

SEPTEMBER 5

From the time we wake up in the morning until we close our eyes at the end of a long day, we're sucking in all that we see. Today's message is a warning to be careful what you allow yourself to see. This is usually a lecture for guys, but girls are subjected to as much.

In your lifetime, you'll be pressured to see and do things harmful to your soul. You may be thinking, "What's the harm in looking? I'm not physically doing anything wrong." That's a false statement. Guys who struggle with overcoming porn addiction will set you straight on that lie. Porn addiction is real, and shockingly on the rise for teen girls.

Scenario: First semester of college, eighteen-years old. Friends were giggling as I walked toward my friend's convertible in the college parking lot. I wondered what was so funny and then Kim flipped a boy porn magazine in front of my eyes. <Gulp!> It threw me off guard. I can still visualize the naked guy wearing nothing but a thick gold chain around his neck (the 80's). There was peer pressure as they teased and tried to force innocence to look as they turned pages. I don't know about them, but it was my first and last experience.

Same as a guys' talk, why is viewing porn wrong? Wait- why is it sinful? Jesus said, *"The eye is the lamp of the body. If your eye is healthy, your whole body will be full of light. But if your eye is bad, your whole body will be full of darkness. So if the light within you is darkness, how deep is that darkness?"* (Matthew 6:22-23 CSB)

Jesus also said, *"But I tell you that anyone who looks at a woman (or man) lustfully has already adultery of the heart with her in his heart."* (Matthew 5:28 NIV)

You should take everything written in the Bible seriously, but especially quotes right out of Jesus' mouth. To paraphrase, He said that gazing at the opposite sex (or same sex) for the purpose of arousing sexual desire is sin (darkness of the heart), and that's the purpose of porn.

Porn is addictive; therefore, it takes control. It's no different than social media addiction. It can't be put down. Try going without social media for a day, week, month, year, or the rest of your life.

Don't look the first time! No porn flicks, magazines, or websites. Protect your eyes, thoughts & soul!

Take5forHIM

SEPTEMBER 6

I grew up being told by my mother, "Nice girls don't." I love my mother dearly, but I'm here to tell you that's the wrong way to communicate to a daughter about premarital sex.

If you're a virgin, YAY! You may be a virgin because you haven't had the opportunity to have sex or because you've made the choice to wait until marriage. Whatever the reason, stay committed. Promise self-control to wait for your husband. It will be so worth it and something you'll never, ever regret. There's nothing sweeter than falling in love with a man who has also waited for you to be his one and only. Pray for it! Don't assume you'll never find a husband who has also made the commitment. God already knows who your husband will be, so pray for your mystery man. Pray for restraint to wait for you, too. It's God's best, and that's what mothers should be teaching their daughters beginning at a young age.

> *"To the unmarried and the widows I say that it is good for them to remain single as I am. But if they cannot exercise self-control, they should marry. For it is better to marry than to burn with passion."*
> *(1 Corinthians 7:8-9 ESV)*

SEPTEMBER 7

If you're not a virgin and feel guilty/ashamed/dirty as you hear lessons on purity, my heart aches for you. Don't be overcome with the hurt and dark emotions. We've all sinned and fallen short of the glory of God (Romans 3:23), and there are all types of sin.

You may have physically lost your virginity, but pledge to God celibacy from this day until your honeymoon night. Humbly ask forgiveness for sexual impurity. God will forgive the past, so bury the hatchet. Next, don't date a guy who doesn't respect your body and faithful abstinence to your future husband. Don't buy into the line, "We love each other and we're going to get married- SOME DAY." Until vows are spoken, rings placed, and the marriage certificate is signed, marriage is not guaranteed. God will honor and bless beyond your imagination if you firmly take the initiative. He forgives and deletes the history.

"Flee from sexual immorality. Every other sin a person commits is outside the body, but the sexually immoral person sins against his own body."
(1 Corinthians 6:18 ESV)

Jesus told the adulterous woman, "Go, and from now sin no more."
(John 8:11 ESV)

Take5forHIM

SEPTEMBER 8

The beauty of the bright blue sky against the new, fresh green leaves in the Spring. The rushing waves controlled by the moon know where to halt on the shoreline. The breathtaking scene of mountains as far as the eyes can see. Rain pouring from clouds that you cannot grab ahold if you tried. Even satellite images of a white puffy, swirling hurricane is an amazing sight, showing God's power and creativity in the sky and ocean. The perfection and fragrance of distinct flowers. No two sets of fingerprints are the same; there are no clones. The individual personalities of pets. How can anyone believe everything we see, touch, and love is an accident?

Deep thoughts of where God was derived; if He has always existed; and if He existed, from where? It's outlandish for the human mind to believe in Him and that He created all, but there's no other explanation as to how it transpired. *"What no eye has seen, nor ear heard, nor the heart of man imagined, what God has prepared for those who love Him." (1 Corinthians 2:9 ESV)* So magnificent. So artistic. So beautiful. So creative.

We'll never have the answers to all questions, but the Bible matches up to believe God is the artisan who has always been. Our minds should be in awe instead of full of rationale negating the historical derivations. We're given the choice whether to believe.

"All things were created through Him, and apart
from him not one thing was created that has been created."
(John 1:3 CSB)

"In His hand are the depths of the earth, and the mountain peaks belong to Him.
The sea is His, for He made it, and His hands formed the dry land."
(Psalm 95: 4-5 NIV)

"The heavens declare the glory of God; the skies
proclaim the work of His hands."
(Psalm 19:1 NIV)

"Listen to this, Job; stop and consider God's wonders. Do you know how God controls the clouds and makes His lightning flash? Do you know how the clouds hang poised, those wonders of Him who has perfect knowledge?"
(Job 37: 14-16 NIV)

Romans 1:20; Psalm 104:24-25, plus more! Don't take His originality for granted.

Take5forHIM

SEPTEMBER 9

For the naysayers who question whether Jesus ever lived. History recognized Jesus' life and death when recording years on the timeline.

B.C. stands for "before Christ." Anno Domini is the Latin phase meaning "in the year of the Lord" and refers to the birth of Jesus Christ- not AFTER DEATH. Developing this system of counting years is very interesting and its origin has been researched by many. For more info, historical articles are easily found on the internet.

Take5forHIM

SEPTEMBER 10

"Serve wholeheartedly, as if you were serving the Lord, not people."
(Ephesians 6:7 NIV)

Whether volunteering or working a part-time job, pray the following prayer based on Ephesians 6:7. "Lord, may I work with enthusiasm and a positive disposition as though I'm working for You rather than people." It will make a difference in work ethic. A long day will fly by with the right perspective to strive to do your best for Him.

SEPTEMBER 11

The effects of the 1962 and 1963 U.S. Supreme Court decisions to remove organized prayer and Bible readings from public schools had the detrimental effects on the country which were feared [by Christians]. The block era of the 1960's was the first decade of mass craziness for the country: three public figure assassinations; Supreme Court ruling to legalize abortions; Vietnam War; the civil rights movement; sexual revolution; public protests and riots. Reviewing the series of events, it's no wonder the removal of prayer is queried as the first step to the marring.

It's difficult to put into words the effects, but sad when America was founded on Christian principles. Home of the free and the land of opportunity are the main attractions for the flock of immigrants to swoon America. I'm exercising freedom of religion and speech and thankful for it, but the country has gone looney tunes. There's very little unity in politics and citizens are divided on many platforms. Life has become complicated and, at times, violent on news talk shows. No one can agree. There are two extremes on every issue and no respect for lawmakers to do their work without backlash. One cannot run for political office without an investigation that may date back to high school. National holidays and catastrophes are the only time Americans pull together in a sentimental hoorah for the nation.

To clarify, Christian clubs and flagpole prayer rallies remain active on public school campuses with the stipulation that it's not held during school hours. Sports teams are also allowed to pray before or after a game. When it's said that prayer was removed from schools, this means there was previously a time (prior to 1963) when schools would pray in the classroom and it was common to begin the day with Bible verses. Later it became known as a moment of silence. What's a moment of silence? It's a politically correct way of saying, "If you're a Christian or whoever you pray to, here's the time to pray to your god without us using the word PRAYER." Let's just say there's a lot of tip-toeing as we've become a SINSITIVE society. Decades have passed, and we'll never know if God's hand would have remained on a thriving country if He'd been allowed in the hearts of students five days per week. Maybe you've never been taught about the Supreme Court rulings in a history class. This is spiritual warfare at its finest. God, have mercy on us.

"Happy is the nation whose God is the Lord-
and the people he has chosen to be his own possession."
(Psalm 33:12 CSB)

"...and my people, who bear my name,
humble themselves,
pray and seek my face,
Take5forHIM

and turn from their evil ways,
then I will hear from heaven,
forgive their sin,
and heal their land.
My eyes will now be open and my ears
attentive to prayer from this place."
(2 Chronicles 7:14 CSB)

"In the same way the Spirit also helps us in our weakness, because we do not know what to pray for as we should, but the Spirit himself intercedes for us with unspoken groanings. And he who searches our hearts knows the mind of the Spirit, because he intercedes for the saints according to the will of God." (Romans 8:26-27 CSB)

"Love the Lord your God with all your heart, with all your soul, and with all your strength. These words that I am giving you today are to be in your heart. Repeat them to your children. Talk about them when you sit in your house and when you walk along the road, when you lie down and when you get up. Bind them as a sign on your head and let them be a symbol on your forehead. Write them on the doorposts of your house and on your city gates." (Deuteronomy 6:5-9 CSB)

Take5forHIM

SEPTEMBER 12

Many of the apostles' books of the Bible end with lovely benedictions, some of which pastors conclude church services and recite at weddings.

> Paul said, "May the Lord of peace himself give you
> peace always in every way. The Lord be with all of you."
> (2 Thessalonians 3:16 CSB)

"Now to Him who is able to strengthen you according to my gospel and the proclamation about Jesus Christ, according to the revelation of the mystery kept silent for long ages but now revealed and made known through the prophetic Scriptures, according to the command of the eternal God to advance the obedience of faith among all the Gentiles- to the only wise God, through Jesus Christ- to him be the glory forever! Amen." (Romans 16:25-27 CSB)

"Finally, brothers and sisters, rejoice. Become mature, be encouraged, be of the same mind, be at peace, and the God of love and peace will be with you. Greet one another with a holy kiss. All the saints send your greetings. The grace of the Lord Jesus Christ, and the love of God, and the fellowship of the Holy Spirit be with you all." (2 Corinthians 13:11-13 CSB)

Take5forHIM

SEPTEMBER 13

Jesus performed oodles of miracles. He raised Lazarus from the dead, healed the sick, fed five-thousand from five loaves of bread and two fish. Today's devo highlights one of many.

Stop. Read John 5:1-16.

Put yourself in the position of the lame man. Have you ever been down for a week with the flu? Injured in a car accident? Hospitalized? You may have watched the sun peek through the curtains; brighten and heat the room; and the room slowly fade to darkness as you laid in a zombie-like state. Time lapses slowly as the clock passes hours. It's a painfully long day as one stares blindly out a window or doorway; too tired to pray, too weak to think. His age was undisclosed but being lame for thirty-eight years must have felt never ending with: frustration, depression, loneliness, and blah days of pining to be active as in the healthy years. They didn't have wheel chairs for self-dependence; home health care agencies for regular hygiene; nor was there a volunteer based daily meal delivery. PT wasn't practiced in Bible times either, so traveling to the pool was a last-ditch effort to rehabilitate. He and other crippled visitors somehow got themselves to the pool which was known as a place of healing.

The pool was likely a legend based on one person's miraculous cure. Keep in mind, the Festival had brought a high traffic of visitors to the city, so a crowd had formed around the pool.

Out of all the eager ones, Jesus zoned in on this one man. He could've put the healing touch on every visitor, but He was drawn to this one man who was struggling to dip in the water. Visualize a paraplegic trying to scoot over the edge with upper body strength. Depending on the depth of the water, maybe there was fear of drowning, too. Jesus sympathized with this one man's attempt to walk again.

> *"'Get up,' Jesus told him, 'pick up your mat and walk.'*
> *Instantly, the man got well, picked up his mat, and started to walk."*
> *(John 5:8-9 CSB)*

The man's life changed on-the-spot. In all probability, he ran and profusely shouted, "I'm healed, I'm healed!" as he laughed, cried, and clamored Jesus' miraculous healing power. He went from bound as a lonely, helpless, disabled man to an exuberant man with a new lease on life. The Jews persecuted Jesus because He was "working" on the Sabbath Day. Ha! God never takes a day off; He's always working.

Take5forHIM

SEPTEMBER 14

Question: Are you amazed when people who are clueless about Christianity suddenly dive in feet first? Is God so real that you would've stepped out on a new faith to believe without a Church or a Bible over 2000 years ago? Do you believe He is the Son of God in 20__? Do you feel Him in your spirit?

Losing excitement happens when distractions cloud our views. That's why it's important to carve out a block of time to get in THE WORD, pray, read faith-filled books, and have some alone time. Today, I encourage you to simply THINK.

"And answering again, Pilate was saying to them, 'Then what shall I do with Him whom you call the King of the Jews?' And they shouted back, 'Crucify Him!' But Pilate was saying to them, 'Why, what evil has He done?' But they shouted all the more, 'Crucify Him!' And wishing to satisfy the multitude, Pilate released Barabbas for them and after having Jesus scourged, he delivered Him to be crucified." (Mark 15:12-15 NAS)

Have you ever wondered if you would have believed Jesus was God's Son if you had been there to witness Him, the uproar of the priests, the people who were talking about His teachings- both favorably and unfavorably? Would you have thought He was a kook, a blasphemer, a liar?

Whether we lived then or now, nothing is different. Those people were given the same opportunity to believe as we are today. If you're a Christian; like Paul, God shed the scales from your eyes and revealed Himself (Acts 9:18). He spoke to your heart, you listened, and prayed to make Him Lord of your life. You believed without visually seeing and touching His nail scarred hands and sides.

After the resurrection, Jesus appeared to the disciples. He showed them the scars where the nails were in His hands and side. Later, the other disciples told Thomas they saw Jesus….

"But one of the Twelve, Thomas, was not with them when Jesus came. So the other disciples kept telling him, "We have seen the Lord!" But he said to them, "If I don't see the mark of the nail in His hands, put my finger into the mark of the nails, and put my hand into His side, I will never believe!" After eight days, His disciples were indoors again, and Thomas was with them. Even though the doors were locked, Jesus came and stood among them. He said, "Peace to you!" Then He said to Thomas, "Put your finger here and see My hands. Reach out your hand and put it into My side. Don't be an unbeliever, but a believer." Thomas replied, "My Lord and my God!" Jesus said, "Because you have seen Me, you have believed. Blessed are those who believe without seeing." (John 20: 24-29 HCSB)

Take5forHIM

SEPTEMBER 15

In an ever-changing world, it's comforting to know God never changes and never will. What He said thousands of years ago in His Word stands true forevermore. You're not old fashioned or behind the times. It doesn't matter if it's 100 A.D. or 20__. God's Word is timeless.

> *"Some take pride in chariots, and others in horses,*
> *but we take pride in the name of the Lord our God."*
> *(Psalm 20:7 CSB)*

SEPTEMBER 16

"Honor your father and your mother." You've heard this your entire life. How long are you required to live by "this rule?" The Bible never says but implies a lifetime commitment. Regardless of the kind of relationship with your parents, the 5th Commandment says you should give them utmost respect.

Parents get a bad rap. Kids think parents are uncool, too strict, and full of "no" answers. Better known as fun-suckers. Opinions will change as an adult- even as you enter the 20's. Parents are always thinking of what's best for you. And, their gut feeling about stuff is usually right. They KNOW! They're not intentionally being vicious dictators. They've lived and see dangers that you do not see. They see stop signs when you see green lights. They're protective because they want to keep you out of harm or from going down the wrong road. The yellow flashing light is parental instinct.

One morning, I heard loud squawking. There's a gigantic camellia bush right outside the sunroom window, so I caught a perfect view. A squirrel was in the bush and two birds were fighting with him. I spotted a nest, and then obvious the mama and papa bird were doing everything they could to protect their chirping babies. They swooped in as close as possible to keep the squirrel from the nest. Minutes passed, and the birds were not going to let anything happen to their precious little ones above. Watching the squirrel, he carefully found a safe place at the base of the tree. He buried his head for a while in the leaves, and then dashed off in a race to save his life. Mama and Papa swooped, screeched and circled him all the way to the opposite end of the yard. They made it clear to NEVER think of coming back to their camellia bush.

And, that's how parents are with children. They have their kid's well-being in mind from the moment they're born. Every decision made, the child is thought of first- even something as menial as, "What's for dinner?" The unconditional love for children never ends, at any age. Bear that in mind when you're worlds apart on issues. God gave them a monumental responsibility to raise HIS CHILDREN, and it's tough.

"Honor your father and mother, which is the first commandment with a promise, so that it may go well with you and that you may have a long life in the land."
(Ephesians 6:2-3 CSB)

"Obey your leaders and submit to them, since they keep watch over your souls as those who will give an account, so that they can do this with joy and not with grief."
(Hebrews 13:17 CSB)

Take5forHIM

SEPTEMBER 17

We live in a fallen world tainted by sin. God created it in His perfection. When Adam and Eve disobeyed, sin entered the world. Sin is contagious like the rotavirus. If we don't surround our world with Christ followers and stay in fellowship with Him, we're setting ourselves up.

Put yourself in a bubble when you feel sin creeping. Stay in communion with Jesus and clutch the Bible like a shield of armor to protect from Satan's trick to separate us from our Father.

"Be strong in the Lord and in the power of His might. Put on the whole armor of God, that you may be able to stand against the wiles of the devil. For we do not wrestle against flesh and blood, but against principalities, against powers, against the rulers of the darkness of this age, against spiritual hosts of wickedness in the heavenly places. Therefore, take up the whole armor of God, that you may be able to withstand in the evil day, and having done all, to stand. Stand therefore, having girded your wait with truth, having put on the breastplate of righteousness, and having shod your feet with the preparation of the gospel of peace; above all, taking the shield of faith with which you will be able to quench all the fiery darts of the wicked one. And take the helmet of salvation, and the sword of the Spirit, which is the word of God; praying always with all prayer and supplication for all the saints." (Ephesians 6:10-18 NKJV)

Duck your head when the darts are flying!

Take5forHIM

One night, my husband and I were brushing our teeth when I said, "What the heck happened to Rebekah?" He said, "Rebekah who?" Me: "Rebekah- as in Isaac and Rebekah. She went wacko." We burst in laughter and toothpaste splattered the mirror.

Rebekah had it all. Genesis 24 is a splendid love story about the arranged marriage to Isaac. Abraham sent his servant to the village where his family originated to find a bride for Isaac. Read this sweet passage in Genesis 24! It was love at first sight when they saw each other the first time. Meant to be.

Rebekah married an incredible guy, arranged by God and Abraham, yet she went nuts. She whined early about infertility, but then blessed with twin sons- Esau and Jacob. Then, she favored Jacob (and he favored Esau). She took extreme measures for her favorite son to receive Isaac's inheritance (Genesis 27).

Time after time, we watch sin take over the best of the best. What can we learn from others' mistakes? First, we all need God because we were born with sinful natures. Next, ask Him to guard us from temptations and for the self-discipline to resist.

"But now apart from the law the righteousness of God has been made known, to which the Law and the Prophets testify. This righteousness is given through faith in Jesus Christ to all who believe. There is no difference between Jew and Gentile, for all have sinned and fall short of the glory of God, and all are justified freely by his grace through the redemption that came by Christ Jesus. God presented Christ as a sacrifice of atonement, through the shedding of his blood- to be received by faith. He did this to demonstrate his righteousness, because in his forbearance he had left the sins committed beforehand unpunished- he did it to demonstrate his righteousness at the present time, so as to be just and the one who justifies those who have faith in Jesus." (Romans 3:21-26 NIV)

SEPTEMBER 19

Mary was a common name back in the day, and it gets confusing in the New Testament with so many Marys. Mary Magdalene was a resident of the village of Magdala, and since there were no last names at the time, many people were identified by first name and the place where they lived or their job title. For example, Jesus of Nazareth, Matthew the tax collector, or Rahab the prostitute. Mary M. was a faithful Christ follower and there's much to learn from her.

"...Jesus traveled about from one town and village to another, proclaiming the good news of the kingdom of God. The Twelve (disciples) were with him, and also some women who had been cured of evil spirits and diseases: Mary (called Magdalene) from whom seven demons had come out; Joanna the wife of Chunza, the manager of Herod's household; Susanna; and many others. These women were helping to support them out of their own means (financially)." (Luke 8: 2-3 NIV)

There are rumors of her lifestyle before becoming a Christ-follower, but there is nothing that confirms it as true. When He healed her from the seven demons (Luke 8: 2), she became a devoted believer. She eagerly followed Him as He spoke to crowds. She stood at the cross with his mother Mary (See Matthew 27: 55-56). She also served by helping Joseph of Arimathea with the burial preparations. Then on the third day, she went to the tomb to put burial oils and herbs on His decaying body, but the tomb was empty.

"After the Sabbath, at dawn on the first day of the week, Mary Magdalene and the other Mary...." (Matthew 28: 1-12 NIV)

She then ran to share the news to the disciples.

"When they came back from the tomb, they told all these things to the eleven and to all the others. It was Mary Magdalene, Joanna, Mary the mother of James (aka mother of Jesus), and the others with them who told this to the apostles. But they did not believe them because their words seemed to them like nonsense." (Luke 24:9-10 NIV)

Take5forHIM

SEPTEMBER 20

Today, read the story of Jesus meeting the Samaritan woman at the well: John 4:1-42.

There was an ethnic divider between Jews and other tribes, so the woman was shocked why Jesus would ask her for a drink of water. Skin color and features must've been the first clue of an ethnic difference. They were labeled: Jew, Gentile, Samaritan, Amorite, Canaanite, etc. Jesus showed kindness although He was asking her to draw water from the well for him. There was no authoritative pompous request coming out of his mouth. First, she called Him a prophet because He was aware of her five husbands and was currently living in sin with a man. When he affirmed He was the Messiah, and then broke the lines of division by saying that a time is coming when all believers will worship the Father in spirit and truth and not on a mountain or a synagogue in Jerusalem- He spoke her language. She knew this guy was special and had to be who He claimed to be- The Messiah. She rushed to tell other Samaritans about Jesus.

He didn't preach law but taught that religious barriers would be broken, and salvation was for all who repented and believed.

His words filled a void which she may have been seeking in a husband. Oh, how fascinating it would be to hear the untold testimonies from the lives of people like the Samaritan woman [because surely, they're not all documented in the Bible]. Did she totally surrender to the Christian life? Did she experience persecution from other Samaritans? Did she leave the man who was not her husband?

"Now many Samaritans from that town believed in Him because of what the woman said when she testified, 'He told me everything I ever did.' Therefore, when the Samaritans came to Him, they asked Him to stay with them, and He stayed there two days. Many more believed because of what He said. And they told the woman, 'We no longer believe because of what you said, for we have heard for ourselves and know that this really is the Savior of the world." (John 4:39-42 HCSB)

Take5forHIM

SEPTEMBER 21

It's common to ask how to know when God is speaking? When you spend quality time getting to know the Father, you'll be in tune to His voice. It may be a thought that cannot be shaken, a song, or a gentle tug. As a Christian, His spirit is living in you, so naturally He'll communicate using various methods as He chooses.

One day while exercising, a memory brought me to tears. I stopped running because I was so upset. I cried at the sidewalk and asked God to help me get through the exertion. That night, I pulled out a devotional book that I rarely read. I intended to turn to "today's" date. I read an out-of-this-world devotional which spoke to my heart and provided comfort relating to the day's struggle. It was tantamount to the situation which amazed me. Then, I glanced at the top of the page—correct date, but wrong month! That's God! He turned me to the page He wanted me to read where He could speak on the day when I least expected.

Take5forHIM

SEPTEMBER 22

Every day is a gift, so relax on this beautiful first day of Fall.

"Lord, our Lord, how magnificent is your name throughout the earth! You have covered the heavens with your majesty. From the mouths of infants and nursing babies, you have established a stronghold on account of your adversaries in order to silence the enemy and avenger. When I observe your heavens, the work of your fingers, the moon and the stars, which you set in place, what is a human being that you remember him, a son of man that you look after him?" (Psalm 8:1-4 CSB)

SEPTEMBER 23

Read 2 Timothy 3 and 2 Timothy 4:1-8.

Does 2 Timothy 3:1-4 sound familiar? Lovers of self, money, boastful, arrogant, deceitful, disobedient to parents, gossips, treacherous, lovers of pleasure instead of lovers of God. These traits surround us daily. It's hard living in the world. Sometimes it stinks because you may wonder what's wrong with everybody. Paul ended Chapter 3 by describing the suffering and persecution he endured for the sake of the gospel. He concluded by encouraging others to keep up their ministry and love for Jesus. Whoah!

Chapter 4 is Paul's anthem that Jesus is worth it all because the world is desperate for a Savior.

Separate your lifestyle apart from the people described in Chapter 3 but share the gospel with them when given a chance. Jesus ministered to the sinners. As followers, let's do the same.

SEPTEMBER 24
The Power of the Mouth

*"And the tongue is a fire, the very world of iniquity; the tongue is set
among our members as that which defiles the entire body,
and set on fire the course of our life, and is set on fire by hell."*
(James 3: 6 NAS)

*"When there are many words, sin is unavoidable,
but the one who controls his lips is wise."*
(Proverbs 10:19 HCSB)

Our mouth is a firearm. Words can do as much damage as a small match in a parched forest. The tongue can be used to encourage and build up or tear down. James 1:19 says, *"But let everyone be quick to hear, slow to speak, and slow to anger." (James 1:19 NAS)* Think before you speak.

Take5forHIM

SEPTEMBER 25

New Christians are amazing to observe when they nose dive into scripture more so than those who've known Jesus for years. In a group setting when asked how one grows in faith during the trials of life, a fairly new believer did not hesitate with the following answer verse.

"And not only that, but we also rejoice in our afflictions because we know that affliction produces endurance, endurance produces proven character, and proven character produces hope. This hope will not disappoint us because God's love has been poured out in our hearts through the Holy Spirit who was given to us."
(Romans 5:4 HCSB)

She had it memorized and didn't stutter as she confidently answered the question. Mouths dropped.

Heresy = false teaching.

How do you distinguish what's true and not true? Whose teaching should you trust? How do you know they're teaching straight up God's TRUTH?

Oh, this is tough because a pastor or leader may be very likeable. You may sincerely enjoy hearing their messages. They may be a family friend, so the thought of murky theology is appalling. New Christians or the biblically unknowledgeable are the most gullible to believe someone they esteem as godly. At minimum, you must know the basics of the Christian faith to recognize heresy. The minute your inner self flinches is a good indicator.

Heresy could be anything. "The devastating tornadoes were a crazy storm pattern-causing massive destruction." Nope. God causes the storms. It's His science, His world, His wind, His power. If you believe He's the creator and sovereign over all, hurricanes and tornadoes aren't blamed on Mother Nature. Instead, you see God's power and mysterious ways at work to bring good in the middle of destruction.

Heresy is also taking one phrase in scripture too far and twisting it. Topics such as prophesying and healing. You cannot add or take away from God's Word.

If you're somewhere and get a strong feeling something's just not right, and everybody's acting a little kooky, you're probably correct. Cultish? Take heed of the unusual personality of the group such as:
-An extreme commitment to its leader regarding beliefs, ideas, and truth.
-Questioning teaching is highly discouraged.
-The group is exclusive and has an intense view of themselves versus others' faith.
- The leadership shuns members if they don't participate in an activity.
-The group is strongly urged to invite certain people into the group whose personal contacts would be beneficial for growth. They're also expect to spend most of their time together- not with outsiders.

It's scary because you still wonder how to know what's slanted. There's a fine line, but beware that false teaching is more common than people want to believe. The best instruction is to do homework so that heresy can be fended off. Stay close to a church with a well-known reputation (or denomination) as sincere Christ followers who preach The Gospel. Pray for God's protection against heresy and the wisdom to know the difference. His Word is a shield.

"But even if we or an angel from heaven should preach to you a gospel contrary to what we have preached to you, a curse be on him!

Take5forHIM

As we have said before, I now say again: If anyone is preaching to you a gospel contrary to what you receive, a curse be on him!"
(Galatians 1:8-9 NIV)

"This is what the Lord Almighty says; 'Do not listen to what the prophets are prophesying to you; they fill you with false hopes. They speak visions from their own minds, not from the mouth of the Lord."
(Jeremiah 23:16 HCSB)

"For the time will come when people will not put up with sound doctrine. Instead, to suit their own desires, they will gather around them a great number of teachers to say what their itching ears want to hear. They will turn their ears away from the truth and turn aside to myths."
(2 Timothy 4:3-4 NIV)

Also read: Acts 20:28-30; 2 Peter 2, 1 John 4:1-6, Matthew 7:15-20, 2 Peter 1:12-21.

Don't' drink the Kool-aid!

Take5forHIM

SEPTEMBER 27

Although dating rules are not mentioned in the Bible, good choices can be made with practical advice.

-Don't go out with anyone you cannot envision marrying. That will eliminate a lot of unnecessary dates. What's the point?

-Evaluate his family life. A guy who's bogged down with dysfunctional family stress will bring it into a dating relationship. Not a good long-term candidate.

-Going out with a non-believer is a huge divider from Day One.

-Dating is healthy, so don't be afraid to date. It helps figure out what characteristics you're looking for in a guy.

-Before the first date, establish physical boundaries.

SEPTEMBER 28

While on a long walk at a weekend retreat, I prayed, "God, does anybody read the Take5 devos?!?! I barely get any responses. I thought _____ admired me yet she never says, 'Miss Rose Marie, I love what you write- like she did when I first started emailing the devotionals.'" I was punching the gut while yearning pats on the back when I heard God say, "It's not about you. It's not about you." This was one instance, but I've heard that countless times. Maybe bonkers in the world's eyes, but I think God's desire for humility was the reason accolades were sparse.

He gave me a vision to begin a weekly devotional ministry to reach a few girls. It was HIM, not my ideas, who gave very specific instructions on what to write, how it should be distributed, the visual of bright multi-colors and fonts, and the name Take5forHIM (right down to how to spell it out). He gives me the topics and sets my fingers to typing. Seriously, I'm the facilitator and He's the writer. I cannot take credit because there's no way I could do this on my own. The Bible is HIS STORY and the devos are about HIS WORK. Our mission is to perk ears to how the Bible relates to you, everyday life, and teaching the richness of God's Holy Word. To God be the glory!

"Little children, let us not love in word or speech but in action and in truth."
(1 John 3:18 CSB)

"Then Jesus said to his disciples, 'If anyone wants to follow after me, let him deny himself, take up his cross, and follow me. For whoever wants to save his life will lose it, but whoever loses his life because of me will find it. For what will it benefit someone if he gains the whole world yet loses his life? Or what will anyone give in exchange for his life?'" (Matthew 16:24-26 CSB)

Take5forHIM

"A rainbow is a meteorological phenomenon that's caused by reflection, refraction and dispersion of light in water droplets resulting in a spectrum of light appearing in the sky which takes the form of a multicolored arc. Rainbows caused by sunlight always appear in the section of sky directly opposite the sun."[20] That's the scientific definition of a rainbow.

The believer's definition is: God's covenant that He will NOT flood the earth again- a rainbow.

People had become wicked and turned away from God. *"Every inclination of the thoughts of the human heart was only evil all the time."* (Genesis 6:5 NIV) In response to the rebellion against Him, God flooded the earth to destroy every living person on the earth except Noah and his family who were faithful to the Lord. The Bible doesn't say Noah was perfect because we're all born sinners, but that he *"was a righteous man, blameless among the people of his time, and he walked faithfully with God."* (Genesis 6:9 NIV) God showed mercy to Noah and his family by saving them from the universal flood.

After all the time Noah spent building the ark, gathering two of every kind of animal plus his family, and then 40+ days and nights in a crowded space with all of them- they must have been relieved to see ground and the sunshine.

Noah worshipped the Lord after the flood by building an altar. He took some of the clean animals and birds and sacrificed burnt offerings on it. This pleased the Lord. The Lord blessed Noah and his sons saying to replenish the earth with babies. (This was the best news the men could hear!) Then, He promised never to flood the earth again.

"Then God said to Noah and to his sons with him, 'I now establish my covenant with you and with your descendants after you and with every living creature that was with you—the birds, the livestock and all the wild animals, all those that came out of the ark with you—every living creature on earth. I establish my covenant with you: Never again will all life be destroyed by the waters of a flood; never again will there be a flood to destroy the earth.'

And God said, 'This is the sign of the covenant I am making between me and you and every living creature with you, a covenant for all generations to come: I have set my rainbow in the clouds, and it will be the sign of the covenant between me and the earth. Whenever I bring clouds over the earth and the rainbow appears in the clouds, I will remember my covenant between me and you and all the living creatures of every kind. Never again will the waters become a flood to destroy all life. Whenever the rainbow appears in the clouds, I will see it and remember the everlasting covenant between all living creatures of every kind on the earth." (Genesis 9:8-16 NIV)

Although the secular world would like us to believe Noah's Ark is a fairytale, Jesus confirmed the reality of the flood when He compared it to the last days (Matthew 24: 37-40). Peter also used the flood as he preached the message of salvation and spoke of the final days before Christ's second coming (1 Peter 3:20 and 2 Peter 2:5; 3:5-6).

Ahhhh....a beautiful rainbow painted on a blue sky canvas. How many times have I almost run off the road craning my neck to see the beauty? When there's a rainbow, people run out of their homes with cameras in hand. They're giddy pointing upward in glee. Even later in the day they remember the sighting, "Hey, did you see the beautiful rainbow over the bay?" It's a beautiful, delightful, priceless gift- whether we've experienced buckets of rainfall or just a sprinkle- it's like seeing a piece of God in the sky. Thousands of years later we hear God's voice saying, *"Whenever the rainbow appears in the clouds, I will see it and remember the EVERLASTING COVENANT between all living creatures of every kind on the earth." (Genesis 9:16 NIV)* A covenant is a PROMISE.

Did you know? The Flood was the first rain. The morning dew moistened the earth.

[20]Rainbow. *Wikipedia.* 2018 . *https://en.wikipedia.org/wiki/Rainbow* .

SEPTEMBER 30
Fanatics for ____

Gooooo Dawgs! Roll Tide! Go Noles! Go Gators! War Eagle! Woo Pig Sooie! Tar Heels! Geaux Tigers! Hotty Toddy! Go Yellow Jackets! Go Knights! Go Bulls! Go Hokies! Fighting Irish! Go Sooners! Go Gamecocks! Go Tigers! Go Vols! Go Eagles! Hail State!

Wearing school colors and team logos is stylin' anytime, anywhere. But, have you ever thought about how people fill up a stadium by the thousands, all screaming for their team? And then when the other team wins, the day/weekend/season takes a nose dive? A game loss totally destroys the mood. There's animosity and sometimes pure hatred towards rivals. One example is when the prized trees at Toomer's Corner on the Auburn University campus were poisoned out of disgust towards the man's rival team, the Auburn Tigers (2010).

I'm not preaching because I pull for my college alma mater and have many orange team rivals. (Friends don't let friends wear ORANGE!) On Fall Saturdays, I hoop, holler, chant a fight song cheer, and cheerleader jump for touchdowns. My heart races when I spot a "G" on another car. My reaction to someone wearing a Georgia shirt is naturally, "Go Dawgs!" I feel at home when I start seeing mailboxes, cars, and flags boasting the "G" after crossing the Georgia line. My heart bleeds red & black.

How often do thousands of people fill up a stadium and scream for Jesus? In many ways, the whole team excessiveness is foolish and absurd. I'm mostly ragging on guys, but do the Ducks become their god, to some extent? Sports fanatics get so elevated about their team, but who gets that excited about the best news ever in the history of the world? *JESUS DIED FOR OUR SINS, WAS RAISED FROM THE DEAD SO THAT WE MAY HAVE EVERLASTING LIFE. "FOR GOD SO LOVED THE WORLD THAT HE GAVE HIS ONLY SON. WHOSOEVER BELIEVES IN HIM SHOULD NOT PERISH BUT HAVE ETERNAL LIFE." (JOHN 3:16 NAS) "And he will send out his angels with a loud trumpet call, and they will gather his elect from the four winds, from one end of heaven to the other." (Matthew 24:31 ESV)* What about the words of Isaiah the prophet in Isaiah 6:5, *"'Woe to me!' I cried. 'I am ruined! For I am a man of unclean lips, and I live among a people of unclean lips, and my eyes have seen the King, the LORD Almighty.'" (Isaiah 6:5 NIV)* What about Revelation 4, the vision of seeing God the Father Almighty. The detailed vision of what we have never seen nor can imagine. A beauty and emotion that's totally different that the goosebumps from our football team storming out on the field while the band is playing the fight song. Far different than the excitement of 100,000 waving pompoms, dressed head to toe in team gear, shouting at the top of their lungs, cheering, & clapping.

Take5forHIM

"'Holy, holy, holy, is the Lord God Almighty, who was and is and is to come!'

Whenever the living creatures give glory and honor and thanks to Him who is sits on the throne and who lives for ever and ever, the twenty-four elders fall down before Him who sits on the throne and worship Him who lives for ever and ever. They lay their crowns before the throne and say:

'You are worthy, our Lord and God, to receive glory and honor and power, for you created all things, and by your will they were created and have their being.'"
(Revelation 4:8-11 NIV)

THERE IS ABSOLUTELY NOTHING WRONG WITH TEAM PRIDE, THE THRILL OF COMPETITION, VICTORY, AND THE AGONY OF DEFEAT. I LOVE IT, but shouldn't we experience the same excitement for our God, His Son, His resurrection, and our eternal future?

It's healthy to think deep, evaluate, wonder, analyze, daydream, ponder about the things of this world, and our role in it.

Take5forHIM

OCTOBER

"There are far, far better things ahead than any we leave behind."

-C.S. Lewis

Take5forHIM

OCTOBER 1

*Paul said, "My goal is that they may be encouraged in heart and united in love,
so that they may have the full riches of complete understanding,
in order that they may know the mystery of God, namely, Christ."
(Colossians 2:2 NIV)*

Goals differ and usually reflect true passions.

Over the years, I've been approached by friends begging me to try pyramid sales marketing for skincare or cosmetics. I couldn't go thru with it because I didn't have the self-confidence, but by golly writing this book and marketing it will be a blast! (There I go with the southern slang again!)

The greatest sales reps are successful because they believe in the product they are selling. The smartest, most academic nerds toil to earn a living if they choose a career that's expected of their intelligence versus motivating interests (i.e. brain surgeon instead of a science teacher).

Paul's passion was to spread the gospel of Jesus and win souls. Find your passion and go for it!

Take5forHIM

OCTOBER 2

Here are three versions of the same verse. God speaks of His judgment regarding sex before marriage and out of marriage. Think twice before sacrificing God's blessings for a few hot & heavy moments.

English Standard Version (ESV)- *"Let marriage be held in honor among all, and let the marriage bed be undefiled, for God will judge the sexually immoral and adulterous."* (Hebrews 13:4 ESV)

New American Standard (NAS)- *"Let marriage be held in honor among all, and let the marriage bed be undefiled; for fornicators and adulterers God will judge."* (Hebrews 13:4 NAS)

Holman Christian Standard Bible (HCSB)- *"Marriage must be respected by all, and the marriage bed be kept undefiled, because God will judge immoral people and adulterers."* (Hebrews 13:4 HCSB)

OCTOBER 3

The Nicene Creed
We believe in one God,
the Father almighty,
maker of heaven and earth,
of all things visible and invisible.
And in one Lord Jesus Christ,
the only Son of God,
begotten from the Father before all ages,
God from God,
Light from Light,
true God from true God,
begotten, not made;
of the same essence as the Father.
Through him all things were made.
For us and for our salvation
he came down from heaven;
he became incarnate by the Holy Spirit and the virgin Mary,
and was made human.
He was crucified for us under Pontius Pilate;
he suffered and was buried.
The third day he rose again, according to the Scriptures.
He ascended to heaven
and is seated at the right hand of the Father.
He will come again with glory
to judge the living and the dead.
His kingdom will never end.

And we believe in the Holy Spirit,
the Lord, the giver of life.
He proceeds from the Father and the Son,
and with the Father and the Son is worshiped and glorified.
He spoke through the prophets.
We believe in one holy catholic and apostolic church.
We affirm one baptism for the forgiveness of sins.
We look forward to the resurrection of the dead,
and to life in the world to come. Amen.[21]

[21]The Nicene Creed. *Trinity Hymnal*, Great Commission Publications, Inc., 1990, 846.

Take5forHIM

OCTOBER 4

"Blessed be the God and Father of our Lord Jesus Christ,
the Father of mercies and God of all comfort,
who comforts us in all our tribulation,
that we may be able to comfort those who are in any trouble,
with the comfort with which we are comforted by God."
(2 Corinthians 1:3-4 NKJV)

Showing compassion cannot be over-drilled. There are countless who are throbbing with physical pain or hanging on their last thread this very minute. Ask God to be His vessel to reach them. Never say, "I'm too busy."

OCTOBER 5

Some weeks are torturous! Here's a little jolt in case you're having a rocky week dealing with girl drama! First, let's start by praying.

Dear Jesus,
I pray for friendships that have taken a dip. Heal the hearts of those who have been saddened by those whom they trusted and respected.

Forgive any one of us if we have wronged, failed, and disappointed someone this week. If we've sinned by speaking, posting or by damaging actions which affect them, convict our hearts. We're responsible for our own behavior and not others, so enlighten us of any misdoings we've been involved. Restore us by drawing us nearer to You, keeping our eyes gazed on the everlasting God. I pray that we'll get a grip by refraining from words & actions that do not honor You so that we live out our faith instead of merely talking it up. Lord, heal stabbed hearts. Amen.

It hurts like ___ on either side when there's conflict.

People change --------> People will disappoint and fail you -------> Even people you love and care about will lie, cheat, backstab, post inappropriate and hurtful things. ------->
God never changes and never will -------> HE WILL NEVER, ever, EVER LEAVE YOU ---->
He will never fail and His word stands forever.

Set boundaries.
Pray for them.
Forgive.
Love them but move on.
Put your faith in Christ NOT people.

"Jesus Christ is the same yesterday. Today, and forever."
(Hebrews 13:8 NKJV)

"Cause me to hear Your lovingkindness in the morning, for in You do I trust;
Cause me to know the way in which I should walk, for I life up my soul to You."
(Psalm 143:8 NKJV)

Take5forHIM

OCTOBER 6

A little white lie or slightly stretching the truth is still a lie with a capital red letter L.

We are guilty of manipulating appearances for own selfish benefit which will get us in T---R---O---U----B----L----E. When a believer sins, God is not going to let you get by with doing wrong. You'll either get caught or feel the heat in some other way. Don't expect the schemed plan to pay off. He disciplines just as parents discipline their children. It's how we learn from mistakes, see our sin, and move toward dependency on Him.

"A righteous man hates falsehood,
but the wicked brings shame and disgrace."
(Proverbs 13:5 ESV)

"For nothing is hidden that will not be made manifest,
nor is anything secret
that will not be known and come to light."
(Luke 8:17 ESV)

Take5forHIM

OCTOBER 7

Girl: "I'm a Christian girl, but my boyfriend is not. He's a great guy and he has a lot of respect for my faith. He was not raised in a Christian home, so all this is new. He comes with me to church sometimes. Is it OK to date him? I think he'll eventually come around."

Me: It's absolutely not OK!

Why the response? There are a lot of caution signs, but the fact that he's not a believer nor been exposed to the faith is reason enough. It's easy to justify and make excuses, but God doesn't want your heart tied up in someone who does not know Him. The heart longs for who it longs for, and your date could become your husband. "I'm 17 years old! Marriage is not on my mind." Umm....the heart gets wrapped....and....it could happen. Marriage is hard enough as it is, so you don't want a marriage with mixed beliefs.

OCTOBER 8

Streets paved of gold (Revelation 21:21), no tears & no pain (Revelation 21:4), reunion with loved ones. There are not a lot of descriptions about what Heaven will be like, but we know God is perfect, creative, glorious, and majestic. Knowing the indescribable beauty of the places on earth, of course He would use the same to create the Paradise of all Paradises. We get caught up in what we can see because we cannot fathom the life that we cannot see.

Afraid? Me too! Over the years I recall nights waking up in the pitch, black dark silence of night. Fear gripped with a cold tightness in my chest. My head rushed as my mind tried to grasp it. We all scramble with the unknown in some way. It's humbling to wonder, "How am I going to die?" "When?" "Will I be in pain?" "Will Jesus' second coming be in my lifetime?" "What will we do in Heaven?" "How will I find the people I love there when it must be a crowded place?" "Will they recognize me?"

Eternity = F-O-R-E-V-E-R, and that can drive us over the edge to try to unravel unless WE BELIEVE JESUS IS WHO HE SAYS HE IS, BELIEVE, SURRENDER, AND KNOW OUR HOME IS IN HEAVEN WITH HIM. This is not home.

Take a deep breath. It's going to be inexpressible! God is in control of you, your fears, and has prepared a great place for your eternal Home. There will be no words to define what it's like to worship Jesus forever and to live in the pure joy and peace that's not found in our current life. It's going to be so crazy awesome that if given the chance to come back, you would not consider it.

"But our citiizenship is in heaven. And we eagerly await a Savior from ther, the Lord Jesus Christ, who, by the power that enables him to bring everythign under his control, will transform our lowly bodies so that they will be like his glorious body."
(Philippians 3:20-21 NIV)

"The I saw a new heaven and a new earth, for the first heaven and the first earth passed away, and the sea was no more. And I saw the holy city, new Jerusalem, coming down out of heaven from God, prepared as a bride adorned for her husband. And I heard a loud voice from the throne, saying, 'Behold, the dwelling place of God is with man. He will dwell with them, and they will be his people, and God himself will be with them as their God. He will wipe away every tear from their eyes, and death shall be no more, neither shall there be mounrning, nor crying, nor pain any more, for the former things have passed away.'" (Revelation 21: 1-4 ESV)

Take5forHIM

OCTOBER 9

*"Hear, O Israel! The Lord is our God, the Lord is one! And you shall love the
Lord your God with all your heart and with all your soul and with all your might.
And these words, which I am commanding you today, shall be on your heart."
(Deuteronomy 6:4-6 NAS)*

Moses commanded these verses to the Israelites. For a while, they walked straight as
arrows, but then some started to wander back "to the desert." God gives us the free
will to make choices. We either choose to serve God or not. Sometimes we must force
happiness, for example, because we decide to be happy. I encourage you to take a
strong-willed stance, "I'm going to serve God." From there, your heart is prepared and
ready. God will do the rest.

OCTOBER 10

On this date in 2018, proofing, edits, and the book cover design were finalized. All devotionals had been written, but on today's date, October 10th, Hurricane Michael hit close to home on Florida's Gulf Coast as a Category 4. Florida's Panhandle and up through Southwest Georgia were devastated as Michael marched through like an atomic bomb. There's no way I could finish Take5 without writing a message after one of the worst hurricanes in American history. Forecasters predicted the storm would take a northeasterly turn as a cold front from the west would push- keeping it east of where I live. On Wednesday morning, we woke up to the news that it strengthened from a CAT 2 to a 4 within 24 hours. Quickly, my husband decided to nail a few extra boards on the windows. We were concerned about safety and what to expect on the west side of a major storm.

As the day progressed, my husband and I busily worked on our computers. I couldn't tell if Mr. Cool was holding it together for me or if he was full of peace. I kept busy and even made a pan of brownies because everything's better with chocolate, right? We depended on local news reports until we breathed a sigh of relief when the worst was over- a few hours of rain and gusty wind.

The next day was most difficult as video footage from drones reeled the devastation. There's no other word to describe the ravenous loss. Photos of trees lodged in living rooms; houses left standing with one room; dead cows on farmland; flattened towns. Our homey small town looked like the town I love with the exception of a large limb by the side of the road or an occasional fallen tree. It felt too normal when east/northeast of us were without power, water, and normalcy. It was a lot to mentally process knowing the cold front saved us from the same depredation.

Days later, sadness, depression, and numbness encompassed with reports of those who lost everything plus a rising death toll. It's humbling when the debris from our yard equaled three trash cans.

So, how does a Christian acknowledge natural disasters?

God is sovereign and controls the wind and the waves- a sign of His divine power. The Bible confirms His deity in all of creation, so His hand in storms cannot be biblically denied. References to Mother Nature or that Satan had a part in sending such a storm is absolutely false. See the below verses on God's creation of storms.

As written in many Take5 devotionals, God's "good" and our definition of "good" are completely different. God will take the elements of the storm and all that has happened to bring about His good. Regardless of how difficult the circumstances of a storm such as this, people of all walks of life come to each other's aid to lend a helping hand. Communities far and wide pull together in catastrophes. Good people rise-up to help neighbors financially, with supplies, and sweat pouring off brows. It's upsetting as the homeless advance from the trenches and note blessings while standing among fragmented pieces they use to call home. A truck delivery of simple supplies brings joyous smiles. Volunteers stop, listen, sympathize, and give needed hugs to complete strangers. And, unlikely ears welcome praying hands and the sound of Jesus' name. It's life-changing for the refugees, the geographically unaffected neighbors, and utility truck drivers who drive across state lines. Destruction brings thankfulness for life rather than material possessions, and priorities are suddenly re-arranged.

"When God fixed the weight of the wind and limited the water by measure, when He established a limit for the rain and a path for the lightning, He considered wisdom and evaluated it; He established it and examined it." (Job 28:25-27 HCSB)

"Praise the Lord from the earth, all sea monsters, and ocean depths, lightning, and hail, snow and cloud, powerful wind that executes His command..."
(Psalm 148:8 HCSB)

Read these verses about God's weather power: Jeremiah 10:13; Job 26:8-9; Job 36:26-33; Psalm 135:7; Psalm 147:8; **Job 37:1-18 (Wow!!); Read Psalm 29 as David wrote about God's almighty power riding the storm!

OCTOBER 11

The next time you're daydreaming in class, fantasize about future in-laws- not the groom or the wedding dresses you've pinned. Sayyyyy whaaaaattt!!!!???

Most likely you are years away from walking down the aisle, but it's not premature to pray now because many marriages suffer because the couple never adopted their mate's parents into the marriage equation. Even worse, they despise their spouse's parents. There's no story that better illustrates sincerely loving your mother-in-law like the story of Ruth and Naomi.

> *"For wherever you go, I will go, and wherever you live, I will live;*
> *your people will be my people, and your God will be my God."*
> *(Ruth 1:16 HCSB)*

The short Book of Ruth (four chapters) is a superb example of family dedication. In summary, Naomi and her husband had two sons and daughters-in-law. Her husband and sons died, and Naomi told the daughters-in-law to go back to their families in Moab. Both wanted to stay, but Naomi urged them to leave. Orpah departed to her Moabite family, but Ruth stuck by her mother-in-law whom she obviously loved the way God wants us to love our mother-in-law.

Naomi needed to be ministered and cared for because she seemed to be sulking in self-pity over the losses of her husband and sons. Ruth had plenty to grieve over herself, but she showed Naomi compassion to the extent that she was called "daughter" in Chapter 2. What a compliment!

The commitment is further declared in Chapter 2 when Ruth met Boaz. They fell in love and Naomi gave her approval to be married. The newlyweds referred to her as "mother-in-law" throughout the remainder of the Book of Ruth. They were so faithful to Naomi that they gave their first-born child to her to love and raise. They named him Obed, and he was the grandfather of David, and in the genealogy line to Mary and then Jesus. And they lived happily ever after!

Take5forHIM

OCTOBER 12

"For by grace you have been saved through faith, and that not of yourselves,
it is the gift of God; not as a result of works, that no one should boast.
For we are His workmanship, created in Christ Jesus for good works,
which God prepared beforehand that we should walk in them."
(Ephesians 2:8-10 NAS)

Many new Christians hit the ground running with eagerness for Jesus. They dive in with excitement and want to do as much as they can to catch up to all they've missed. They furiously work at proving their new faith so that everyone around will take note of the life changes.

Recurrently, new Christians backslide because living the "perfect life" of a model Christian is unattainable. Re-read the verses again. For by grace you have been saved through faith, NOT BY WORKS. There's nothing to prove to anyone.

Take5forHIM

OCTOBER 13

One of the most over-used phrases is, "GOD IS GOOD ALL THE TIME." Yes, He is, but it's normally acknowledged ONLY in a recent celebration: job promotion, cancer healing, money tree bloomed, love of their life entered the room. Is He NOT GOOD when life is on the downhill? Is He NOT GOOD when there's a cancer diagnosis? Girls, He's good EVEN when life is sinking.

In general, God's not praised off the lips in the desolate moments, but He's still working. Dismal events may not appear in our favor because we've determined life is good ONLY in health, happiness, wealth, travel, joyous family vacations, and when there are no conflicts whatsoever.

Our ways are not His ways; our thoughts are not His thoughts. His ways are mysterious, but He is good in all times.

"For He will conceal me in His shelter in the day of adversity:
He will hide me under the cover of His tent; He will set me high on a rock."
(Psalm 27:5 HCSB)

"For my thoughts are not your thoughts, and your ways are not My ways.
This is the Lord's declaration. For as heaven is higher than earth,
so My ways are higher than your way,
and My thoughts than your thoughts."
(Isaiah 55:8-9 HCSB)

"The Lord is good, a stronghold in a day of distress;
He cares for those who take refuge in Him."
(Nahum 1:7 HCS)

"I will make an everlasting covenant with them; I will never turn away
from doing good to them, and I will put fear of Me in their hearts so they
will never again turn away from Me."
(Jeremiah 32:40 HCSB)

Read Psalm 145.

Take5forHIM

OCTOBER 14

"No servant can serve two masters, for either he will hate the one
and love the other, or he will be devoted to the one and despise the other.
You cannot serve God and money."
(Luke 16:13 ESV)

We need money for necessities and pleasure, but don't let it dictate your thoughts. Don't let money become what motivates you.

OCTOBER 15

The death of a young person is startling and usually a result of a car or freak accident. Newspaper articles may leave readers assuming the deceased was a bad kid who stirred up trouble in the middle of the night or was texting while driving. There are always hearsay rumors about the death, but he/she was a son/daughter, a brother/sister, and a friend to many. The person may have honestly been at the wrong place at the wrong time, ending life tragically.

On the reverse side, a large community of friends praises the deceased's outstanding qualities. An obituary defends what's spoken by those who knew him/her well and all that matters at this point- their legacy. Accolades that he/she was a friend to all he/she met, had an award-winning smile, and a pleasure to be around. It grips a mom's heart to think of a family enduring such pain which forever changes family, friends & acquaintances immeasurably. Their loved one was one of a kind.

What will be your legacy? What would your parents write in the obituary? In a world full of confused thoughts about Christianity, full of hate, terrorism, political chaos, selfishness, corrupt living- our greatest legacy would be to leave a mark just the opposite. Aspire to be known as a Proverbs 31 type woman, godly, kind, loving, compassionate, joyful, a friend to all, honest, non-judgmental, genuine, encouraging, giving, a friend to all. These wash out any rumors of negativity. Others will cite how you affected their lives, what you believed & stood for, and what a difference you made.

"I am the way, the truth, and the life.
No one comes to the Father except through Me."
(John 14:6 CSB)

"His master said to him, 'Well done, good and faithful servant."
(Matthew 25:33 CSB)

Take5forHIM

OCTOBER 16

Isn't it amazing how often females gossip? Others relish in talking about what's going on in others' lives. More often than not, it's total fabrication passed down a long line of folks; therefore, what's true is questionable. People are fascinated with scandals, but their lives are not anyone's business. All the while, they would NEVER admit to gossiping.

There's a fine line between having a conversation regarding someone versus defamation. It's imperative to be subconsciously wise to know the difference before you open your mouth. Using good judgment increases trust as you are entrusted with important info.

"You must not spread a false report.
Do not join the wicked to be a malicious witness."
(Exodus 23 CSB)

"If anyone thinks he is religious without controlling his tongue,
his religion is useless and he deceives himself."
(James 1:26 CSB)

OCTOBER 17

Not happy with your church or student ministry? Don't feel guilty or anguished. People change with varying intervals of spirituality. It's a personal decision. Find a new place where you can be fed spiritually while enjoying the worship style and people.

Locked in your family's church membership? Discuss concerns with your parents. Perhaps you can attend the Sunday morning church service as a family, but a Bible Study or group elsewhere.

OCTOBER 18

We get caught up on whether someone has backslidden in faith when there's talk of partying and/or sex. They're judged and frowned upon. There is reason for concern. There are many ways to fall yet, partying, weed, drugs, or sex is how a set-back is measured.

What about disrespecting parents, cussing, bitterness, lust, backstabbing, a foul attitude, gossip, lying, sending nudes for boys' "vaults," cheating on a test, or pride? In God's eyes, these things are sinful and just as harmful. The truth is- everybody sins. It doesn't make any of the above acceptable, but God doesn't classify one over the other as worse. Tears fall from His face (figuratively speaking) when we sin in any way because we've greatly disappointed. He calls us to be an example.

"All of us have become like something unclean, and all our righteous
acts are like a polluted garment, all of us wither like a leaf,
and our iniquities carry us away like the wind."
(Isaiah 64:6 CSB)

"The one who conceals his sins will not prosper,
but whoever confesses and renounces them will find mercy."
Proverbs 28:13 CSB)

"If we walk in the light as he himself is in the light,
we have fellowship with one another,
and the blood of Jesus his Son cleanses us from all sin.
If we say, 'We have no sin,'
we are deceiving ourselves, and the truth is not in us.
If we confess our sins,
he is faithful and righteous to forgive us out sins and
to cleanse us from all unrighteousness."
(1 John 1: 7-9 CSB)

Take5forHIM

OCTOBER 19

"Humble yourselves, therefore, under God's mighty hand,
that he may lift you up in due time.
Cast all your anxiety on him because he cares for you."
(1 Peter 5:6-7 NIV)

Jesus knows the qualms of your circumstances. Whatever you're facing right now, He can change the situation at any given moment. Or, He'll provide the strength and direction to pull you out. Don't submit to despair.

OCTOBER 20

"The Hiding Place" by Corrie Ten Boom is a must read. The book is Corrie's recount of how their cookie cutter Christian life in a Dutch small town was rocked during the Holocaust. The book's emphasis is not on the gory aspects, but what their family endured, the relationships that were formed, and how faith prevailed. Their family's foundational faith is aspiring. The Holocaust is a perfect example of why it's essential to build your life on Christ. Faith matters in hard times. The Holy Spirit and The Word sustains until the storm clouds pass and the sun shines again.

In the 1940s, Europe suffered the effects of Hitler's Nazis. The TenBooms were a devoted family who thought their world was far removed from the evil against Jewish Germans. They lived a simple life above their family's watch shop in a quaint Holland town. When soldiers invaded their town, people mysteriously disappeared. It was quiet and eerie. Their ministry began when Jewish acquaintances and friends began knocking on their door for a safe place to stay for protection from soldiers.

The father and two old maid sisters were eventually captured, but God kept Jewish friends safely tucked behind the TenBoom's walls (literally, they were hiding behind the walls). The sisters were transferred from one training camp to the next. Sister Betsie's faith shined in a way Corrie had never seen. Together they clung to the Bible they secretly carried. They ministered to the women all around as fear gripped daily with disease, death, and torture although the sisters were repeatedly spared.

Corrie's quote deserves #lifegoals:

> But as the rest of the world grew stranger, one thing became increasingly clear. And that was the reason the two of us were here. Why others should suffer we were not shown. As for us, from morning until lights-out, whenever we were not in tanks for roll call, our Bible was the center of an ever-widening circle of help and hope. Like waifs clustered around a blazing fire, we gathered about it, holding out our hearts to its warmth and light. The blacker the night around us grew, the brighter and truer and more beautiful burned the word of God. 'Who shall separate us from the love of Christ? Shall tribulation, or distress, or persecution, or famine, or nakedness, or peril, or sword?'.....Nay, in all these things we are more than conquerors through him that loved us.' I would look about us as Betsie read, watching the light leap from face to face (of other women). More than conquerors. It was not a wish. It was a fact.[22]

[22]Ten Boom, Corrie with John and Elizabeth Sherrill. *The Hiding Place*. New York, Toronto, London, Sydney, Auckland, Bantam Books by arrangement with Fleming H. Revell Company, 1971, p. 194.

Take5forHIM

OCTOBER 21

"And so, as those who have been chosen of God, holy and beloved, put on a heart of compassion, kindness, humility, gentleness and patience; bearing with one another, and forgiving each other, whoever has a complaint against anyone, just as the Lord forgave you, you should also forgive. And beyond all these things put on love, which is the perfect bond of unity. And let the peace of Christ rule in your hearts, to which indeed you were called in one body; and be thankful." (Colossians 3:12-15 NAS)

We'd be living paradise on earth if we stuck to these verses. It seems so easy as the text is read. The more dependent on Jesus; the less self-focused you'll be. The more in love with Jesus; the less you'll love the things of this world but love the people of the world more than yourself.

OCTOBER 22

"A lady was asked what it was like to be a Christian. She was caught off guard and didn't know how to answer; but when she looked up, saw a jack-o-lantern and said: "It's like being a pumpkin." She explained, "God picks you from the patch and brings you in and washed off all the dirt on the outside that you got from being around all the other pumpkins. Then He cuts off the top and takes all the yucky stuff out from inside. He removes all the seeds of doubt, hate, greed, etc. Then He carves you a smiling face and puts His light inside of you to shine for all to see. It is our choice to either stay outside and rot on the vine or come inside and be something new and bright."[23] –Author Unknown

"Behold, I stand at the door and knock. If anyone hears My voice and opens the door, I will come in to him and dine with him, and he with Me."
(Revelation 3:20 NKJV)

"Then I will sprinkle clean water on you, and you shall be clean;
I will cleanse you from all your filthiness and from all your idols.
I will give you a new heart and put a new spirit within you;
I will remove your heart of stone and give you a heart of flesh."
(Ezekiel 36:25-27 NKJV)

"For it is the God who commanded light to shine out of darkness,
who has shone in our hearts to give the light of the knowledge of the
glory of God in the face of Jesus Christ."
(2 Corinthians 4:6 NKJV)

[23]Christians & Pumpkins. *DLTK's Bible Crafts for Kids.* 2018. http://www.dltk-bible.com/p.asp?p=http://www.dltk-bible.com/phow_a_christian_is_like_a_pumpki.asp

OCTOBER 23
The Great Commission

Before Jesus ascended into heaven, these were his parting words to the eleven disciples (FYI- Judas had hung himself after betrayal).

"The eleven disciples traveled to Galilee, to the mountain where Jesus had directed them. When they saw Him, they worshiped, but some doubted. Then Jesus came near and said to them, 'All authority has been given to Me in heaven and on earth. Go, therefore, and make disciples of all nations, baptizing them in the name of the Father and of the Son and of the Holy Spirit, teaching them to observe everything I have commanded you. And remember, I am with you always, to the end of the age.'" (Matthew 28:16-20 HCSB)

Missionaries have these lines memorized. Jesus spoke with authority that it was their (our) responsibility to spread the gospel out into the world so that others will know Him, The Father God, and the Holy Spirit.

Take5forHIM

OCTOBER 24

The hundred years or less you live is a tiny speck on a timeline. Make the most of the speck. Enjoy it. Live BIG. Have unrealistic dreams, and don't be afraid to bite the pie in the sky. If there's something you're convicted to do, go after it. Brainstorm historical events that made marks on the timeline in history books.

Life is short.
"Teach us to number our days carefully so that we may develop wisdom in our hearts."
(Psalm 90:12 CSB)

Life is a vapor.
"Come now, you who say, 'Today or tomorrow we will travel to such and such a city and spend a year there and do business and make a profit.' Yet you do not know what tomorrow will bring- what your life will be! For you are like vapor that appears for a little while, then vanishes. Instead, you should say, 'If the Lord wills, we will live and do this or that.' But as it is, you boast in your arrogance. All such boasting is evil. So it is sin to know the good and yet not do it." (James 4:13-17 CSB)

OCTOBER 25

Thomas is nicknamed Doubting Thomas. Movie viewers shield eyes during the scene of the ravens plucking out Thomas' eyes. It's hard to watch the images of a man who drove himself insane with guilt over the denial of Jesus, so he committed suicide. Therefore, no one likes to admit their doubts out of fear of a lightning bolt strike.

Doubt is typical. Any human cannot deny it's dubious. In a paragraph...eons ago there was no existence of anything? Nothing yet God was here? From where did He come? Then, God created the world, the galaxies, animals, the moon, sun, flowers, grass, bodies of water, and Adam and Eve? Then, they sinned and changed the course of the paradise He created? From Adam and Eve, they populated the earth until God wiped out all people except Noah, his wife, sons, daughters-in-law, and one male and female animal of all kinds? They floated in a manmade ginormous boat for months? Humanity was destroyed except those few, so they re-populated the earth? Then all kinds of things happened throughout history like the parting of the Red Sea, wars, calamities, prophecies of a future King? Then this baby was born in a stable who some believed to be God's Son? He supposedly lived a sinless life which we know is impossible? He spoke these crazy parables that no one understood, but they were visuals of God's principles? He raised a man to life who had been dead for four days? He rubbed mud on a blind man's eyes and then he could see? He walked on water? Are these tales or truth? There was a division between the people who believed and those who rejected Him? He was put to death on a cross and walked out of the grave three days later? Thousands of years later, there are people who worship Him. They raise hands singing about death having no sting because if you believe in Him, you'll die and walk into His presence to live an eternal life without pain, sorrow, sickness, stress, and worship God the Father Almighty forever and ever??

One sleepless night, I stumbled to the kitchen. As I drank water and a sleep aid, I peered out the window. The sky was clear and bright. The moon was a night light and the stars were twinkling. It was so peaceful that I walked back into the kitchen five minutes later for another look. My cognizance was attracted to the beauty as I thought, "There's no way the stars glisten, and the moon can glow without a perfect Creator. And, the earth rotates creating day and night every 24 hours as the earth revolves around the sun every 365 days to bring different seasons. Clouds wisp the sky as if they're painted. Storm systems are developed from overly formed clouds which bring rain for the parched ground and crops to provide food for all living things." For me, God's story is so unbelievable that it's believable!

If the jury's still out, it's OK. We're given brains to form our own conclusions. Make a rational decision by starting in Genesis and slowly reading through to the very end of

Take5forHIM

Revelation. It's common to raise eyebrows, but it's a personal verdict whether you're sold out on God's story.

Read the Bible and pray, "God, if You're real and this Book is living truth, please reveal Yourself to knock out uncertainties. Give me the backbone to stand firm to be a believer and not a morally good person."

OCTOBER 26

"'Do not judge, so that you won't be judged. For with the judgment you use, you will be judged, and with the measure you use, it will be measured to you. Why do you look at the speck in your brother's eye but don't notice the log in your own eye? Or how can you say to your brother, 'Let me take the speck out of your eyes, and look, there's a log in your eye? Hypocrite! First take the log out of your eye, and then you will see clearly to take the speck out of your brother's eye. Don't give what is holy to dogs or toss your pearls before pigs, or they will trample them with their feet, turn, and tear you to pieces.'" (Matthew 7:1-6 HCSB)

Calling all hypocrites to the table! Hypocrites are too big for their own britches. A hypocrite doesn't see her/his own sin but points out the defects of others. In the passage, the specks and logs are faults. Judgy and hypocritical people are elated in others' losing moments, trials, weight-gain, acne, bad hair day, break-ups. It's sick, but there are busy-bodies who thrive on others' specks when they have their own set of logs. These people are either "holier than thou" or suffer from insecurities.

Today, assess if Jesus could insert your name in Matthew 7.

OCTOBER 27

"Beware of false prophets who come to you in sheep's clothing but inwardly are ravaging wolves. You'll recognize them by their fruit. Are grapes gathered from thorn bushes or figs from thistles? In the same way, every good tree produces good fruit, but a bad tree produces bad fruit. A good tree can't produce bad fruit; neither can a bad tree produce good fruit. Every tree that doesn't produce good fruit is cut down and thrown into the fire. So you'll recognize them by their fruit.

Not everyone who says to Me, Lord, Lord! will enter the kingdom of heaven, but only the one who does the will of My Father in heaven. On that day many will say to Me, 'Lord, Lord, didn't we prophesy in Your name, drive out demons in Your name, and do many miracles in Your name?' Then I will announce to them, 'I never knew you! Depart from Me, you lawbreakers!'" (Matthew 7:15-23 HCSB)

Whoah! It's easy to get stymied with deceivers who twist the gospel for their benefit or their church's. Some (not all) television and street evangelists are guilty, and those wrapped up in cultish theology. Jesus is the ultimate judge, and He will condemn false teachers on Judgment Day. Let Him do the convicting.

OCTOBER 28

What's your testimony? Today, spend time writing a draft. Your story may not be an earth-shattering journey of how you were pulled out of the depths of a black hole, but you're His masterpiece and have a beautiful memoir. When written, you'll be prepared if asked to speak publicly or if inquired by someone's curiosity.

OCTOBER 29

A 1960's band turned this passage into a classic.

"There is an occasion for everything and a time for every activity under the heaven: a time to give birth and a time to die; a time to plant and a time to uproot; a time to kill and a time to heal; a time to tear down and a time to build; a time to weep and a time to laugh; a time to mourn and a time to dance; a time to throw stones and a time to gather stones; a time to embrace and a time to avoid embracing; a time to search and a time to count as lost; a time to keep and a time to throw away; a time to tear and a time to sew; a time to be silent and a time to speak; a time to love and a time to hate; a time for war and a time for peace." (Ecclesiastes 3:1-8 HCSB)

"He has made everything appropriate in its time. He has also put eternity in their hearts, but man cannot discover the work God has done from beginning to end. I know that there is nothing better for them than to rejoice and enjoy the good life. It is also the gift of God whenever anyone eats, drinks, and enjoys his efforts. I know that all God does will last forever; there is no adding to it or taking from it. God works so that people will be in AWE of HIM. Whatever is, has already been, and whatever will be, already is. God repeats what has passed." (Ecclesiastes 3:11-16 HCSB)

Time and seasons are bewildering, and we'll undergo most of the life experiences in the passage. With God by our side, we can handle the positive and the negative; the joys and the sadness; the mountain tops and the trials.

Take5forHIM

OCTOBER 30

Regarding the breakup with an old boyfriend vs. a new boyfriend, a girl said she figured out why it didn't work with the ex. "_____ wasn't a Christian and in the back of my mind it bothered me, and I knew I couldn't trust his actions. Now, dating _____ is a different experience because he's a radical Jesus freak."

It's bizarre that regardless of how a believer hears she should not date a non-believer, she's still attracted by chemistry. If faith is so important, why would a girl date a guy who doesn't embrace Jesus as Lord? Labeling himself a Christian because his parents are followers or let's say his family doesn't deny Christ. Maybe he's a "good" guy, but that should not fit your high standard requirement.

Legalistic? That's not the motive, but your thought process needs reversing if you believe it's acceptable. Sever your connection like cutting a tight rope with scissors. Make it a clean break. Go separate ways without second guessing. Being a Christian isn't easy, but you are called to be choosy when it comes to boys. Hard but best.

OCTOBER 31

Is it wrong to celebrate Halloween? Coming from a Halloween Birthday Girl, no! Are you participating in seances, witchcraft, worshipping false gods, and other wicked games on Halloween? It would be practiced year-round- not just one day per year. Extremists get on a high horse around Halloween that it's the witch's holiday. I don't agree with crimson decorations, but lean towards harvest, pumpkins, candy, and non-scary costumes. Tombstones on lawns, a naked baby doll marked with red for blood stains hanging by a tree limb, and other creepy decorations are disturbing.

Historical Background: The holiday originated over 2,000 years ago as a Celtic festival. People lit fires and wore costumes to ward off evil spirits. In the eighth century, Pope Gregory III designated November 1 as a time to honor the dead. Today, some denominations memorialize those who have passed away within the year on "All Saints Sunday" which is the first Sunday of November.

"When you enter the land of the Lord your God is giving you, do not learn to imitate the detestable ways of the nations there. Let no one be found among you who sacrifices their son or daughter in the fire, who practices divination or sorcery, interprets omens, engages in witchcraft, or casts spells, or who is a medium or spiritist or who consults the dead. Anyone who does these things is detestable to the Lord; because of these same detestable practices the Lord your God will drive out those nations before you. You must be blameless before the Lord your God." (Deuteronomy 18:9-13 HCSB)

"Abstain from every form of evil."
(1 Thessalonians 5:22 ESV)

"Therefore be careful how you walk, not as unwise men, but as wise, making the most of your time, because the days are evil."
(Ephesians 5:15-16 NAS)

If you celebrate the innocence of handing out candy to toddlers dressed as princesses and cowboys, as a Christian, you'll be challenged. The topic of controversy will arise.

Take5forHIM

NOVEMBER

"When one door of happiness closes, another opens; but often we look so long at the closed door that we do not see the one which has been opened for us."

-Helen Keller

Take5forHIM

NOVEMBER 1

"In this world, nothing can be said to be certain, except death and taxes."
Benjamin Franklin

Do you grab a paper bag to inhale/exhale because CHANGE causes immediate hyperventilation? Do you resist it or go with the flow? Many fray at the ends with the least bit of change, even a shift of a plant in a room. Others struggle with more intense situations such as moving, job changes, and life transitions. It's normal to experience anxiety, increased heart rate, and ugly cry tears. There are good, dramatic, and negatively perceived changes. CHANGE is a part of life, and we will ALWAYS experience change. Nothing stays the same, so we must learn how to manage it in our own way or we'll be a walking wreck.

Find peace in scripture endorsing God as the One who holds your future and the little things. He's in the center of it all, and the way you reply is a reflection of trusting Him with the big and the little.

"Casting all your cares on him, because he cares about you."
(1 Peter 5:7 CSB)

"Cast your cares on the LORD, and he will sustain you;
he will never let the righteous be shaken."
(Psalm 55:22 NIV)

"Therefore, with your minds ready for action, be sober-minded,
And set your hope completely on the grace to be brought to you
at the revelation of Jesus Christ."
(1 Peter 1:13 CSB)

"Let the peace of Christ rule in your hearts,
since as members of one body you were called to peace.
And be thankful."
(Colossians 3:15 NIV)

"Now may the Lord of peace himself give you
peace at all times and in every way.
The Lord be with all of you."
(2 Thessalonians 3:16 NIV)

Take5forHIM

NOVEMBER 2

Emotions stir at the final football game of the season. It's a blow to the football team. Practically all year, the guys pump iron and drink protein shakes to build muscle. At the beginning of Summer practices, they're only thinking of themselves as they strive to impress the coaches for first-string positions. After the long and humid summer, the adrenaline flows as they burst through the banner looking like rock star champs running across the field after training hours weekly. So many hopes for big wins and a long season to make it to "State."

Every year the team make up is a little different. Brotherhood, as they call it, is formed. They over-analyze wins and losses. There are long bus rides home after losses recalling plays and what "coulda, shoulda, wish I woulda" done. In a rough and tough player's own way, they console those who blame themselves. They take a knee when someone is hurt, and a sigh of relief when the injured teammate staggers off the field. They unify in the locker rooms, as stone faced cool dudes at pep rallies, fried chicken dinners on game days, and participate in "football trash talk." By the end of the season, whether playing or standing on the sidelines, they're cheering each other with high fives and chest bumps.

When the season ends, 16-18-year-old smelly football guys are hugging and crying their eyes out. It's brutal on Monday morning when the coaches yell, "Turn in your uniforms! Everybody clean-up the locker room, get your stuff, and Seniors---GOOOOO to study hall!" No more practices, no more weightlifting, it's just plain over! The team splits. Time together from that moment becomes "back in the day when..." They'll never all be together again, but they still have that inner bond of brotherhood.

Working together and encouraging one another builds a team, and so it is with the Body of Christ. We can call it the brotherhood or sisterhood of Christ, but people need people to point them to the champion.

"Now may the God of patience and comfort grant you to be like-minded toward one another, according to Christ Jesus, that you may with one mind and one mouth glorify the God and Father of our Lord Jesus Christ."
(Romans 15:5 NKJV)

"For as we have many members in one body,
but all members do not have the same function, so we, being many,
are one body in Christ and individually members of one another."
(Romans 12:4-5 NKJV)

Take5forHIM

NOVEMBER 3

In the Old Testament, there are numerous stories of people worshipping false gods, statues, the god of sun and moon, and even a donkey statue. There is only one true God, but all religions promise(d) an after- life (or paradise) after death.

The only true living God, creator of all things, created Heaven and Hell. Throughout the Old Testament, God says not to worship other gods. "There shall be no other gods before me."

Young and old want their eternal destination to be in Heaven, but the only way is to personally accept Jesus Christ as Lord and Savior. No one can make the decision for you, and no one can take it away.

"And there is salvation in no one else, for there is no other name
under heaven given among men by which we must be saved."
(Acts 4:12 ESV)

"Jesus answered him, 'Truly, truly, I say to you,
unless one is born again he cannot see the kingdom of God.'"
(John 3:3 ESV)

"Jesus said to her, 'I am the resurrection and the life.
Whoever believes in me, though he die, yet shall he live,
and everyone who lives and
who believes in me shall never die...."
(John 11:25-26 ESV)

"This is the bread that comes down from heaven,
so that one may eat of it and not die.
I am the living bread that came down from heaven.
If anyone eats of this bread, he will live forever.
And the bread that I will give for the life of the world is my flesh.'"
(John 6:50-51 ESV)

Take5forHIM

NOVEMBER 4

Know anyone who's wallowing in pride? So full of themselves that they're effortful to bear? Self-promoting, self-exalting, self-absorbed in self, self, self? They're a walking billboard. We all know at least *one*. They brag and/or continuously post on social media their perfect life: best boyfriend, best friends, best family, best moments, best everything <Cringe>.

While we should be happy for others, it's hard to share the excitement if it's puffed up. Before tempted to bash braggadocious behavior, bite your tongue. It's hard to connect with boastful people because they intimidate our "meek little lives." Most likely- if they feel the need to publicize- there's a void to fill, neediness, something to prove, a motive, or even low esteem. They could be laughing on the outside and crying on the inside, so show 'em a little grace.

Hopefully that didn't hit a nerve. Guilty of any of the above? Maybe you've ignored your own self-centeredness. When we put ourselves on a pedestal, we're making an idol of ourselves instead of glorifying the Father. A daily self-check: Did I put myself on the throne today? Did I serve myself today or did I serve God? Do I put God and others ahead of my needs? Pride is one of the worst battles with the flesh. That's why Paul talked so much about it throughout his writings.

Life Lesson: We all have jubilant moments when we're bursting at the seams to share it but beware not to develop the "all about me" mentality.

"He must increase, but I must decrease."
(John 3:30 CSB)

"God resists the proud,
but gives grace to the humble."
(James 4:6 CSB)

"Let the one who boasts boast in the Lord."
(1 Corinthians 1:31 NIV)

"Then He said to them all, 'If anyone wants to come with Me, he must deny himself, take up his cross daily, and follow Me. For whoever wants to save his life will lose it, but whoever loses his life because of Me will save it. What is a man benefited if he gains the whole world yet loses his soul."(Luke 9:23-25 HCSB)

Take5forHIM

NOVEMBER 5

Today is a challenge. You can do this! Find someone who's sitting alone in the cafeteria. Ditch your friends and ask if you can sit with him/her. Strike up a conversation. If this is not do-able, talk to someone in a classroom whom you've never spoken before. Let the conversation be about them and not about you. Vow to keep up the kindness with this person. Pray for him/her even if you have no idea what to pray regarding. Pray he/she will know Jesus. By praying, you'll develop a heart and gradually a relationship will form. Reach out. There's a world full of lonely people.

"She opens her mouth in wisdom,
and the teaching of kindness is on her tongue."
(Proverbs 31:26 NAS)

"Each of us must please his neighbor for his good, to build him up."
(Romans 15:2 HCSB)

"Rejoice with those who rejoice, weep with those who weep."
(Romans 12:15 HCSB)

NOVEMBER 6

Fornication. <country voice> Do you know what for—ni—ca—tion means? The Bible speaks a lot about adultery and fornication. Adultery is a married person having sex with someone other than their spouse. Fornication is an unmarried couple having sex. Casual or sex with a current love interest is fornication. God calls sex outside the bond of marriage between a man and woman- sin. This is a hail and brimstone message, but some are oblivious about what's right and wrong. Breaking away from fornication is extremely difficult when you're infatuated or in love, but much easier if it's casual sex because there's no love adrenaline. If you're fornicating and attending Bible Study, posting verses, and living the double life depending on the day of the week or who you're with- STOP going to Bible Study and acting like Christy Christian. Don't go back until you decide to quit fornicating! Living two faces gives this thing called Christianity a bad rap. There's absolutely nothing in the Bible that gives God's blessing on fornication- under any circumstance. Whether the translation uses the word fornication or sexual immorality, it's always pertaining to sin and the eternal effects. Phrases such as, "Flee from sexual immorality," express the urgency to evacuate. God will repeatedly speak to the inner conscience of poor choices. It's somber to see the joy vanish from a Christian girl's eyes as a result of hooking up. Deep down, she knows.

"No temptation has overtaken you except what is common to humanity.
God is faithful, and He will not allow you to be tempted beyond what you are able,
but with the temptation He will also provide a way of escape,
so that you are able to bear it."
(1 Corinthians 10:13 HCSB)

"Therefore, consider the members of your earthly body as dead to immorality,
impurity, passion, evil desire, and greed, which amount to idolatry."
(Colossians 3:5 NAS)

"If we confess our sins, He is faithful and righteous to forgive us our sins
and to cleanse us from all unrighteousness."
(1 John 1:9 NAS)

"For know and recognize this: Every sexually immoral or
impure or greedy person, who is an idolater, does not have an
inheritance in the kingdom of the Messiah and of God."
(Ephesians 5:5 HCSB)

Take5forHIM

NOVEMBER 7

Jesus said, "Go therefore and make disciples of all the nations,
baptizing them in the name of the Father and of the Son and of the Holy
Spirit, teaching them to observe all that I commanded you;
and lo, I am with you always, even to the end of the age."
(Matthew 28:19-20 NAS)

Short term mission trips are an immense opportunity to see God's work globally, and participants hope to make a difference in seven days. While lots of hands are needed on mission trips to complete chores, full-time missionaries are the ones who reap of the harvest as it usually takes time and relationship building. NEWS FLASH: There's a mission field waiting in your backyard.

We're in a culture of mixed beliefs that every day is mission work. Even nominal Christians are in need of a "local missionary" to share the Good News. Others need someone to provide concrete answers on what God's Word says regarding social issues. The world is broken, and various forms of media are confusing truth from lies. There are poverty-stricken areas in our hometowns with leaky roofs, hungry children, and family members sleeping in the same bed or on floors.

Sure, there's excitement and glamour in hopping on a plane to a third world country, but let's not forget to love our neighbors right where we are. Sweat a little; show love; give hope.

Take5forHIM

NOVEMBER 8

What's heavy on your mind today? Is there a family concern, financial stress, a health crisis, dire straits? How long has it been since you spent a heap of time in prayer? "I know I should, but I don't have time." "I'll pray later." Stop procrastinating. Recluse to a bathroom or closet. Fall on your knees as a prayer warrior for those you've nonchalantly said, "I'll pray for you," but never get around to it. Spill it out to Jesus. There's no need to scramble for eloquent speech. God doesn't mind poor grammar and long-winded sentences. He enjoys time with you just the way you are. Five minutes can easily become an hour, but the quality is more significant than quantity.

Prayer is a crucial faith builder. Be blessed.

"But when you pray, go into your private room, shut your door, and pray to your Father who is in secret. And your Father who sees in secret will reward you."
(Matthew 6:6 HCSB)

"The righteous cry out, and the Lord hears,
and delivers them from all their troubles."
(Psalm 34:17 HCSB)

Take5forHIM

NOVEMBER 9

Sickening nausea saturates deep in the gut when there's news of a suicide. It's a deep-seated sadness more than any other type of death. It devastates not only the closest friends and family, it stretches far into a community. It's difficult for those on the outside to understand why, and everyone wants answers. Not only why, but how and what method accomplished the suicide buzz on the phone lines. Sadness and grief overcome as we silently think through what may have been the scenario leading up to the finality. Hard hearts may brush it off by saying, "It's their life. They can end it if they choose." NOOOOOO, it's wrong and unnatural!

There are many who shout, "JESUS IS THE ANSWER!" While we'd love for everybody to put their faith and hope in Jesus, not everybody is going to accept HIM. That's not a popular statement, but it's common sense reality. Many think counseling is preventive because "he/she needs a professional who deals with life-ending emotions on a regular basis." And, many believe awareness is the best platform.

We all have personal issues, and we must learn to love the skin [and soul] we're in. Nobody can convince you to love yourself but YOU. The toughest part of counseling (especially a teenager) is to convey that their current life circumstances will not last forever. A bad situation today can completely resolve in 2 weeks, 6 months, or down the road. Teenagers tend to look at the present and cannot see into the future.

There are tons of heartwarming testimonies from successful, happy adults with stories of the worst childhoods imaginable who broke the cycle in their adulthood. Someone may have endured an abusive life thus far but pull out of the foxhole to be an amazing, caring, compassionate, attentive wife and mom someday. Someone may live in a dingy, run down, filthy trailer with a dirt yard and no bed of their own, but as an adult clean-up with hygiene and thrift store clothing to obtain the best paying job she can get. If home life is rough, there may only be a few years before there's complete independence. Money can be spent wisely, so there's a rainy-day savings plan in hardships. In other words, SEE BEYOND THE PAST AND HOPELESS PRESENT, AND BELIEVE YOUR LIFE HAS VALUE.

Many people assume a victim was depressed and friendless with comments such as, "Oh, if she had just known how many people loved her." That's not necessarily the case. One can be lonely in a crowded room. It's another opinion, but I believe suicide would decline with self-esteem and by looking beyond the dark hour towards a hopeful future.

Be aware of warning signs. If a friend or family member says they want to end their life, don't take it lightly. TELL SOMEONE WHO CAN INTERVENE.

Take5forHIM

If you ever, ever, ever have suicidal thoughts, do not carry the heaviness alone. PLEASE talk to a parent, a well thought of adult, or friend. Over time, circumstances change, and problems are relieved. Life is worth living and nothing is so unbearable. Every single life that has ever lived has value and purpose in YOUR CREATOR God's eyes!

Now, as Christians, we know God's Word offers the best hope & encouragement at our lowest points. He's our hope for abundant life on earth.

"Are not five sparrows sold for two pennies? And not one of them is forgotten
before God. Why, even the hairs of your head are all numbered.
Fear not; you are of more value than many sparrows."
(Luke 12:6-7 ESV)

Paul prayed and pleaded three times to take away his suffering
and then proclaimed: "But He said to me, 'My grace is sufficient for you,
for my power is made perfect in weakness. Therefore, I will boast all the more
gladly of my weaknesses, so that the power of Christ may rest upon me.
For the sake of Christ, then, I (Paul) am content with weaknesses, insults,
hardships, persecutions, and calamities. For when I am weak, then I am strong.'"
(2 Corinthians 12:9-10 ESV)

"But you, O Lord, are a shield about me (David),
my glory, and the lifter of my head."
(Psalm 3:3 ESV)

Take5forHIM

NOVEMBER 10

Praise songs are a far cry from the depth and meaning behind hymns. Sadly, your generation is not familiar with many hymns other than "Amazing Grace." As churches are leaning to contemporary worship, hymns may become obsolete over time. There are so many lessons about the vastness of our God and the depth of our dependence by reading a hymnbook. The story behind "It is Well with My Soul" is a great example of penning your emotions to paper whether it's in a journal or to music.

In the early 1870s, Horatio and Anna Spafford were a young, wealthy Chicago couple with five children. They lost their business in the Great Fire of Chicago, but he was a smart businessman who rebuilt it back to success. In the same year, their young son died of pneumonia. A couple of years later, Charles stayed in Chicago while Anna and their four daughters took a trip on a French ocean liner to Europe. The ship wrecked into another vessel in the middle of the Atlantic Ocean. Within a few minutes, over 226 passengers including the four daughters drowned. A sailor spotted Anna floating on a small piece of wreckage. When she made it safely to Wales nine days later, she sent a telegraph message to her husband, "Saved alone, what shall I do?" He immediately left on the next available ship to join her in Europe to grieve their losses together.

Four days into the trip, the ship's captain notified Horatio when they reached the area where the shipwrecked waters had succumbed his daughters. He looked over the dark billowy water and expressed his loss by writing "It is Well with My Soul" during the journey. I can picture Horatio looking out into the sea bawling his eyes out as he mourned for his baby girls. Random thoughts must have raced through his head, but his faith pointed him to Christ.

> When peace, like a river, attendeth my way, when sorrows like sea billows roll; whatever my lot, thou hast taught me to say, 'It is well, it is well with my soul'.

> Though Satan should buffet, though trials should come, let this blest assurance control, that Christ has regarded my helpless estate, and has shed his own blood for my soul.

> My sin---O the bliss of this glorious thought! — my sin, not in part, but the whole, is nailed to the cross, and I bear it no more; praise the Lord, praise the Lord, O my soul!

> O Lord, haste the day when the faith shall be sight, the clouds be rolled back as a scroll, the trump shall resound and the Lord shall descend, 'Even so'--- it is well with my soul.

Take5forHIM

It is well with my soul; it is well, it is well with my soul.[24]
By Horatio G. Spafford, 1873

The family was blessed with three more children but lost another son to a brief illness. The family endured unbearable loss of life. It's hard to believe after such tragedy had struck their lives, but their church wrongly proclaimed it was "divine punishment." They were deeply hurt by the condemnation of their Christian friends at a time when they needed them most. The Spaffords spent the remainder of their lives in Jerusalem, forming the group "The Overcomers" which loved & served all people, regardless of their religious denomination. They ministered to suffering people in soup kitchens and hospitals.[25] Through heartache, they focused their eyes on Christ, and God gave them a heart to serve His people.

"And the peace of God, which surpasses every thought,
will guard your hearts and minds in Christ Jesus."
(Philippians 4:7 HCSB)

[24]Spafford, Horatio G. "It is Well with My Soul". *Trinity Hymnal*, Great Commission Publications, Inc., 1990, 691.
[25]It is Well with My Soul. *Wikipedia.* 2018.
https://en.wikipedia.org/wiki/It_Is_Well_with_My_Soul *(all information for this devotional was gathered from this website)*

Take5forHIM

NOVEMBER 11

In the early 1900's, Adelaide Pollard was an old maid who devoted her life to serving and evangelizing. She had an affection for Africa after going on a short-term mission trip before WWI. Years later, she attempted fundraising to return, but to no avail. She was distraught over it. As an elderly woman, she attended a prayer meeting and was touched by a friend's prayer for Adelaide's unsettled distress that she could not get back to Africa due to funding and poor health. She went home that evening and wrote the hymn, "Have Thine Own Way, Lord," inspired by Jeremiah 18.

"The word that came to Jeremiah from the Lord: 'Arise, and go down to the potter's house, and there I will let you hear my words.' So I went down to the potter's house, and there he was working at his wheel. And the vessel he was making of clay was spoiled in the potter's hand, and he reworked it into another vessel, as it seemed good to the potter to do. Then the word of the Lord came to me: 'O house of Israel, can I not do with you as this potter has done? Declares the Lord. Behold, like the clay in the potter's hand, so are you in my hand, O house of Israel.'" (Jeremiah 18:1-6 ESV)

The analogy of the potter (God) and the clay (believers) is also referenced in: Isaiah 64:8; Romans 9:21; 2 Corinthians 4:7. It's a gorgeous comparison as it describes yielding our desires to God's will. Adelaide identified well as she was bummed because missionary work should always be pleasing to the Lord, right? God said, "no." *(See the January 25th devo on disappointments.)* Adelaide relinquished her aspiration that evening as she wrote, "Have Thine Own Way." Perhaps God used Adelaide's letdown to console others' through song?

"Have Thine own way, Lord! Have Thine own way! Thou art the potter, I am the clay: mold me and make me after Thy will, while I am waiting, yielded and still."[26]

[26]Pollard, Adelaide A. "Have Thine Own Way, Lord!" *Trinity Hymnal,* Great Commission Publications, Inc. 1990, 688.

NOVEMBER 12

As a young girl, you may remember a grandmother clasping your child-size hands, guiding pointer fingers to form a steeple and slowly saying, "This is the church. This is the steeple. Open the doors and there's all the people." There were giggles as you wiggled fingers to represent the people inside the church. Childhood memories!

The steeple may represent a visual image, but church is not about a steeple or beautiful stained-glass windows. The CHURCH is the people who are outside the walls of a formal brick building. Sometimes the church is a retreat, Bible Study, hanging out with friends at sunset on the beach, reaching out to someone in need, or living life. Being the church means living outside walls as the Body of Christ.

Take a moment to reminisce a weekend retreat's depiction of THE CHURCH, and how campers left spiritually bonded and renewed. It can be a lifechanging experience for some as they emerge into spiritual giants. Think about someone who attended a faith-filling event who's not currently living the Christian life. Send a text or PM. Open up the conversation with, "Hey, I just watched a video from Sabbath and caught a glimpse of you. Checking in…." Reminisce about the camp's toast (it's like a brick), Gold Bond powder on the mattresses (to keep the bugs away), no cell service, and the Capture the Flag competition. It won't be offensive nor misunderstood because old friends appreciate being remembered. Deep down, Jesus is living inside even though she/he may not have visited HIM in a long while. It's subtle.

That's being THE CHURCH. Smile upon the memories, stick together through the bumps of life, and meet back up later if time lapses. Jesus is the common denominator.

Be the church. Be intentional. Be the Light of Christ. NEVER GIVE UP ON ANYONE.

"For this reason also, since the day we heard of it, we have not ceased to pray for you and to ask that you may be filled with the knowledge of His will in all spiritual wisdom and understanding, so that you will walk in a manner worthy of the Lord, to please Him in all respects, bearing fruit in every good work and increasing in the knowledge of God; strengthened with all power, according to His glorious might, for the attaining of all steadfastness and patience; joyously giving thanks to the Father, who has qualified us to share in the inheritance of the saints in Light. For He rescued us from the domain of darkness, and transferred us to the kingdom of His beloved Son, in whom we have redemption, the forgiveness of sins." (Colossians 1:9-14 NAS)

Go after that one lost sheep!

Take5forHIM

NOVEMBER 13

"We have so much to be thankful for," is glibbed throughout Turkey Month. There are so many blessings, but I challenge deeper thinking than the standard responses: family, friends, God, freedom, a roof, food, health. Get specific and write a list.

We take for granted that God has blessed us with more reasons to be thankful than there are lines on a sheet of notebook paper. Our lives are braided, and you'll find what's most grateful cannot be bought on Black Friday. Often, it's the people who have been placed in our lives.

NOVEMBER 14

Ever hear people say, "Heaven gained a new angel" (when someone dies) or "My guardian angel was watching over me?" Have you ever seen ladies wearing a little cherub pin as a purposeful reminder that their guardian angel is watching over them? God (not an angel) is in control although, according to the Bible, He sends angels to do His work on earth at appointed times. Personally, I've had four instances that I question whether it was an angel who came to the rescue.

At five years old, I got lost from my family when we were on a business trip. While taking a walk around the lake at a Disney World hotel, I got separated from the other day camp kids. I wandered to another group who was boarding a boat to ride to the other side of the lake. When I got off the boat, the monstrous hotel seemed like such a long way to walk, but I started walking as I cried for my family. A man wearing a white jumpsuit and working alone on the beach asked why I was crying. He safely walked me to the hotel front desk. I was reunited with my frantic family a few hours later. When my parents questioned the man's identity, there was no explanation as to why a worker wearing white clothing would have been on the beach that day. Was he an angel?

Early in marriage, my husband & I were on a vacation when his convertible started shaking. The car sputtered to the nearest gas station. He knew nothing about car repairs but lifted the hood to check the engine's oil and water. He tried to crank it, but it trembled and conked out. A man walked up and said he'd take a look. He touched a few wires and said, "Now try." The man walked away as the car cranked right up. When my husband got out of the car to thank him and lower the hood, the man was gone. Unexplainable.

After Christmas, we left the grandparents' house on a cold, windy evening. Santa Claus loaded us up with so many gifts that we had to secure the luggage on top of the van. Looking like gypsies, we were traveling on a rural four lane highway about an hour from home when the wind gusted. Boom, boom, boom! The luggage fell off as we were driving at least 60 miles per hour. We pulled off to the side of the road. Right before my husband got out of the van, a semi-truck plowed by and hammered one of the suitcases. The contents scattered in all directions. The road was quiet without a car in sight as he scrambled to pick up a shoe, a shirt, a pajama bottom, etc.- without a flashlight. I watched a car drive past and make a U-turn at the next median. The car came back, parked, and two men got out of the car. They had a flashlight and started helping him without barely saying a word, and then took off. When the car drove past, I noticed-- NO CAR TAG! When we got back on the highway, we both commented how traffic on both sides of the road suddenly picked up. We were shaken but thankful. Angels?

Take5forHIM

Lastly, I was running five minutes late for my daughter's doctor appointment. Since the medical office closes for an hour lunch break and she was the first patient scheduled after the break, the parking lot was empty except one car in the circular driveway. I caught a glimpse of a man with a long ponytail who appeared to be helping someone in or out of the passenger side of the car. As I was huffing & puffing about being late, I jerked open the door. I was wearing 3" chunk heel, thong sandals. The height of the sandal was just the exact height, and my foot was in just the wrong place that I opened the door over my right foot. My foot got stuck under the heavy glass door. I gasped for breath and looked down. Blood was gushing. I screamed to the lady at the front desk, but she stood jaw-dropped & paralyzed. In the quick moments, I knew attempting to move my foot could rip the skin right off. I panicked! The receptionist ran out screaming, "EMERGENCY!" In the corner of my eye, I still saw the man with the ponytail. Aloud I said, "If only the door could be lifted up a tad. I cannot move it [my foot]." Suddenly, a pair of masculine hands came across my mid-section and firmly gripped the door. I didn't see his face, but I saw the ash brown, braided ponytail. The lady said, "Can you move your foot now?" I slid it from underneath, and she clutched me as we started slowly walking inside. The pain was excruciating, and a trail of blood followed my path. Immediately nurses and the doctor ran out into the waiting area. I said, "Please go tell that man thank you. He lifted the door to free my foot." The receptionist ran out and returned exclaiming, "He wasn't there. The parking lot is empty! I don't know where he went so quickly." It couldn't have been more than 30-45 seconds since the incident, but he was gone. Without a doubt, this had to be a divine intervention of some sort. Have you ever tried "lifting" a hinged door? They are set tight and don't budge. An angel?

Angels appear in the Bible as adult size male-looking figures in visual accounts. (Genesis 18- Abraham had three male visitors appear before him.) (Daniel 3:25- Shadrach, Meshach and Abednego were in the blazing fire and a fourth man who may have been the Son of God.) (Matthew 1:20-23; Luke 2:9-15; Luke 1:11-20; Luke 1:26-38- angels appearing in Jesus' birth.) (Matthew 28:1-7; Mark 16: 1-7; Luke 24:1-8- Resurrection Day) (Acts 12:6-18- An angel released Peter from prison.)

Scripture speaks of angels as created beings (Matthew 22:29-30), and also referred as messengers and ministering spirits (Hebrews 1:13-14 and Luke 24:37-39).

Do they have wings? Sometimes/sometimes not (Genesis 18-19; Isaiah 6- Isaiah saw the Lord seated on a throne with six-winged angels surrounding Him with six wings.)

There's no biblical mention that angels are assigned to specific people. Jesus is our ever-present help in a day of trouble (Psalm 46:1). He may send an angel for a special mission, but He's ultimately the one with the power to save us spiritually and physically.

Take5forHIM

NOVEMBER 15

When Jesus foretold of His second coming, and when John had visions which resulted in the Book of Revelation, followers thought the time was near. Two thousand years have passed, and people mention that the "end is coming" or there are "signs of the end times."

It's not the end for Christians; it's a celebration. Secondly, people can make predictions and theories, but Jesus said no one- not even the angels in heaven- know the day and time. We do know Jesus said the rapture will be like a thief in the night (1 Thessalonians 5:2,4). It may/may not happen in your lifetime, but always be expectant and prepared.

"For the Lord himself will descend from heaven with a shout, with the archangel's voice, and with the trumpet of God, and the dead in Christ will rise first. Then we who are still alive, who are left, will be caught up together with them in the clouds to meet the Lord in the air, and so we will always be with the Lord. Therefore, encourage one another with these words." (1 Thessalonians 4:16-18 CSB)

Take5forHIM

NOVEMBER 16

In 1620, the Pilgrims' sail to new land was a HUGE act of faith. Over a hundred passengers crammed onto the Mayflower for nine weeks on a slow path to the New World. There was sickness, disease, and rough experiences while traveling. Many second guessed if this was a good idea. It was a rugged voyage but landing in Cape Cod and starting fresh was even rougher. There were forty-seven deaths in their first winter due to poor diet, cold weather, and disease. When Spring came, they feared when Indians approached their camp. Surprisingly, the Indians were friendly, especially two leaders- Samoset and Squanto. They spoke English well and befriended the Pilgrims, providing farming and hunting tips. The Pilgrims felt like God sent Squanto to their aid as he was such a help by showing them how to fish, hunt, farm, and use herbs for medicinal purposes. That Fall, their first harvest provided enough food to last through the winter. The Pilgrims hosted a great feast to celebrate with their new friends. The Indians brought wild turkeys and deer. The three-day celebration was the first Thanksgiving as the two groups joined in peace, love, and appreciation for one another.

In historical writings, God was central in their leap of faith from the beginning to early years on new soil where they literally came with only the clothes on their backs. They lived primitively as they gradually engineered a culture. With strong conviction that God was leading them across the Atlantic, He was their ROCK for daily strength as life wasn't all rosy as portrayed in a kindergarten play.

Being a Squanto: Read Matthew 25:35-40.

"And my God will meet all your needs according to the
riches of his glory in Christ Jesus."
(Philippians 4:19 NIV)

Take5forHIM

NOVEMBER 17

Day One: Samson

Historical Background: Inhabited by the Canaanites, Joshua ushered the Israelites into the Promised Land which was reserved for God's chosen people. When Joshua died, they lacked a good leader to rid the territory of those opposing God. He appointed the tribe of Judah to the leadership seat, but they failed. As punishment for their actions, God put the Philistines in charge for 40 years.

We've studied several births of baby boys: Abraham and Sara's Isaac, Hannah's Samuel, and Moses. Judges 13 tells the story of Samson's birth. Maybe an anticipated glimpse of the most special baby boy ever to be born hundreds of years later?

Samson's parents were faithful Israelites in the tribe of Dan. His mother was barren. Get this…An angel appeared to Samson's mother and told her she'd give birth to a son. Familiar? The angel issued a strict diet of prohibited foods and stated that "no razor shall come upon his head." Samson's mighty strength due to uncut hair is his signature fame. Imagine a muscular, manly, buff, long-haired dude.

"'Now please be careful not to drink wine or beer, or to eat anything unclean;
for indeed, you will conceive and give birth to a son.
You must never cut his hair because the boy will be a Nazirite to God from birth,
and he will begin to save Israel from the power of the Philistines.'"
(Judges 13:4-5 HCSB)

Strength was a plus, but women were his downfall. He was strong-willed, determined, and had an attitude that could conquer the world. In Chapter 14, he performed absurd acts such as killing a lion with bare hands and scooping honey from the lion's bee-filled carcass. He married a Philistine girl despite the plea by his parents not to marry outside the tribe. At the marriage feast, he arrogantly puzzled guests with a riddle. He was irritated when the men begged his wife for the meaning. She whined asking for clues. His anger burned when she snitched the meaning after seven days of nagging, so he killed thirty of the men. When he returned home, his father-in-law had given his wife to one of his friends to marry. He fumed, so he did another ludicrous act. Ready for this one? Keep in mind: fearless and gutsy. He caught three hundred foxes, tied their tails together, set their tails afire, and released them in a field of grain. The Philistines were irate because the crop was destroyed, so they burned the father-in-law and wife to death. Samson sought revenge by slaughtering more Philistines.

The Philistines then captured Samson, but the Spirit of the Lord allowed him to bust the flax rope used to tie him down. After that, he had no problem killing a thousand men with a dead donkey's jawbone! The Lord appointed him as a judge of Israel for twenty years. The Philistines still ruled, but Samson was a respected leader in the Israelite community. God blessed Samson with super hero strength to drive out the Philistines. Recall the territory had not been cleaned out after Joshua's death.

Who votes Samson as the most bizarre, outrageous character in the Bible? Read Judges 13-16 for the details.

NOVEMBER 18

Day Two: Samson and Delilah, a power couple?

As acknowledged, women were Samson's weakness. The first line of Chapter 16 begins with Samson having sex with a harlot. Then, he fell in love with Delilah. For some reason, society has an obsession with Samson and Delilah as if they represent a model couple. It's quite the opposite. The Philistines offered Delilah eleven hundred pieces of silver to discover the source of Samson's strength. For three days, he answered silly ways he could be bound, so she would give it a try while he slept. He easily burst out each time as she screamed, "The Philistines are here!" Like his first wife, she wailed how she felt unloved and deceived.

> *"Because she nagged him day after day and pleaded with him until she wore*
> *him out, he told her the whole truth and said to her, 'My hair has never*
> *been cut, because I am a Nazirite to God from birth. If I am shaved, my strength will*
> *leave me, and I will become weak and be like any other man.'"*
> *(Judges 16:16-17 HCSB)*

Delilah was a trader. The poor guy sought love and couldn't find a woman who pledged trust and devotion for his out of the ordinary attributes. He was a novelty who raised snooping from the bad guys. In both instances, his wife and Delilah caved instead of standing by their man.

Read today's lesson in Judges 16. Men don't appreciate a nagging woman. There's an old saying, "Behind every successful man is a great woman." A woman who's adoring, supportive, encouraging, and faithful, gives a man the confidence to do great things. It's not the gospel, but it's true. While the four chapters in Judges describes several defeats against the Philistines, Samson's personal life is the umbrella. In the years to come, be reminded of this perspective of Samson's relationship with women. May it dissuade future nagging.

Take5forHIM

NOVEMBER 19

"And He said to them, 'Where is your faith? And they were fearful and amazed, saying to one another, 'Who is this, that He commands even the wind & the water, and they obey Him?'"
(Luke 8:25 NAS)

When we pray boldly and consistently but we're not seeing God move, it's unsettling. The answer seems obvious, yet God is not intervening. You wonder why He is allowing ___ to continue or why there's not a breakthrough when you're praying diligently. You pray at least once daily yet He's silent. You believe nothing is impossible with God (Matthew 19:26), so it would be so easy for Him to say "yes" to your tiny little request when there are much worse situations in life.

There are times when you have to throw your hands up in the air and give up. Not give up as in GIVE UP, buttttttt give it all to Him. God is working even when we don't see the results after hard core prayer. It doesn't matter how many times we pray or how loud we scream out. We are not God, He is. His ways are not our ways. *"For my thoughts are not your thoughts, neither are your ways my ways," declares the LORD."* *(Isaiah 55:8 NAS)* He reigns, so rely on Him, & let Him be God—even when our souls battle against relinquishing.

The silent shut door may be temporary, or it may be dead bolt locked. Let your new prayer be: "God, I have answered the call to faithfully pray for ___. Give me the peace to lay it at Your feet. Take it off my shoulders and into Your hands. You're in control. Let it be well with my soul how you move in hearts and situations. Work the quandary in Your own way, in Your timing."

If He healed the sick, raised Lazarus from the dead, walked on water, calmed the storm, was crucified and rose from the grave three days later-- why should we question His authority to rightly ANSWER PRAYERS IN A WAY THAT IS ORDAINED AND BEST [on my behalf and others']??? Ahhhhh, it is well with my soul!

Take5forHIM

NOVEMBER 20

No condemnation. ~ Those who live according to the Spirit are about the things of the spirit. ~ The mind set on the Spirit is life and peace. ~ The spirit of God lives in you. ~ All those led by God's spirit are God's sons and daughters. ~ Received the spirit of adoption. ~ Abba, Father! ~ The glory that is going to be revealed to us. ~ But the spirit Himself intercedes for us with unspoken groanings. ~ All things work together for good of those who love God. ~ If God is for us, who is against us? ~ Nothing can separate us from the love of God.

This is Romans 8. Familiar truths are in this chapter. It's specific regarding the contrast between living in the flesh and the life of salvation. It seems too good to be true. Adopt it as TRUTH.

Tip: Writing down highlights from a chapter is a great way to learn instead of rushing through it, barely comprehending what's been read.

NOVEMBER 21

Baptism is a sign of repentance. Some denominations sprinkle the head, and some insist on immersing the body in water. Whether babies are sprinkled, or a new Christian is baptized in a pool of water is a complicated debate that cannot be theologically solved by this writer. It's a matter of preference according to what Christian denomination a child's parents attend or when a person is converted to faith.

Theologian John Piper's teachings are highly respected on many issues. His website "Desiring God" is recommended when searching for solid biblical answers such as, "Why should I be baptized?"

> Baptism is not man's idea. It was God's idea. It is not a denominational thing. It is a Biblical thing. It started with John the Baptist at the beginning of our gospels. He came, verse 11 says, to "baptize with water for repentance." It continued in the ministry of Jesus himself. John 4:1 says, "Jesus was making and baptizing more disciples than John," although it was the disciples, not Jesus who did the actual immersing (John 4:2). And the practice was picked up by the church not because of their own wisdom, but because of the command of the Lord. At the end of his earthly ministry Jesus said, "Go therefore and make disciples of all the nations, baptizing them in the name of the Father and the Son and the Holy Spirit" (Matthew 29:18). So Jesus made baptism part of his ministry and part of our mission.[27]

Baptism was not mentioned in the Bible until John the Baptist. It's believed that some sectors of the Jewish faith were baptizing as a sign of repentance, but baptism became more common in the New Testament.

"John appeared, baptizing in the wilderness and proclaiming a baptism of repentance for the forgiveness of sins. And all the country of Judea and all Jerusalem were going to him and were being baptized by him in the river Jordan, confessing their sins." (Mark 1:4-5 ESV)

John baptized Jesus:
"In those days Jesus came from Nazareth of Galilee and was baptized by John in the Jordan. And when he came up out of the water, immediately he saw the heavens being torn open and the Spirit descending on him like a dove. And a voice came from heaven, 'You are my beloved Son; with you I am well pleased.'" (Mark 1:9-11 ESV)

The early church baptized new converts:

Take5forHIM

"'How can we who died to sin still live in it? Do you not know that all of us who have been baptized into Christ Jesus were baptized into His death?'" (Romans 6:2-3 ESV)

Have you been baptized? Were you baptized by a sprinkling of water as an infant? Or, dunked in a lake or baptismal pool? If you have not been baptized, but you've become a believer, take the step to make the public profession of faith by baptism.

Go deeper. Also read 1 Peter 3:18-22.

[27]"I Baptize You with Water." *Desiring God.* 26 September 2018. www.desiringgod.org/messages/i-baptize-you-with-water .

Take5forHIM

NOVEMBER 22

Metaphorically speaking, one cannot sit on the fence and sometimes breathe Christianity and sometimes not. Are you going to be a hot or cold Christian? Or, are you going to be lukewarm by sitting on the fence?

It's convicting, but God despises the lukewarm who are straddling.

"I know your works: you are neither cold nor hot.
Would that you were either cold or hot! So, because you are lukewarm,
and neither hot nor cold,
I WILL SPIT YOU OUT OF MY MOUTH."
(Revelation 3:15-16 ESV)

NOVEMBER 23

Do you sometimes think God and this thing called Christianity isn't working for you? That's the reply a girl gave when told to pray about a black cloud hanging over her head. "I've tried praying and it doesn't work for me. I swear I think God hates me." When someone has this frame of mind it's hard to know how to respond except to say, "You cannot go to God only when you're in a frenzy."

Seek Him first. Be dependent on Him instead of self-reliant. Submit to His authority. Open eyes to see Him in everything. Give Him the glory when good things happen, but also praise Him in pandemonium.

Read 1 Timothy 2:1-15.

NOVEMBER 24

Some youth group leaders have the philosophy that it's acceptable to bounce back & forth because teens are trying to figure out life- a carefree idea that students have to go through junk to recognize their desperation for God. Dismally, most youth testimonies are full of admissions to alcohol, drugs, sex, porn, and domestic violence. It's the same ole, same ole with a few different details of twists. Faithful teens abstain from testimonies on stage because it's a snoozer without big punches such as getting arrested for shoplifting a fifth at the big box liquor store. This youth leader contends the faithful are the wiser.

I've known gorgeous girls who struggled to walk the straight and narrow because the world loves their style, boys love their figures, and popular peers invite them to parties. The yo-yo from Christian friends to the popular is tiresome and confusing. It's lonely being the only sober one with a house full of drunks, so she tries the cup holder technique hoping no one will notice. After a while, "What the heck, it's Prom Night." Or, "It's Initiation Weekend." A special occasion makes the next weekend more tempting and before you know it.... It's a crying shame because there was a potential statement maker. "I'm different. I'm living for God." It's doubtful a girl would be ousted from the Greek Community, but greatly blessed by God. The quality of friends would come if she planted her feet in cement.

Sadly, the fictitious character resembles many readers. We love worldly adventures and the attention that comes with it. The popularity high is loved more than The Most High. The buzz from rum shots is favored over the Prince of Peace. At the moment, the tangible is more valuable than the invisible. The Almighty God is pushed aside while she lives what the world calls her prime.

The Old Testament reveals the jealous character of God's adoration for His devoted children. His vast love is the choice trait rather than judgment. The soft term "consequences" is preferred instead of wrath for enjoying worldliness over the Holy One who was invited in her soul to be Lord.

"In their case the god of this world has blinded the minds of the unbelievers,
to keep them from seeing the light of the gospel of the glory of Christ,
who is the image of God."
(2 Corinthians 4:4 ESV)

Also, look up 1 John 2:15-1; James 4:4.

Take5forHIM

NOVEMBER 25

Thanksgiving messages abound. My favorite holiday, it's a sweet day with very little commercialism except grocery store ads. It's a celebration as moms and grandmothers break out the fine china for a feast fit for a king. What an awesome day for a family to stuff themselves to the gullet, and then nap while watching college football. Ahhhhhhhh!

Thanksgiving should be celebrated year-round telling others how much they're appreciated. Above all, thank God daily for all He has done in our lives. Sometimes life stinks but give Him praise regardless of how life is treatin' ya. ALL THINGS WORK FOR THE GOOD OF HIS PEOPLE.

"Rejoice always, pray without ceasing, give thanks in all circumstances; for this is the will of God in Christ Jesus for you."
(1 Thessalonians 5:18 ESV)

Also, read Psalms 18:1; 1 Chronicles 16:34; Ephesians 5:20.

Take5forHIM

NOVEMBER 26
Giving Thanks by Showing Gratitude

"Please" and "thank you" are the magic words taught at an early age. Parents have great intentions as children are given gifts to prompt a verbal "thank you" when opening a gift, and many train kids to send thank you notes to gift givers. I taught my own children to write thank you notes for birthday and Christmas gifts as soon as they learned to write. I pestered for years by placing cards on the kitchen table and reminding, "OK, everybody, write thank yous." For the longest, I sat at the table coaching what to write, and I addressed envelopes to speed up the agonizing time spent at the table. It was a proud moment when my college-age daughter asked for addresses because, on her own, she purchased and wrote birthday thank you notes. It had become a learned ritual, and gift givers adore receiving snail mail (NOT EMAILED OR TEXTED). It's old fashioned, but a handwritten note for a birthday, Christmas, or graduation gift is treasured.

For the giver, it's satisfying. It shows appreciation that he/she took the time to thoughtfully shop and spend hard earned money for the perfect gift. Regardless of the gift's value, no matter how expensive [or how small], a handwritten note is priceless. Not only is it etiquette, it's a display of gratefulness.

Make someone smile by your gratitude- especially this time of year! Add a few kind verses to a thank you card...

"(I)We give thanks to God always for you all,
making mentioned of you, in our prayers."
(1 Thessalonians 1:2 NKJV)

"The Lord bless you and keep you;
The Lord make His face shine on you,
And be gracious to you;
the Lord lift up His countenance on you,
And give you peace."
(Numbers 6:24-26 NAS)

"Grace and peace to you from God our Father and the Lord Jesus Christ,
I thank my God every time I remember you. In all my prayer for all of you,
I always pray with joy because of your partnership with the gospel from
the first day until now that he who began a good work in you will carry it
on to completion until the day of Christ Jesus."
(Philippians 1:2-6 NIV)

Take5forHIM

NOVEMBER 27

Dear God, I pray this reader will feel Your presence and embrace biblical truths. May Your Holy Spirit overpower her thoughts. Fill her with head knowledge for success but refrain academic assignments from encompassing the space of time to forget what's most important. I pray she will have faith to move mountains and defeat any weaknesses or adversities. Tear down the wall of insecurities.

I pray she will glorify You in all areas of her life: home, friends, classmates, work. Provide accountability partners for friends. Protect them against feuds that can send relationships down the tube.

May she dodge the paths that lead to destruction but race down the straight path to Your everlasting arms. Place Your righteous right hand of protection to guide her safely. In Jesus' precious name. Amen.

Take5forHIM

NOVEMBER 28

Do you serve in a church ministry, non-profit, or Christian related ministry? It could be sorting through clothes at a thrift shop, disaster relief clean-up, serving at a soup kitchen for the homeless, a church greeter, or nursery volunteer. Find a place where you can show God's love and be blessed in return. Get involved!

"God is not unjust; he will not forget your work and the love you have shown him as you have helped his people and continue to help them."
(Hebrews 6:10 NIV)

NOVEMBER 29

"Stand firm, and you will win life."
(Luke 21:19 NIV)

"As I sit here this morning, I am amazed at the goodness of our God. I had the privilege of sharing my testimony last night at a student ministry but honestly, it was just a chance to declare God's faithfulness. To share how my journey has allowed me to meet with Jesus not only on the good days, but in the most painful and challenging areas of my life...and how continuing to walk with Him has been (and will be) the most beautiful journey I ever take.

The roots grow first, but the fruit WILL come-and multiply! Embrace the seasons where you feel hidden, hurt, or confused....your Heavenly Father will meet you there and bring restoration and LIFE like never before! Continue, my friends. Press on. Stand firm in the waiting. His heart is here."

Written by Meredith F., college friend and budding author.

NOVEMBER 30

We have no idea what God may call us to do. It could be as far-fetched as when God told Noah to build an ark. It had never rained before the forty days of flooding, so people thought Noah had lost his cotton pickin' mind!

Or, can you imagine wanting a baby as much as Hannah that you would desperately pray that if God answered with a baby, to vow to give him up to serve the Lord?

Or, what about God calling Abraham to start a new life in a new land?

These are just a few who were willing to do whatever God asked of them. Would you be willing to marry a missionary and move to a third world country or _____?

Take5forHIM

DECEMBER

"The best time to plant a tree was 20 years ago. The second best time is now."

-Chinese Proverb

Take5forHIM

DECEMBER 1

"In the beginning was the Word, and the Word was with God, and the Word
was God. He was in the beginning with God. All things were made through him,
and without him was not anything made that was made. In Him was life,
and the life was the light of men. The light shines in the darkness,
and the darkness has not overcome it."
(John 1:1-5 ESV)

There's the truth about who Jesus is in these five verses. God sent His son as a baby to live on this earth for thirty-something years. He was born to die, but His death gave us life.

DECEMBER 2

Which is the most important event- Jesus' birth or the resurrection? Over a month is spent preparing for Christmas Day, so many would answer "the immaculate conception and birth." While it's dear to our hearts, the miracle of the resurrection far outweighs the birthday.

Years ago, I attended a Christmas Party in which everyone shared a holiday tradition. A wise elderly woman shared that she puts a large rusty nail tipped with red paint at the top of the Christmas tree signifying that without Jesus' death we would have nothing to celebrate. I fell in love with the idea, so I've given many rusty, red tipped nails with red satin ribbon wrapped around the top, as a way to share the gospel perspective at Christmas with others. It's an unexpected surprise to receive such an unusual tree ornament. He was born to die for our sins and give us the hope of eternal life in Heaven with Him and our Heavenly Father.

"For in bringing many sons to glory, it is entirely appropriate that God - all things exist for Him and through Him - should make the source of their salvation perfect through sufferings. For the One who sanctifies and those who are sanctified all have one Father. That is why Jesus is not shamed to call them brothers saying: 'I will proclaim Your name to my brothers; I will sing hymns to You in the congregation.' Again, 'I will trust in Him.' And again, 'Here I am with the children God gave Me.' Now since the children have flesh and blood in common, Jesus also shared in these, so that through His death He might destroy the one holding the power of death - that is, the Devil - and free those who were held in slavery all their lives by the fear of death. For it is clear that He does not reach out to help angels, but to help Abraham's offspring. Therefore, He had to be like His brothers in every way, so that He could become a merciful and faithful high priest in service to God, to make propitiation for the sins of the people. For since He Himself was tested, and has suffered, He is able to help those who are tested." (Hebrews 2:10-18 HCSB)

"Therefore, as He was coming into the world, He said: 'You did not want sacrifice and offering, but You prepared a body for Me. You did not delight in whole burnt offerings and sin offerings. Then I said, 'See- it is written about Me in the volume of the scroll- I have come to do your will, God!'" (Hebrews 10:5-7 HCSB)

Take5forHIM

DECEMBER 3

"For a child will be born to us, a son will be given to us;
And the government will rest on His shoulders;
And His name will be Wonderful Counselor, Mighty God,
Eternal Father, Prince of Peace. There will be no end to the
increase of His government or of peace."
(Isaiah 9:6 NAS)

Isaiah was a prophet over 600 years before Jesus' birth. Scanning through the Book of Isaiah, there are numerous prophesies of Jesus' birth, death, and resurrection.

Other prophetic verses were handed down for generations to Jesus' day. For example, John 19:36-37 said prophecy was fulfilled in that not a bone would be broken (Jesus'), and He would be pierced. Girls, nobody could make this stuff up! God's Word is the truth, real and perfect!

DECEMBER 4

Matthew Chapter One's long genealogy list of Jesus' family tree is skimmed over as readers skip to the Christmas story. However, the line is a vital chunk connecting all that was written in the Old Testament to the Messiah. Here's a brief synopsis of the key names in the family tree.

Abraham > Isaac > Jacob and Leah > Judah > Rahab > Ruth > David > Joseph > JESUS

Jesus' stealthy ancestors were God's historical patriarchs who made a mark for the kingdom of God whether they knew it at the time or not. Many had sinful flaws and didn't always live for God, but their stories go far deeper than a five-minute read.

Did you know?
Abraham was the first descendant after The Flood recognized in the Bible as the chosen father of a multitude of nations, and kings came from him. God established a covenant with Abraham and his descendants to be their God and give all of the land of Canaan. (Genesis 17:1-9)

Obediently, Abraham and Isaac walked up the hill carrying wood [for the dad to sacrifice his son]. God provided a perfect ram in the thickets right before Abraham slayed his son. This is a foreshadowing illustration of Jesus who would someday carry the cross up a hill to be sacrificed as the perfect lamb for our sins. God knew Abraham fully trusted Him at that point, and it was a turning point in Abraham's walk. (Genesis 22:1-12)

Jacob's unloved first wife is in the lineage to Jesus NOT his first love Rachel who was the mother of Joseph (as in the favored son with the beautiful coat of colors) and Benjamin. Although God used Joseph in a totally different way, Leah and Jacob's son Judah carried the blood line to the Savior.

Rahab was a prostitute in Jericho (the city in Canaan which was surrounded by a stone wall). Joshua, the leader of the Israelites, after Moses died, sent two men to spy around Jericho to check it out. The king got news that the men were hiding at Rahab's. He thought there was going to be a takeover. She hid the men on the rooftop, so they couldn't be found. She wholeheartedly believed the spies were God's men, the Israelites whom she'd heard. She put her faith in them to protect her parents and family from being harmed. God indeed protected her family, and she was blessed with Boaz (see below) who was documented fourteen generations to Jesus. (Joshua 2)

Ruth's story is of love and dedication to her mother-in-law after their husbands died. Ruth later married Boaz, and they were the grandparents of King David. (Book of Ruth)

Take5forHIM

David was a shepherd boy who bravely fought Goliath [the giant] and later became King of Israel. While on the run for his life from King Saul, he wrote Psalms. The Psalms have inspired people for thousands of years when in despair, joyful, thankful, or praising God. David was known to be a "man after God's own heart" (1 Samuel 13:14) yet he lived many highs and lows. His adventurous life and royal reign can be read in 1 Samuel 16 thru the end of 2 Samuel.

Joseph wasn't Jesus' father by blood but by marriage. Mary was legally in the family line of the House of David which justified the prophesy that the Messiah would be born in the lineage of Abraham, Isaac, Jacob, & King David. (Isaiah 7:14, Jeremiah 23:5, & Isaiah 11:1-10)

Jesus, 100% man/100% God, was birthed from a family tree of familiar and unknowns. Jesus' birth was prophesied in the Old Testament and fulfilled 41 generations after God promised Abraham (and his grandson Jacob) that He would bless him with as many descendants as the stars in the sky.

While biblical customs differ from the cozy American life, THE WORD bridges the gap for understanding His story of love, forgiveness, and redemption despite rampant sin since Adam and Eve. Sometimes He uses believers to do His work; sometimes not. God's gonna shine either way.

"The scepter will not depart from Judah, nor the ruler's staff
from between his feet, until he to whom it belongs shall come
and the obedience of the nations shall be his."
(Genesis 49:10 NIV)

"Therefore, the Lord himself will give you a sign: The virgin will
conceive and give birth to a son and will call him Immanuel."
(Isaiah 7:14 NIV)

"A shoot will come up from the stump of Jesse;
from his roots a Branch will bear fruit.
The Spirit of the LORD will rest on him—
the Spirit of wisdom and of understanding,
the Spirit of counsel and of might,
the Spirit of the knowledge and fear of the LORD—
and he will delight in the fear of the LORD.....
(Isaiah 11:1-10 NIV)

Also read Jeremiah 23:5.

Take5forHIM

DECEMBER 5
Who was she?

A pregnant woman, in even the best circumstances, is flooded with emotions. Mary was not in a sweet spot as an engaged teenage girl when given the news, by the angel Gabriel, that she had found favor with the Lord and was expecting a baby boy, God's son. But, she ended the angelic encounter by declaring, *"Behold, the Lord's servant; be it done to me according to your word." (Luke 1:38 NAS)* As only imagined, household tension and a multitude of questions sent her on a three-month getaway to visit her cousin Elizabeth who was also pregnant [with John the Baptist]. In those days, unwedded pregnancies were shunned, and a girl could be stoned (Deuteronomy 22:20). However, Elizabeth didn't question Mary's conception, but affirmed her as a blessed woman who carried the child of her Lord. Elizabeth revealed herself as an encourager, comforter, and a great woman of God (Read Luke 1: 39-45).

Following the pep talk, Mary must have been empowered that God would take care of the societal and family pressures of the unknown. She prayed what's sometimes referred to as "Mary's Song," praising God the Father.

"And Mary said: 'My soul exalts the Lord. And my spirit has rejoiced in God my Savior. For He has had regard for the humble state of His bond slave; for behold, from this time on all generations will count me blessed. For the Mighty One has done great things for me; and holy is His name. And His mercy is upon generation after generation toward those who fear Him. He has done mighty deeds with His arm; He has scattered those who were proud in the thoughts of their heart. He has brought down rulers from their thrones and has exalted those who were humble. He has filled the hungry with good things; and sent away the rich empty-handed. He has given help to Israel and His servant, in remembrance of His mercy, as He spoke to our fathers, to Abraham and his offspring forever. And Mary stayed with her about three months and then returned to her home." (Luke 1: 46-56 NAS)

Surely there were moments of fear and anxiety, but God chose sweet, humble, young Mary to be the mother of His only son. She wasn't raised in a palace, but her heart for God and virginity honored her to be the Messiah's mother. Purity placed her in a position to be blessed. Second Timothy 2:21 says, *"Therefore if anyone cleanses himself from the latter, he will be a vessel for honor, sanctified, and useful for the Master, prepared for every good work."(NKJV)* Mary was pure in obedience to God and physically pure for her fiancé. When faced with the unexpected, she relied on her Heavenly Father for the journey that was much different than dreams to marry Joseph, have three kids, and live happily ever after. Life wasn't easy because the parenting challenges were much different than raising any other child. The only glimpse of Jesus' childhood is the story of Him wandering into the temple (Luke 2:39-52). God's plan for Mary's (and Joseph) life was total dependence for the huge responsibility to be Jesus' earthly parents.

Mother Mary is a perfect example of God using the least likely to fulfill His work. She wasn't royalty, an angel sent down from heaven, or a flawless human being, but the one chosen to be The Holy's MOM.

DECEMBER 6

Much of Jesus' birth story is left to the imagination. I love a good story but wish to know more about the people who were/were not mentioned. I want to know more about Elizabeth's birth to John the Baptist. What did the grandparents say? Was Mary kept inside for nine months or casted out? What were people whispering about them, and how was the pregnancy explained? How long did the wise men and shepherds stay at the stable? Have you ever wondered why His birth was under those circumstances instead of in a palace with servants as He deserved?

He was born for all the people. He was born to live, walk, and breathe with the people and to live a humble life.

"And the word became flesh, and dwelt among us,
and we beheld His glory,
glory as of the only begotten from the Father,
full of grace and truth."
(John 1:14 NAS)

DECEMBER 7

True story. A 70-year old lady was walking her dog around 8 a.m. when she tripped on her shoelaces. She stumbled chest down. She couldn't get up at first, so she took a few moments to figure the best way to stand. As she laid face down on the curb, five cars drove by. She reported that a couple of cars raced by while others steered a wide semi-circle as they passed. She was understandably miffed that out of the five neighborhood cars, no one stopped to ask if she was alright or to offer help. She was banged-up and scraped but managed to hobble home. She lives in what's considered a friendly area, but she was more emotionally hurt than physically that a Good Samaritan didn't come to aid. The term Good Samaritan is traced to the Bible.

In Luke 10, an expert in Jewish laws interrogated Jesus with several questions including who will inherit eternal life. He then inquired about the neighbor Jesus kept stating to love. He replied with the Parable of the Good Samaritan which has been an adopted rule of thumb for thousands of years to lend a hand to someone on the spur of the moment when urgently needed.

Read the story of the Good Samaritan in Luke 10:25-37.

> *"'The one who showed mercy to him,' he said.*
> *Then Jesus told him, 'Go and do the same.'"*
> *(Luke 10:37 CSB)*

Take5forHIM

DECEMBER 8

Generally a happy natured person, I hit rock bottom without warning when we moved in 2005. Things slowly got better. Even then, darkness would creep back causing an "unhappy Mommy" who spent many afternoons and early evenings crawling in the bed. I cried a lot, and the least little thing irritated me. Unfortunately, my family suffered through my problems. I smiled to the outside world as I did all of the "right things": taught Sunday School, volunteered at school, kept the house and clothes clean, cooked, and obsessed with exercising. I was on an up and down roller coaster, and my poor family never knew what to expect.

A few years back, depression reared its ugly head around Christmas time. Once again, I did all the "right things": decorated the house, made my traditional cinnamon candy, yet felt blah! For so long, I had prayed for a joyful heart. I didn't understand why I had bursts of happiness and then crashes. Where was God and why wasn't He answering my prayers?

On Christmas Day, we were flooded with gifts at my mother-in-law's home. I plastered on a smile, for the day, as I knew the gifts would bring temporary happiness. I muddled through unwrapping gifts, and then opened a bag that contained three folksy, distressed angels inside. One held a star-shaped sign that said "LOVE," another "PEACE," and the third one "JOY." I stared at the "JOY" angel's eyes. Although she held the "JOY" sign, her eyes gripped mine with sadness. She wasn't smiling like the other two angels. The crackled-painted wood made her smile look upside down. No one was paying attention as I stared into the angel's eyes. She looked the same way I felt—hiding behind a sign, wearing a fake smile. "S-A-D," "MISERABLE," or "DEPRESSED" would have been a more appropriate label..

I quickly stuffed the three angels back inside the gift bag. I felt like I had seen a ghost but painted on a smile to get through the night.

I wish I could say I experienced a Christmas Miracle like a movie ending, but I did not. Time passed, and I really can't say a new season came depression-free until God turned my lukewarm life around at a youth retreat in 2015. Even though I had been a Christian since childhood, I screamed out to God on the last night of worship at the retreat. The music was blaring as I turned a rusty, metal folding chair into an altar. I felt someone wrap arms around me as I screamed (!), cried, confessed, and begged God to work in my marriage/our finances/my family, and to make me His vessel. I fully surrendered to make Him Lord over my life. I'll never know, but I'm not so sure that it was a person who placed arms around me that night. It may have been the arms of My Father comforting me as I gave Him my all. I didn't leave the retreat feeling changed, *but I made changes* as I started reading the Bible like I never had before, praying about everything, and becoming Christ-focused. I gave up on perfectionism

Take5forHIM

(trying to be somebody I'm not and trying to fix things). He gave me the JOY I had craved for years. He set me on a new path.

"Be joyful in hope, patient in affliction, faithful in prayer."
(Romans 12:12 NIV)

"The Lord your God is with you, the Mighty Warrior who saves.
He will take great delight in you;
in his love he will no longer rebuke you,
but will rejoice over you with singing."
(Zephaniah 3:17 NIV)

"When anxiety was great within me,
your consolation brought me joy."
(Psalm 94:19 NIV)

DECEMBER 9

With mixed feelings, a new Bible is on my Christmas list. I've had mine for 20+ years, and I'd like an updated translation. My Bible's pages are marked and tattered. So, is it time for a new one?

Recently, I tossed and turned all night fretting over a situation. The next morning, I woke up exhausted. Though I couldn't find the particular verse I needed for comfort, I started crying as I flipped pages of underlined and highlighted verses. Strong assurances popped off the pages and assured me that what kept me from sleeping was going to iron itself out. God sits on His throne, and I need to allow Him to be God. Tears and peace poured from my eyes.

God, I cling to Your living word. It speaks to me. I need it. Thank you for speaking Your Word to me over and over again.

A new Bible will be bittersweet!

"All people are like grass, and their faithfulness is like the flowers of the field. The grass withes and the flowers fall, because the breath of the Lord blows on them. Surely the people are grass. The grass withers and the flowers fall, but the word of our God endures forever."
(Isaiah 40:6-8 NIV)

Take5forHIM

DECEMBER 10

*"Now may the God of hope fill you with all joy and peace in believing
that you may abound in hope by the power of the Holy Spirit?"*
(Romans 15:13 NAS)

Think of a few who are considered joy-filled. Being joyful doesn't mean laughing, smiling, and floating on air all the time on a Jesus freak high. You can have joy without being bubbly. Part of having joy is being content in life, having faith that God is in control, loving others, and having the hope of eternity with Jesus. We all have different personalities, so don't confuse personality traits with joy.

DECEMBER 11

Someone once said that different denominations draw similar personalities. Comparatively, the same can be said with respect to different ways of worship. Not everybody's inclined to raise hands in the air when worshipping just as others are lulled to sleep while singing from a hymn book. You're not less of a Christian if it's awkward rocking out in a contemporary worship service but prefer to keep hands at waistline and eyes wide open. Don't ever let anyone guilt you into thinking otherwise. There are varying worship styles and people express their heartfelt love for Jesus diversely.

"Then the prophetess Miriam, Aaron's sister, took a tambourine in her hand, and all the women came out following her with tambourines and dancing. Miriam sang to them: 'Sing to the Lord, for he is highly exalted; he has thrown the horse and its rider into the sea.'"
(Exodus 15:20-21 CSB)

"David was dancing with all his might before the Lord wearing a linen ephod. He and the whole house of Israel were bringing up the ark of the Lord with shouts and the sound of a ram's horn."
(2 Samuel 6:14-15 CSB)

"About midnight Paul and Silas were praying and singing hymns to God, and the other prisoners were listening to them."
(Acts 16:25 NIV)

"Yours, Lord, is the greatness and the power and the glory and the majesty and the splendor, for everything in heaven and earth is yours. Yours, Lord, is the kingdom; you are exalted as head over all."
(1 Chronicles 29:11 NIV)

JESUS. Worthy of every song we sing to HIM.

Take5forHIM

DECEMBER 12

"Some people are rich, and they don't even know it." I remember the sweet elderly lady who looked at our three young children running around like monkeys in my husband's office. She saw a wealth that money cannot buy.

We get persuaded that money is our answer to happiness when some of the wealthiest people attest to the stress and complexity of their lives. More money and more stuff cause more time to take care of the stuff. The best things in life cannot be purchased in a store or online. What things in your life can you appreciate as priceless gifts without a price tag?

"Every good gift and every perfect gift is from above,
coming down from the Father of lights
with whom there is no variation of shadow due to change."
(James 1:17 ESV)

"And He said to me, 'It is done. I am the Alpha and the Omega,
the beginning and the end. To the thirsty I will give from the spring
of the water of life without payment."
(Revelation 21:6 ESV)

"A joyful heart is good medicine..."
(Proverbs 17:22 NAS)

"Behold, children are a heritage from the Lord,
the fruit of the womb a reward."
(Psalm 127:3 ESV)

"For physical training is of some value, but godliness has value for all things,
holding promise for both the present life and the life to come."
(1 Timothy 4:8 NIV)

"My son (and daughter), pay attention to what I say; turn your ear to my words.
Do not let them out of your sight, keep them within your heart; for they are life
to those who find them and health to one's whole body."
(Proverbs 4:20-22 NIV)

"Gracious words are a honeycomb, sweet to the soul and healing to the bones."
(Proverbs 16:24 NIV)

I'm filthy rich. How about you?

Take5forHIM

DECEMBER 13

Jesus' birth is exactly the way His Father planned- even the innkeeper having no vacancies at the inn! But, there was no room for the savior of the world? Would it have made a difference if he had known who was asking for a room to rest for the night?

To this day, multitudes have had the choice to know Jesus yet slam the door shut as if there's no room. He's the King of Kings, Lord of Lords, Prince of Peace, and so much more yet even as believers we don't always make room for Him in our day. Days can lead into months without inviting Him in our hearts. He's worthy to be praised!

> *"Then she gave birth to her firstborn Son, and she wrapped*
> *Him snuggly in cloth and laid Him in a feeding trough—*
> *because there was no room for them at the lodging place."*
> *(Luke 2:7 HCSB)*

DECEMBER 14

God is so perfect and awesome. He could have sent His Son to earth as a full-grown man wearing a cloak, crown, a staff & scepter proclaiming, "I AM GOD. BOW DOWN TO ME. I AM HERE TO REIGN IN A BIG CASTLE IN JERUSALEM. I AM KING, so listen up you HEATHENS!" Instead, He came quietly as a sweet little baby born into the world in the same way as all of us. He was a cute, precious baby who gripped Mary & Joseph's hearts as with all parents who gush over their baby. Hyperbolized for Christmas plays, we love Christmas so much that it takes over a month to get ready. We decorate, shop, cook, and eat party food yet Biblically, it's not the most important event in history. Matthew and Luke condensed the story to a few chapters each because it really isn't the most important piece of Jesus' life story.

The basics of the story are: the perfection of His genealogical lineage (1st Chapter of Matthew); the angels appearing to Mary and Joseph; the virgin conceiving God's Son; Elizabeth carrying John the Baptist in her old age and him leaping for joy in her womb when Mary told Elizabeth she was carrying a baby; Mary (on a donkey) & Joseph traveling for the census; no room in the Inn; the stable; the birth; the star; the shepherds and three wise men. Then, the Bible jumps to Jesus as an adolescent boy, and then to His adult life ministry.

So, why are we so captivated by Christmas? Because, He was born as a BABY, and we love babies! It's a cherished story, but it wasn't a Christmas Pageant. He came humbly and quietly. Probably a huge reason why His birth wasn't announced with a megaphone was because He had to be protected from King Herod. The wise men were excited about His birth, so they went to the King and asked the Messiah Child's location. The Messiah, known to be the future King of the Jews, was a threat to Herod's throne. So, Jesus' birth was hushed. Following Jesus' birth, the King had every baby boy killed to ensure his royalty for years to come.

Then, it skips to his boyhood. Once again, the Bible leaves a lot to our imagination as to what the times were like. How did Mary and Joseph explain Jesus to their parents and relatives? Did their families know this baby was super special? How did the government explain the killing of baby boys? Did Herod think he had solved his problem by the killings? Did he have restless nights regretting his order to kill innocent babies? Did the shepherds and wise men go around telling people who told others, who told more, who told even more of this momentous birth that changed the world?

There's so much to treasure regarding His birth: His perfection, His goodness, His divine nature, and holiness in the Christmas story. So, go read it beginning in Matthew and then thumb over to Luke. God's perfect plan: the holy baby born in an imperfect, tumultuous world!

Take5forHIM

DECEMBER 15

You may be skeptical whether situations are God's maneuvering or by chance. When God began working in me after a youth retreat in 2015, there's one story that's well worth sharing.

At the retreat, there was a girl who I knew by name and face only except an occasional "hello," but that was the extent of a conversation. Youth leaders mumbled rumors about this girl's romance with a much older boy when she was a freshman. It rubbed under my skin when hands were cusped, and ladies would gossip about "what they had heard." When she was cleaning off a table at lunchtime, I smiled and asked if she was having a good weekend. She pleasantly answered. At the end of the retreat as everyone was saying goodbye after unloading the bus, she walked past me and another youth leader, hugged each of us, and said thank you for a great weekend. I looked at my friend and said, "I'm going to pray for that girl." As the days passed, I recalled our eye-to-eye contact and the scrutiny of the busy-body gossipers. As adults, where was the "there is therefore now no condemnation for those who are in Christ Jesus" and empathy when none of us are blameless without faults? As I reminisced the weekend with my husband, I expressed my heart for this particular girl.

The next Sunday at church, it was unusual when a line of girls filed in and sat a few rows ahead. They were at the retreat and I spotted the girl immediately. At the end of the service, I leaned over to my husband, pointed her out, and said, "I'm going to dash out of the row to catch _____ to tell her I've felt called to pray for her and offer encouragement to cling to the faith." He raised eyebrows and said, "Ok, do what you've gotta do, but she's going to think you're a little crazy." I wove through the crowd, said hello to the other girls, and then looked her in the eye and said what I needed to say. She had a serious look but smiled and said thanks. I didn't give it a lot of thought until I received a text hours later. "Hello, this is _____. It took my breath away when you said you had been praying for me. It just so happens that I've been praying since the retreat for you to be a mentor or my small group leader." I clutched my chest, "OH MY GOODNESS!"- the wave of emotions. I didn't know how to respond at first but replied that I was flattered and if she ever needed someone to talk to I'd be available. She then quickly wrote, "How about tomorrow?" Floored by her anxiousness, we met the next afternoon. I was nervous as I got out of the car but said a quick, "Lord, bless this conversation. I don't know what's on her mind. Give me the right words." She was in a booth waiting at the fast food restaurant. When I walked in, she stood up with open arms as I walked towards her. We didn't know each other, so we talked about my intuition and her text. When asked to tell me about herself, she spilled her background and life story. I discovered a beautiful and kind young woman with an appreciation for family, friends, faith, and a promising future. And

Take5forHIM

then I shared my own testimony. It was "Day One" of an endearing friendship. We met often to talk, share, advise, or get something off our chest, so to speak. Time has passed and now she's in college. We continue to text although busy schedules prohibit one-on-one time spent. I laugh that she's my first adopted daughter but through our long conversations, I've learned much about the life of a teenage girl in this day and age. She represents the typical girl who loves the Lord, but struggles keeping on the path. Who doesn't? Like anyone, she needs reminders, guidance, and an adult mentor.

She's socially and academically swamped, and lives hours away. As time passes, physical distance isn't a barrier because God gave me a heart to pray for her, and I do. That "God could only bring us together" encounter secured us, and we'll keep in touch for the duration. Over my lifetime, God has brought me together with friends I least expected to hit it off with, and I testify it's a bonafide God thing. As a believer, nothing's perceived as a coincidence.

Back story info: Wonder how she obtained my cell number? She kept it from over a year prior when the youth took an amusement park trip. I was the emergency contact leader assigned to her group. While I had long deleted those girls' numbers, she had stored mine.

Final Point: Don't judge a book by its cover; be empathetic. Empathy is sharing mutual feelings as one whose walked in the same shoes. Read Matthew 7:1-5.

"Therefore, there is now no condemnation for those in Christ Jesus,
because the law of the Spirit of life in Christ Jesus
has set you free from the law of sin and death."
(Romans 8:1-2 CSB)

"Iron sharpens iron, and one person sharpens another."
(Proverbs 27:17 CSB)

DECEMBER 16

The bitter truth hurts, but the world does not revolve around you. We know, but we do not live it. We live in a ME-concentrated society. We cannot get past ourselves, what we want, and what we can do to make "Number 1" get ahead. It's like we're running a race to look the best, appear to be the smartest, wisest, most popular, most put together person we know. Who are we fooling? As a Christian, we should put HIM first, family and friends second, and then "me."

Be less self-centered, less self-serving, and more like Jesus.

DECEMBER 17

Christmas music begins to play around Halloween. It may be a plot to boost the economy or to spur excitement for the upcoming season, but "Jingle Bell Rock" is a numbing background noise that gets old quickly. That may be true but listening to a soprano belt out "O Holy Night" was far from my favorite carol as it seemed like an excuse to show off vocal talent. Recently, I embraced the lyrics as the congregation sang it one Sunday morning.

O Holy Night!
The stars are brightly shining
It is the night of the dear Savior's birth!
Long lay the world in sin and error pining
Till He appeared and the soul felt its worth.
A thrill of hope the weary soul rejoices
For yonder breaks a new and glorious morn!

Fall on your knees
Oh hear the angel voices
Oh night divine
Oh night when Christ was born
Oh night divine
Oh night divine

Led by the light of faith serenely beaming
With glowing hearts by His cradle we stand
So led by light of a star sweetly gleaming
Here come the wise men from Orient land
The King of Kings lay thus in lowly manger
In all our trials born to be our friend.

Truly He taught us to love one another
His law is love and His gospel is peace
Chains shall He break for the slave is our brother
And in His name all oppression shall cease
Sweet hymns of joy in grateful chorus raise we,
Let all within us praise His holy name.
Christ is the Lord. O praise His name forever. His power
and glory ever more, ever more proclaim.[28]

Take5forHIM

While "Jingle Bells" and "Rudolph" are reminiscent of childhood, "O Holy Night" reminds us of the everlasting reason for the season. Jesus never gets old and boring to Christians. "Let all within us praise His holy name. Christ is the Lord. O praise His name forever. His power and glory ever more, ever more proclaim." The GREAT I AM.

"And He was saying to them, 'You are from below, I am from above;
you are of this world, I am not of this world.'"
(John 8:23 NAS)

"While I am in the world, I am the Light of the world."
(John 9:5 NAS)

"Jesus therefore said to them again,
'Truly, truly, I say to you, I am the door for the sheep.'"
(John 10:7 NAS)

"Do you say of Him, whom the Father sanctified and sent into the world,
'You are blaspheming,'
because I said, 'I am the Son of God'?"
(John 10:36 NAS)

"In Him was life, and the life was the light of men."
(John 1:4 NAS)

More verses proclaiming Jesus' identity: John 6:35; John 8:58; John 11:25; John 13:13; John 14:6; John 15:1; Revelation 1:8; Revelation 1:17.

[28]Author: Cappeau, Placide (1847). Translator: Dwight, John Sullivan. *Hymnary.org*. 2018. "Oh, Holy Night."
https://hymnary.org/text/o_holy_night_the_stars_are_brightly_shine.

Take5forHIM

DECEMBER 18

Without a change of heart, one cannot genuinely convert to Christianity. When we fess up to our sin, brokenness, bitterness, anger, rebellion and repent- that's when true conversion occurs.

I looked for inspiring quotes about changing hearts for today's devo, but they were all empty, lifeless, heartwarming phrases. No famous person's quote can beat the Bible's.

"Therefore, if anyone is in Christ,
he is a new creation;
old things have passed away,
and look, new things have come."
(2 Corinthians 5:17 HCSB)

"I will give them a heart to know Me, that I am Yahweh.
They will be My people, and I will be their God
because they will return to Me with all their heart."
(Jeremiah 24:7 HCSB)

"No, a person is a Jew who is one inwardly;
and circumcision is circumcision of the heart, by the Spirit,
not by the written code. Such a person's praise
is not from other people, but from God."
(Romans 2:29 NIV)

"Create in me a clean heart, O God,
and renew a steadfast spirit within me."
(Psalm 51:10 NKJV)

"For the godly sorrow produces repentance leading to salvation,
not to be regretted; but the sorrow of the world produces death."
(2 Corinthians 7:1 NKJV)

Take5forHIM

DECEMBER 19

The wise men are presumed to be godly figures who were following the star to find God's infant son. They are props in the nativity scene, right? Bible scholars say the men were just the opposite. The magi (a.k.a. wise men) were astrologists with black magic and probably not God followers of any sort, but they were on a mission to follow the eastern start to find the Messiah.

"You are worn out with your many consultations. So let the astrologers stand and save you- those who observe the stars, those who predict monthly what will happen to you. Look, they are like stubble, fire burns them. They cannot rescue themselves from the power of the flame. This is not a coal for warming themselves, or a fire to sit beside!" (Isaiah 47:13-14 CSB)

The three gifts from the wisemen had symbolic meanings. We're accustomed to giving monogrammed burp towels, but these were fine gifts commonly presented to royalty. Gold is a fine precious metal symbolizing kingship because Jesus is the King of Kings. Frankincense is a very peculiar smelling incense given as a symbol of deity and Jesus' priesthood. Myrrh is a resin-like oil used as an embalming oil in ancient times which symbolized that Jesus would die for our sins. Both frankincense and myrrh were used to cover the smell and preserve dead bodies. We can make sense of giving gold, but other two gifts were odd. Assuredly, there was deep thought for the best and most appropriate gifts to give a king.

The Christ child's first contact with humans was not with "holy and righteous priests," but with pagans just as He was drawn to minister to the same as an adult. Wow! What an amazing God!

Take5forHIM

DECEMBER 20

The history of Santa Claus is quite amusing. St. Nicholas was a monk who lived around the 3rd century A.D. in modern day Turkey. He generously shared his wealth with the poor. Over time, there were numerous legends about his charitable kindness. Good 'ole America popularized the figure of Santa Claus at the end of the 18th century. Between a New York author, the Salvation Army, and Clement C. Moore writing "An Account of a Visit from St. Nicholas" (later known as "Twas the Night Before Christmas"), Santa Claus' popularity grew like wildfire. Department Stores capitalized on the story with images of Santa Claus in their holiday advertisements. Around the world, America's Santa Claus became a phenomenon such as in Germany and Switzerland with Kris Kringle who delivered gifts to well-behaved children. Kris Kringle is derived from the word Christkind.[29] Clement C. Moore's imagination can be applauded for Santa's total package illustration.

That which started as a legend of a generous monk, quickly spread as the replica of Christmas. Santa Claus fueled the world back to celebrating Jesus' birthday. While it's a season of excessive giving and benevolent contributions, reading the background of this fictitious character caused me to question why we bought into the jolly old elf. As a child, I was devastated when I found out it was all made up, but that didn't detain my husband and me from playing Santa with our own kids. It's part of childhood fun at Christmas. I recall telling our children that Santa Claus comes as long as they believe and left it at that. The truth didn't seem earth-shattering when they discovered it. As adults, we tease that Santa Claus only comes if they still "hear the bell."

Extreme conservative Christians argue that kids may grow up thinking God is a lie, because they've been taught Santa is real up to the age of knowledge. That's hogwash! There's a healthy way to raise children to enjoy the magic of gifts delivered by a fat, red-suited, grandfather-like figure who comes down the chimney. It depends on what angle the parents and grandparents play out Santa and the elf versus teaching Jesus' birthday being the center of the home's month-long festivities. Santa Claus shouldn't skew the image of God.

Thinking deeper: The devil creeps in innocently. I wouldn't classify myself as one of those extreme conservatives, but I'm baffled about how "over the top" Christmas has become. It also jumped out that the word Satan, scrambled up, is Santa. What started as a tale blew up as a pot of gold for retailers. Generally speaking, do nonbelievers know as much about Baby Jesus as they know about Santa Claus? Reminisce about your childhood years of Christmas mornings. How did you find out the Santa was make-believe? Were you angry? Did it affect your image of God? Will you buy into Santa Claus when you're a mom? How will Christmas be observed in your home?

Take5forHIM

"With whom, then, will you compare God? To what image will you liken him? As for an idol, a metalworker casts it, and a goldsmith overlays it with gold and fashions silver chains for it. A person too poor to present such an offering selects wood that will not rot; they look for a skilled worker to set up an idol that will not topple." (Isaiah 40:18-20 NIV)

"All who make idols are nothing, and the things they treasure are worthless. Those who would speak up for them are blind; they are ignorant, to their own shame. Who shapes a god and casts an idol, which can profit nothing? People who do that will be put to shame; such craftsmen are only human beings. Let them all come together and take their stand; they will be brought down to terror and shame." (Isaiah 44:9-11 NIV)

"'She will give birth to a son, and you are to give him the name Jesus, because he will save his people from their sins.' All this took place to fulfill what the Lord had said through the prophet: 'The virgin will conceive and give birth to a son, and they will call him Immanuel.'" (Matthew 1:21-23 NIV)

[29]Santa Claus. Author: History.com Editors. *History*. A&E Television Networks. 2010. https://www.history.com/topics/christmas/santa-claus .

Take5forHIM

DECEMBER 21
Set Apart

You are set apart, and don't ever forget it. We're called to be different, act differently, and live differently because we serve Yahweh, the one true God. A Christian's normal is not the world's normal. Some may call us peculiar.

"But you are a chosen race, a royal priesthood, a holy nation,
a people for his own possession, that you may proclaim the excellences
of him who called you out of darkness into his marvelous light."
(1 Peter 2:9 ESV)

"If you were of the world, the world would love you as its own;
but because you are not of the world, but I chose you out of the world,
therefore the world hates you."
(John 15:19 NAS)

"For we are his workmanship, created in Christ Jesus for good works,
which God prepared beforehand,
that we should walk in them."
(Ephesians 2:10 ESV)

"I have been crucified with Christ. It is no longer I who live, but Christ who lives in me.
And the life I now live in the flesh I live by faith in the Son of God,
who loved me and gave himself for me."
(Galatians 2:20 ESV)

"For you are a people holy to the Lord your God, and the Lord has
chosen you to be a people for his treasured possession, out of all the
peoples who are on the face of the earth."
(Deuteronomy 14:2 ESV)

"But to all who did receive him, who believed in his name, he gave the right to
become children of God, who were born, not of blood nor of the will
of the flesh nor of the will of man, but of God."
(John 1:12-13 ESV)

"But know that the Lord has set apart the godly for himself;
the Lord hears when I call to him."
(Psalm 4:3 ESV)

Take5forHIM

DECEMBER 22

The devotional on Santa Claus, a few days ago, wasn't meant to be a Debbie Downer message, but one to get you thinking. Everyone wants to believe in God, but nobody wants to believe Satan is alive and well. Everybody wants to go to heaven but shutter the idea that hell exists. It's insightful to get out of the box to sense what may be Satan's scheme to lure minds from God. Thoughts of Santa Claus, pop culture's lyrics and videos, social stances, political agendas, and participating in "innocent" gossip are all ways Satan makes a move. Be on the alert.

"Be sober-minded; be watchful. Your adversary the devil prowls
around like a roaring lion, seeking someone to devour."
(1 Peter 5:8 ESV)

"Whoever makes a practice of sinning is of the devil,
for the devil has been sinning from the beginning.
The reason the Son of God appeared was to destroy the works of the devil."
(1 John 3:8 ESV)

"Moreover, he must be well thought of by outsiders,
so that he may not fall into disgrace, into a snare of the devil."
(1 Timothy 3:7 ESV)

Take5forHIM

DECEMBER 23

"'Come, all you who are thirsty,
come to the waters;
and you who have no money,
come, buy and eat!
Come, buy wine and milk
without money and without cost.
Why spend money on what is not bread,
and your labor on what does not satisfy?
Listen, listen to me, and eat what is good,
and you will delight in the richest of fare.
Give ear and come to me;
listen, that you may live.
I will make an everlasting covenant with you,
my faithful love promised to David.
See, I have made him a witness to the peoples,
a ruler and commander of the peoples.
Surely you will summon nations you know not,
and nations you do not know will come running to you,
because of the Lord your God,
the Holy One of Israel,
for he has endowed you with splendor.'
Seek the Lord while he may be found;
call on him while he is near.
Let the wicked forsake their ways
and the unrighteous their thoughts.
Let them turn to the Lord, and he will have mercy on them,
and to our God, for he will freely pardon.
'For my thoughts are not your thoughts,
neither are your ways my ways,'
declares the Lord.
'As the heavens are higher than the earth,
so are my ways higher than your ways
and my thoughts than your thoughts.
As the rain and the snow
come down from heaven,
and do not return to it
without watering the earth
and making it bud and flourish,
so that it yields seed for the sower and bread for the eater,
so is my word that goes out from my mouth:

Take5forHIM

It will not return to me empty,
but will accomplish what I desire
and achieve the purpose for which I sent it.
You will go out in joy
and be led forth in peace;
the mountains and hills
will burst into song before you,
and all the trees of the field
will clap their hands.
Instead of the thorn bush will grow the juniper,
and instead of briers the myrtle will grow.
This will be for the Lord's renown,
for an everlasting sign,
that will endure forever.'"
(Isaiah 55 NIV)

How does this relate to Christmas? EVERYTHING about this passage presents Christmas. Without our thirst to worship the baby who was the answer to salvation, Christmas is solely a pagan holiday with gifts. Isaiah 55 is a prophetic invitation to all who are thirsty for the quenching satisfaction of knowing Jesus.

Take5forHIM

DECEMBER 24

*"Now after Jesus was born in Bethlehem of Judea in the days of Herod the king,
behold, wise men from the East came in Jerusalem, saying,
'Where is He who has been born King of the Jews?
For we have seen His star in the East, and have come to worship Him.'"*
(Matthew 2:1-2 NKJV)

*"And having heard the king, they went their way; and lo, the star, which they had
seen in the east, went on before them, until it came and stood over where the Child
was. And when they saw the star, they rejoiced exceedingly with great joy. And they
came into the house and saw the Child with Mary His mother; and they fell down and
worshiped Him; and opening their treasures they presented to Him gifts of gold and
frankincense and myrrh."* (Matthew 2:9-11 NAS)

What's the significance of the star? For centuries, astronomers have tried to figure
out an astronomical event to explain the Star of Bethlehem. Was it an explosive star,
a meteorite, the conjunction of two planets, or a bright comet? I don't believe
smarties will ever pinpoint the star God placed in the sky specifically to guide the wise
men and shepherds to the Christ Child. The star moved in the same fashion as the
pillar of cloud that lead the Israelites to the safety of the wilderness (Exodus 14:19-
20). Stars don't move, so brainiacs are unable to assess them the same as solar
eclipses which occur every X number of years.

The star was a compass to lead the magi and shepherds, because they needed
direction. That's akin to our dependence on Jesus to lead us in the dark instead of
muddling through life running circles in a dry desert. Thank God we're not searching
for a big sign in the sky- a revelation that He's near. He's the captain, and the Bible is
the guide, to knowing the Baby Jesus who was born in a stable and died on a cross.
Our magnificent God sent His only son to be born and die in humble means. That
speaks so much of the character of our Lord. No wonder the Bible says, *"God opposes
the proud but shows favor to the humble."* (James 4:6 NIV) That's the life Jesus lived
on earth.

There are so many life lesson parallels in the Christmas story such as following the
star. Don't obliterate the Christmas story when the holidays are over. It's a
demonstration of how God came down and brought love to the earth by living and
breathing WITH THE WORLD.

Take5forHIM

DECEMBER 25

"For unto us a Child is born, unto us a Son is given, and the government will be upon His shoulder. And His name will be called Wonderful, Counselor, Mighty God, Everlasting Father, Prince of Peace."
(Isaiah 9:6 NKJV)

The more I read the Bible, the more in awe of how perfectly it's woven. Old Testament prophesies of Jesus' coming are hinted from Genesis to Malachi. Isaiah 9 is one of the most familiar prophesies, but it's one of many. Specifically, from the time the Israelites were freed, until His birth [about 1500 years later], people were waiting for the Expected One. He wasn't born in the lineage of royalty as the people expected. His character and life story were not what people expected, either. He came humbly, lived among us, worked as a carpenter with Joseph, ate/drank/slept as we do, and prayed to His Father. He didn't fit the royal mold, so many people rejected Him. As Christians, it's hard for us to imagine the repudiation.

There are a multitude of descriptive names for Jesus throughout the Bible. Here are just a few:

Prince of Peace ~ King of Kings ~ Lord of Lords ~ Emmanuel ~ Righteous One ~ Savior ~ Name Above All Names ~ Wonderful Counselor ~ Mighty God ~ Everlasting Father ~ Christ ~ Advocate ~ The Everlasting God ~ The Highest ~ The Alpha and the Omega ~ Son of God ~ Son of David ~ Man of Sorrows ~ Lamb of God ~ Word of God ~ The Good Shepherd ~ Comforter ~ The Vine ~ Bread of Life ~ The Way ~ Light of the World ~ I AM ~ The Rock ~ Cornerstone ~ Suffering Servant ~ Redeemer ~ Salvation ~ The Author and Finisher of Faith ~ Lord of Lords ~ Holy One ~ The Risen Lord ~ Messiah ~ Jesus

How can anyone dispute the validity of His Word?! No human is brilliant enough to weave the stories of the Bible so impeccably or so illustrative about the nature of the Son of God. It's absolutely too perfect to be a book of lies.

He is who He said He was, and He is the one true God who is the same yesterday, today and forever (Hebrews 13:8). His character never changes. Preaching truth!

Merry Christmas to all!

Take5forHIM

DECEMBER 26

While Adam was born a perfect man, he fell to sin in the Garden of Eden. Other great men came along such as Abraham, Isaac, Jacob, Samuel, King David, Solomon, and Job. Women such as Esther, Ruth, Elizabeth, and the Marys also made an impression on God's kingdom. But, none of them were stainless. Along with every single human, who's ever lived, they had times when they honored God and moments when they erred. Jesus is the ONLY one who has ever lived a sin-free life. The world around Him was not flawless, but He never sinned. The Israelites had kings who they probably suspected was the Messiah, because they looked the part but were proved wrong as blemishes flared. This year we've studied umpteen biblical figures, and none of them compare to the distinctness of Jesus. Other religions worship false gods whose characters are incomparable to Jesus. He is the image of perfection. He alone is worthy to be praised. Jesus! Oh, what a name!

"Who committed no sin, nor was any deceit found in his mouth."
(1 Peter 2:22 NAS)

"For we do not have a high priest who is unable to sympathize with our weaknesses, but one who in every respect has been tempted as we are, yet without sin."
(Hebrews 4:15 NAS)

"He made the one who did not know sin to be sin for us, so that we might become the righteousness of God in Him."
(2 Corinthians 5:21 HCSB)

"For God has done what the law, weakened by the flesh, could not do. By sending his own Son in the likeness of sinful flesh and for sin, he condemned sin in the flesh..."
(Romans 8:3 ESV)

"So all this was done that it might be fulfilled which was spoken by the Lord through the prophet saying: 'BEHOLD, THE VIRGIN SHALL BE WITH CHILD AND SHALL BEAR A SON, AND THEY SHALL CALL HIS NAME IMMANUEL,' which is translated, 'GOD WITH US.'"
(Matthew 1:22-23 NKJV)

Take5forHIM

DECEMBER 27

Did you know Jesus was a Jew? It's OK if you didn't know or have never thought about it. The fact that his lineage is rooted in the Jewish faith, may be the lost puzzle piece as to why it's said, "Jesus died on the cross as the final ultimate sacrifice for our sins." His shed blood is also referred to as "the perfect Passover Lamb." The soldiers who mocked him by nailing the sign "King of the Jews" above the cross were also acknowledging his Jewish faith.

Back then, you were either a Jew or a Gentile. A Gentile was anyone who wasn't of Jewish descendent- born from the family line of Abraham, Isaac, and Jacob.

Is Jesus his first name and Christ his last name? Silly question? It's a common question but no, Christ is one of the many names describing Jesus' identity. So, "Messiah" and "Christ" are transliterated words for the same thing. These words mean "anointed one" in their original languages.

In the realm of it all, the particulars aren't important but helpful to understand that the magnificence of God the Creator is unfathomable. You were made to worship Him. You were put on this earth to worship the Baby Jesus who as an adult (around 33 years old) died on the cross as the final sacrifice for our sins. He walked on this earth, was thirsty and drank, was hungry and ate to nourish His body. He had emotions. He performed miracles. He had one-on-one conversations with everyday ordinary sinners like us. He preached to thousands. He didn't condemn but showed love to sinners. He is altogether man and the infinite God. We were not put on this earth to be cheerleaders or basketball players or doctors or lawyers. We were put on this earth to worship Jesus, the King of the Jews, the King of Kings, the Lord of Lords. While we live life, and enjoy all of the activities and opportunities available, our first priority is to serve the Lord. So much emphasis is placed on the earthly, and so little time is spent getting to know our Creator, serving Him, and worshipping the One we will spend eternity.

Jesus celebrated all the Jewish festivals and prayed in the synagogue yet was rejected by His own religious leaders. Read John 10:22-42.

Take5forHIM

DECEMBER 28

"Through Him we have also gained access by faith into his grace in which we now stand. And we boast in hope of the glory of God. Not only so, but we also glory in our sufferings, because we know that suffering produces perseverance, and perseverance produces character, and character, hope. And hope does not put us to shame, because God's love has been poured out into our hearts through the Holy Spirit, who has been given to us." (Romans 5:2-5 NIV)

Suffering is a dreadful thought that produces uneasiness. Anxiety is the better term. What kind of suffering will be endured in a lifetime? Will it be tragedy, sickness, financial hardship, or lost relationships? The above verse is backwards mentality. Is this some type of reverse psychology? Not necessarily. There are non-believers who testify that hard times made them stronger individuals. Trials can cause people to pull themselves up by their bootstraps. For the believer, we grow in faith during tribulations because we know God is our only hope. Prayer happens in the car, in the bathroom, and everywhere (at any moment) when relief is sought. As time goes by, hope will become second nature when life's storms are raging. Ask for the Lord's guidance to mature and prepare for what's ahead.

DECEMBER 29
Hall of Fame- Ummmm...Hall of FAITH!

Before we close the year, you've gotta read Hebrews 11. Many of the people I've written about during the year are listed in the "Hall of Faith" chapter of Hebrews. People who lived in ancient times didn't have computers or modern-day papers to refer back to for historical information. The stories of the Old Testament were written on scrolls, taught in temples, and re-told for generations. Hebrews is in the New Testament, but Chapter 11 recalls acts of faith of people who lived centuries beforehand. The Bible is the inspired, inerrant Word of our Father who appointed writers to write it down for you and me. Simply ah-mazing!

"Now faith is confidence in what we hope for and assurance about what we do not see. This is what the ancients were commended for.

By faith we understand that the universe was formed at God's command, so that what is seen was not made out of what was visible.

By faith Abel brought God a better offering than Cain's. By faith he was commended as righteous, when God spoke well of his offerings. And by faith Abel still speaks, even though he is dead.

By faith Enoch was taken from this life, so that he did not experience death: 'He could not be found, because God had taken him away.' For before he was taken, he was commended as one who pleased God. And without faith it is impossible to please God, because anyone who comes to him must believe that he exists and that he rewards those who earnestly seek him.

By faith Noah, when warned about things not yet seen, in holy fear built an ark to save his family. By his faith he condemned the world and became heir of the righteousness that is in keeping with faith.

By faith Abraham, when called to go to a place he would later receive as his inheritance, obeyed and went, even though he did not know where he was going. By faith he made his home in the Promised Land like a stranger in a foreign country; he lived in tents, as did Isaac and Jacob, who were heirs with him of the same promise. For he was looking forward to the city with foundations, whose architect and builder is God. And by faith even Sarah, who was past childbearing age, was enabled to bear children because she considered him faithful who had made the promise. And so from this one man, and he as good as dead, came descendants as numerous as the stars in the sky and as countless as the sand on the seashore.

Take5forHIM

All these people were still living by faith when they died. They did not receive the things promised; they only saw them and welcomed them from a distance, admitting that they were foreigners and strangers on earth. People who say such things show that they are looking for a country of their own. If they had been thinking of the country they had left, they would have had opportunity to return. Instead, they were longing for a better country—a heavenly one. Therefore, God is not ashamed to be called their God, for he has prepared a city for them.

By faith Abraham, when God tested him, offered Isaac as a sacrifice. He who had embraced the promises was about to sacrifice his one and only son, [18] even though God had said to him, 'It is through Isaac that your offspring will be reckoned.' Abraham reasoned that God could even raise the dead, and so in a manner of speaking he did receive Isaac back from death.

By faith Isaac blessed Jacob and Esau in regard to their future.

By faith Jacob, when he was dying, blessed each of Joseph's sons, and worshiped as he leaned on the top of his staff.

By faith Joseph, when his end was near, spoke about the exodus of the Israelites from Egypt and gave instructions concerning the burial of his bones.

By faith Moses' parents hid him for three months after he was born, because they saw he was no ordinary child, and they were not afraid of the king's edict.

By faith Moses, when he had grown up, refused to be known as the son of Pharaoh's daughter. He chose to be mistreated along with the people of God rather than to enjoy the fleeting pleasures of sin. He regarded disgrace for the sake of Christ as of greater value than the treasures of Egypt, because he was looking ahead to his reward. By faith he left Egypt, not fearing the king's anger; he persevered because he saw him who is invisible. By faith he kept the Passover and the application of blood, so that the destroyer of the firstborn would not touch the firstborn of Israel.

By faith the people passed through the Red Sea as on dry land; but when the Egyptians tried to do so, they were drowned.

By faith the walls of Jericho fell, after the army had marched around them for seven days.

By faith the prostitute Rahab, because she welcomed the spies, was not killed with those who were disobedient.

And what more shall I say? I do not have time to tell about Gideon, Barak, Samson and Jephthah, about David and Samuel and the prophets, who through faith conquered kingdoms, administered justice, and gained what was promised; who shut the mouths of lions, quenched the fury of the flames, and escaped the edge of the sword; whose

Take5forHIM

weakness was turned to strength; and who became powerful in battle and routed foreign armies. Women received back their dead, raised to life again. There were others who were tortured, and refused to be released so that they might gain an even better resurrection. Some faced jeers and flogging, and even chains and imprisonment. They were put to death by stoning; they were sawed in two; they were killed by the sword. They went about in sheepskins and goatskins, destitute, persecuted and mistreated— the world was not worthy of them. They wandered in deserts and mountains, living in caves and in holes in the ground.

These were all commended for their faith, yet none of them received what had been promised, since God had planned something better for us so that only together with us would they be made perfect." (Hebrews 11 NIV)

Take5forHIM

DECEMBER 30
Year-end Reflection

As I reflect on the year, I recall special occasions, events, changes, happiness, heartaches, and a few speed bumps. Our goal should be to count every circumstance and every trial as JOY. Experiences are faith markers.

In a moment, life can take a quick turn of events. On a Friday morning, our day was packed as we toured a college campus with our sons and family friends. At the end of the long day, we went to a restaurant for an early dinner. I was starving, since I had not eaten all day. I was laughing and very chatty. Suddenly, I felt tightness in my chest, and I was light-headed. My husband and a friend, simultaneously, looked worried and concerned as they recognized that something was wrong. The next thing I remember was trying to wake up, but I could not. Then, EMTs asked questions as they transported me via ambulance to the hospital.

Various tests, including tests on my heart, were performed because my heart rate had fallen to 40 beats per minute at the restaurant. After hours of testing, I was diagnosed with a severe case of dehydration. My body had shut down, since I had not eaten all day and only drank a half cup of coffee at 6 a.m.

Though I left with a simple prescription cure– "DRINK A LOT"-- I was emotionally exhausted. I've often thought about how I went from laughing to falling out of my chair- heavy, limp, clammy, and lifeless- within 5 minutes. Once the IV kicked in, I was not furiously praying for recovery. I had a certain degree of peace, yet it bothered me later that I did not PRAY. My husband reminded me that the Holy Spirit lives in me. My heart belongs to HIM, and I've given my life to Him; therefore, my spirit trusted Him without desperation of prayer.

At the snap of a finger, our fragile lives can change. Celebrate the freedom of trusting God, so when out of control events happen, you don't cry for HELP. Your spirit will TRUST, because it has become your way of life.

"Why, you do not even know what will happen tomorrow. What is your life?
You are a mist that appears for a little while and then vanishes."
(James 4:14 NIV)

Also read: Psalm 39:5, Psalm 78:39, Psalm 112:7, Psalm 144:4, Proverbs 27:1; James 5:7-12.

Take5forHIM

DECEMBER 31

Dear Heavenly Father,

We're at the end of the year. I thank you for the privilege You've given me to teach this beautiful young woman Your Word and who You are. I pray this year has been an eye opener. I pray that she has become renewed, excited, and a changed woman after a year of Bible stories and rich passages. I pray that she has become more knowledgeable about Biblical history and common church practices that aren't always explained - sort of taken for granted that "everyone just knows." Lord, I pray these devotionals have helped her figure out what it looks like to be a Christian girl on a high school/college campus/team/workplace. Let any notions that the Bible is boring be dispelled, and any doubts be resolved that the Bible is THE TRUTH.

Life is tough, and we need guidance. Thank you for speaking through me, letting my fingers do the talking, giving me the passion to teach this generation. I've learned so much, and it's been such a joy to thumb through the Bible and soak it up. This has not been a chore or a job; it has been a pleasure and an honor to write for You. May this devotional book be an aid to the reader, then used as a reference and later passed on to a friend who needs an easy to understand way to be inspired. I pray that the readers will flee from sin, walk by Your ways, seek what's best for them, and not let the world infiltrate secular ideals in their brains. Come alive!!! God, open doors for Bible studies. Equip these girls to study and teach. Let them rise up to spread the gospel on campuses and in communities. Grow them into adult women who never let the fire burn out but aspire to dig more, show your love to the world, and radiate with the joy of knowing the risen Savior. Each one of them is beautiful in Your sight. God, do Your work in each life. They are YOUR daughters. Let the voice of our consciences be loud when we're out of your will. I pray they'll see You as their King and Lord over their lives. Lastly, let them see You, Christ, in everything, every day! *"Now to Him who is able to do above and beyond all that we ask or think, according to the power that works in us-- to Him be the glory in the Church and in Christ Jesus to all generations, forever and ever. Amen." (Ephesians 3:20-21 HCSB)*

In Your Precious Name,
Amen

Take5forHIM

Notes

January 1
[1]Wilkinson, Katie B. "May the Mind of Christ, My Savior." *Trinity Hymnal*, Great Commission Publications, Inc., 1990, 644.

January 16
[2]*Facing the Giants*. Dir. Alex Kendrick. Perf. Alex Kendrick, Shannen Fields, Tracy Goode, James Blackwell, Bailey Cave, Jim McBride, Jason McLeod. Samuel Goldwyn Films, Destination Films, 2006. DVD.

January 22
[3]Bush, Barbara. *Barbara Bush a Memoir*. New York, London, Toronto, Sydney, Tokyo, Singapore, Lisa Drew Books, Charles Scribner's Sons, ©1994.

January 27
[4]"Salty." *Urban Dictionary*, 2011, /www.urbandictionary.com/define.php?term=Salty.

February 22
[5]*The Hobbit, The Desolation of Smaug*. Dir. Peter Jackson. Perf. Ian McKellen, Martin Freeman, Richard Armitage, Benedict Cumberbatch, Evangeline Lilly, Lee pace, Luke Evans, Stephen Fry, Ken Stott, James Nesbitt, Orlando Bloom. Warner Brothers Pictures, December 2013.

[6]*The Hobbit: The Battle of the Five Armies*. Dir. Peter Jackson. Perf. Martin Freeman, Ian McKellen, Richard Armitage, Evangeline Lilly, Lee Pace, Luke Evans, Benedict Cumberbatch, Ken Stott, James Nesbitt, Cate Blanchett, Ian Holm, Christopher Lee, Hugo Weaving, Orlando Bloom. Warner Brothers Pictures, December 2014.

March 15
[7]Bennett, Arthur (Editor). *The Valley of Vision: A Collection of Puritan Prayers and Devotions*. The Banner of Truth Trust, 1975, 2002, 2003. Print.

March 25
[8]Rosen, Ceil and Moishe. *Christ in the Passover: Why is this night different?*. Moody Press. 1978, 31-32.

March 26
[9]Rosen, Ceil and Moishe. *Christ in the Passover: Why is this night different?*. Moody Press. 1978, 28-30.

Take5forHIM

[10]Rosen, Ceil and Moishe. *Christ in the Passover: Why is this night different?*. Moody Press. 1978, 70.

March 27.
[11]Rosen, Ceil and Moishe. *Christ in the Passover: Why is this night different?*. Moody Press. 1978, 7.

April 13
[12]The Apostles Creed. *Trinity Hymnal*, Great Commission Publications, Inc., 1990, 845.

May 19
[13]Niebuhr, Reinhold (1934). *Wikipedia*. 2018. https://en.wikipedia.org/wiki/Serenity_Prayer.

May 27
[14]Newton, John. "Amazing Grace!". *Trinity Hymnal*, Great Commission Publications, Inc., 1990, 460.

May 28
[15]Amazing Grace. *Wikipedia*. 2018. https://en.wikipedia.org/wiki/Amazing_Grace.

August 7
[16]Rainbow. *Wikipedia*. 2018. *https://en.wikipedia.org/wiki/Rainbow*.

August 22
[17]Atonement. Elwell, Walter A. *"Entry for Atonement'. "Evangelical Dictionary of Theology"*. 1997. *Bible Study Tools*.
www.biblestudytools.com/dictionary/atonement/).
[18]Redemption. *Google*. www.google.com/search.
[19]Redemption. *GotQuestions.org*. 2018. www.gotquestions.org/redemption,html.
[20]Scrupulosity. *Wikipedia*. 2018. https://en.wikipedia.org/wiki/Scrupulosity.

October 3
[21]The Nicene Creed. *Trinity Hymnal*, Great Commission Publications, Inc., 1990, 846.

October 20

[22]Ten Boom, Corrie with John and Elizabeth Sherrill. *The Hiding Place.* New York, Toronto, London, Sydney, Auckland, Bantam Books by arrangement with Fleming H. Revell Company, 1971, p. 194.

October 22

[23]Christians & Pumpkins. *DLTK's Bible Crafts for Kids.* 2018. http://www.dltk-bible.com/p.asp?p=http://www.dltk-bible.com/phow_a_christian_is_like_a_pumpki.asp.

November 10

[24]Spafford, Horatio G. "It is Well with My Soul." *Trinity Hymnal,* Great Commission Publications, Inc., 1990, 691.
[25]It is Well with My Soul. *Wikipedia.* 2018. https://en.wikipedia.org/wiki/It_Is_Well_with_My_Soul.

November 11

[26]Pollard, Adelaide A. "Have Thine Own Way, Lord!" *Trinity Hymnal,* Great Commission Publications, Inc. 1990, 688.

November 21

[27]"I Baptize You with Water." *Desiring God.* 26 September 2018. www.desiringgod.org/messages/i-baptize-you-with-water.

December 17

[28]Author: Cappeau, Placide (1847). Translator: Dwight, John Sullivan. *Hymnary.org.* 2018. "Oh, Holy Night." https://hymnary.org/text/o_holy_night_the_stars_are_brightly_shin.

December 20

[29]Santa Claus. Author: History.com Editors. *History.* A&E Television Networks. 2010. https://www.history.com/topics/christmas/santa-claus .

Take5forHIM

Topic Search

Take5forHIM

Take5forHIM